STUDIES IN THE MEDICINE OF ANCIENT INDIA

OSTEOLOGY OR THE BONES OF THE HUMAN BODY

BY

A. F. RUDOLF HOERNLE, C.I.E.

PH.D. (TÜBINGEN), HON. M.A. (OXFORD),

LATE PRINCIPAL, CALCUTTA MADRASA

CONCEPT PUBLISHING COMPANY, NEW DELHI 110059

ISBN 81-7022-137-4

First Published 1907
Reprinted in India 1984
Second Reprint 1994

Published and Printed by
Ashok Kumar Mittal
Ccncept Publishing Company
A/15-16, Commercial Block, Mohan Garden
NEW DELHI 110059 (INDIA)

PREFACE

OUR knowledge of the Medicine known to the ancient Indians is at present extremely limited. I was made painfully aware of this fact in the course of preparing my edition of the two old Indian medical tracts preserved in the well-known Bower Manuscript of the fifth century A.D. The exigencies of that edition led me to a closer study of Indian Medicine, and the present treatise on its osteological doctrines is one of the firstfruits of that study.

Probably it will come as a surprise to many, as it did to myself, to discover the amount of anatomical knowledge which is disclosed in the works of the earliest medical writers of India. Its extent and accuracy are surprising, when we allow for their early age—probably the sixth century before Christ—and their peculiar methods of definition. In these circumstances the interesting question of the relation of the Medicine of the Indians to that of the Greeks naturally suggests itself. The possibility, at least, of a dependence of either on the other cannot well be denied, when we know as an historical fact that two Greek physicians, Ktesias, about 400 B.C., and Megasthenes about 300 B.C., visited, or resided in Northern India.

No satisfactory knowledge of human anatomy can be attained without recourse to human dissection. Of the practice of such dissection in ancient India we have direct proof in the medical compendium of Suśruta, and it is indirectly confirmed by the statements of Charaka. It is worthy of note, however, that in the writings of neither of these two oldest Indian medical writers is there any indication of the practice of animal dissection.[1] Whatever

[1] The only mention of an animal subject is in connexion with training in surgery. Thus 'puncturing' is to be practised by the medical pupil 'on the veins of dead animals and on the stalks of the water-lily'; similarly, 'extracting,' on the pulp of various kinds of fruit and 'on the teeth of dead animals'.

knowledge of the structure of the human body they possessed would seem to have been derived by them from the dissection of human subjects. And, whether or not cases of such dissection were frequent, their surprising proficiency in osteology argues a considerable familiarity with the bones of the human body. As to the Greeks there is indubitable evidence that an extensive practice of human dissection, on dead, and even on living subjects, prevailed in the Alexandrian schools of Herophilos and Erasistratos in the earlier part of the third century B.C. But their knowledge of anatomy appears in some particulars, such as the nervous and vascular systems, so much in advance of that of the early Indians, that, if there was any borrowing on the part of the latter from the Greeks, it must have taken place at a very much earlier period, in the time of Hippokrates and his immediate followers—that is to say, in the second half of the fifth century B.C.

This conclusion is confirmed by the chronological indications, no doubt more or less vague, given to us by the Indian tradition which places the earliest Indian medical schools of Ātreya and Suśruta at some time in the sixth century B.C., a date supported by the Vedas. This being so, and considering that we have no direct evidence of the practice of human dissection in the Hippokratic school, but know of the visit, about 400 B.C., of Ktesias to India, the alternative conclusion of a dependence of Greek anatomy on that of India cannot be simply put aside. On the other hand, there is some indirect evidence that the Hippokratics were not entirely unfamiliar with human dissection[1]; and once admitting the practice of such dissection among both the early Greeks and the early Indians, the general similarity of standard in their knowledge of human anatomy may well be conceived without the hypothesis of an interdependence. In order to be able to verify a dependence of either upon the other, we require the evidence of agreement in points which are both peculiar and essential in the respective systems. It

[1] On this and other points touching Greek anatomy, see Dr. Puschmann's *History of Medical Education.*

is, in part at least, with this object that the present essay on the osteology of the ancient Indians has been prepared. It presents the Indian side of the evidence with respect to that particular department of anatomy. The Greek side of it yet remains to be exhibited; and in the absence of it, as well as of my competence for the task, I have entirely abstained from complicating my subject with references to any ancient osteology other than Indian, lest the presentment of the latter should be unduly biased.

I am tempted, however, to offer one or two passing observations. No summary of osteological doctrine, such as we find in the writings of Charaka and Suśruta, appears to exist in any of the known works of the earlier Greek medical schools. If this is the case—and I am writing under correction—it greatly adds to the difficulty of making any satisfactory comparison. There exists, however, a somewhat similar osteological summary in the Talmud (see the Note, p. viii); and as the Talmudic anatomy is admittedly based on the anatomy of the Greeks, the summary in question may perhaps be taken to reflect the contemporary Greek doctrine on the subject. It is ascribed to the first century A.D.; but certain points in it, such as the inclusion of 'processes' and cartilages to make up its total of 248 bones, seem to point to its being rather a survival of the system of the Hippokratic school. In any case, however, in its method and details of classification it differs materially from the Indian; and if it may be taken in any way as a representative of Greek doctrine, it is difficult to believe in any connexion of the latter with the Indian. In this connexion a statement of Celsus, who is a fair exponent of the Greek osteology of the first century B.C., may be noted. Referring to the carpus and tarsus, he says that they 'consist of many minute bones, the number of which is uncertain', but that they present 'the appearance of a single, interiorly concave, bone'; and with reference to the fingers and toes, he says that 'from the five metacarpals the digits take their origin, each consisting of three bones of similar configuration' (beginning of Book VIII). In the latter numeration of fifteen joints in the hands and feet, Greek osteology agrees with the Talmudic and Indian. As to the carpus and tarsus, the two views of 'a number of small bones' and of 'a single bone' are also found in the Indian osteological summaries of Suśruta and Charaka respectively; the Talmudic summary implies a reckoning of eight small bones.

Another object of the present treatise is to vindicate the true form of the osteological summaries of Charaka and Suśruta. The former is at present in imminent peril of total displacement and oblivion in favour of a well-meant but very ill-considered substitute, to which the otherwise meritorious first edition of Charaka's Compendium by Gangādhar has given general currency. But in this matter Indian medical history is only repeating itself. For, many centuries ago, the same misfortune overtook the osteological summary of Suśruta, the true form of which is now totally lost from all manuscripts owing to its supersession by a falsified substitute which gained general acceptance through the great authority, apparently, of Vāgbhaṭa I, who once held a position in India somewhat analogous to that of Galen in the mediaeval medicine of the West. At a very early period in the history of Indian Medicine, owing to the ascendancy of Neo-brahmanism, which abhorred all contact with the dead, the practice and knowledge of anatomy very rapidly declined, and concurrently anatomical manuscript texts fell into great disorder. Attempts were made from time to time to restore and edit such corrupt texts, but divorced from and uncontrolled by practical knowledge of anatomy, they could not but prove unsatisfactory The earliest example of such an attempt which has survived is what I have called the Non-medical Version of the summary of the osteological system of Ātreya, which may be referred to the middle of the fourth century A.D. A more conspicuous example is the falsification of Suśruta's osteological summary, under the authority of Vāgbhata I, probably in the early part of the seventh century A.D.

The latest example is presented in Gangadhar's invention, not quite thirty years ago, of what professed to be the osteological summary of Charaka. In this last-mentioned case, owing to the modernity of the substitute, it is not difficult, by an appeal to the consensus of still existing manuscripts, to expose and prove its baselessness. But that remedy is not available in the case of the osteological summary of Suśruta, the genuine form of which has now disappeared from all available manuscripts, and can be recovered only by a laborious application of textual criticism combined with an appeal to practical anatomy. But what has occurred in the case of the osteological summaries may have happened also to other parts of the ancient Indian texts concerned with anatomy and surgery. These texts require careful scrutiny before they can be trustfully accepted and cited as evidence. The present dissertation is offered as a first example of such an investigation. Of its success I must leave others to judge, only hoping that it may induce more competent hands than mine to take up and continue the inquiry.

. . . .

It only remains for me to offer my cordial thanks to the scholars who have given me their help in various ways: to Dr. W. Osler, Regius Professor of Medicine, who gave his valuable support to the publication of my monograph by the Delegates of the University Press; to Dr. Arthur Thomson, Professor of Human Anatomy, who most kindly gave me the benefit of his skilled judgement on several difficult points; to Dr. P. Cordier, of the French Colonial Medical Service, to whose letters and publications I owe several useful hints; but especially to Dr. J. Jolly, Professor of Sanskrit and Comparative Philology in the University of Würzburg, and Dr. Hamilton Osgood, of Boston, formerly Lecturer at Jefferson College, Philadelphia, U.S.A.,[1] who both did me the favour of carefully reading the whole of my manuscript, and supplying me with some valuable corrections and suggestions in the Text-critical and Anatomical Sections respectively. My thanks are due also to the authorities of the India Office for their liberality in granting a subvention towards the cost of publication. For most of the illustrations in the Text I am indebted

[1] His lamented death occurred on the 10th July, 1907, while these pages were passing through the Press.

to the skilful hand of my son. A few of them are borrowed, by permission, from Professor A. Thomson's *Handbook of Anatomy for Art Students.* The execution of the whole is another example of the well-known high standard of the work of the Clarendon Press.

A. F. R. H.

OXFORD: JULY, 1907.

NOTE

THE Talmudic osteological summary, referred to on p. v, is given in the *Jewish Encyclopedia, s.v.* Anatomy, as follows:

'The Rabbis declared that there were 248 members (bones) in the human body; namely, 40 in the tarsal region and the foot (30+10=40); 2 in the leg (the tibia and fibula); 6 in the knee (including the head of the femur and the epiphyses of the tibia and fibula); 3 in the pelvi. (ilium, ischium, and pubes); 11 ribs (the 12th rib, owing to its diminutive size, was not counted); 30 in the hand (the carpal bones and the phalanges); 2 in the forearm (radius and ulna); 2 in the elbow (the olecranon and the head of the radius); 1 in the arm (humerus); 4 in the shoulder (clavicle, scapula, caracoid process, and acromion)—which makes 101 for each side, or 202 for both; 18 vertebrae; 9 in the head (cranium and face); 8 in the neck (7 vertebral, and the os hyoides); 5 around the openings [*sic*] of the body (cartilaginous bones); and 6 in the key of the heart (the sternum).' (OH. I. 8.)

The identifications within brackets appear to be those of the writer of the article on Anatomy. Dr. Bergel, in his *Studien über die naturwissenschaftlichen Kenntnisse der Talmudisten,* hesitatingly identifies the last two items as genitals and cardiac appendices (*Herzanhang,* appendix auricularis?). The identifications that I would suggest may be seen from the subjoined tabular statement.

The Talmudic osteology does not, like the Indian, divide the body into three, but into two parts; namely, (1) the trunk, inclusive of the four extremities, and (2) the neck and head. The trunk, again, is divided, (1) sagittally, into the two sides, right and left; and (2) coronally, into the back and the front. Hence arises the subjoined scheme:

I. Trunk and Extremities.

A. The Two Sides

1. Lower Limb

a. phalanges	15	40 (foot, tarsals)	
b. metatarsals	5		
c. tarsals	8		
d. malleoli	2		
e. unidentified	10		
f. leg (tibia, fibula)	2	(leg)	
g. patella	1	6 (knee)	
h. inner and outer tuberosities	4		
i. femur	1		
k. ilium	1	3 (pelvis)	
l. ischium	1		
m. pubes	1		

2. Middle

ribs	11	(ribs)	

3. Upper Limb

a. scapula	1	4 (shoulder)	
b. clavicle	1		
c. acromion process	1		
d. caracoid process	1		
e. humerus	1	(humerus)	
f. olecranon process	1	2 (elbow)	
g. capitellum of humerus	1		
h. radius and ulna	2	(forearm)	
i. styloid processes	2	30 (hand)	
k. carpals	8		
l. metacarpals	5		
m. phalanges	15		
Total	101 × 2 = 202		

B. Back, or spinal column (exc. cervix)

a. dorsal vertebrae	12	18 (vertebrae)
b. lumbar vertebrae	5	
c. sacrum, coccyx	1	

C. Front, or breast

a. sternum and		6 (key of heart)
b. costal cartilages		
Total of Trunk and Extremities		226

Brought forward 226

II. Head and Neck.

A. Head

1. Cranium

a. frontal bones . . .	2		
b. parietal bones . . .	2		
c. occipital bone . . .	1	9 (head)	
d. temporal bones . . .	2		
e. malar bones	2		

2. Openings

a. mouth (maxillaries) . .	2	
b. ear (pinna)	2	5 (openings)
c. nose (cartilage) . . .	1	

B. Neck

a. vertebrae	7	8 (neck)
b. windpipe	1	

Total of Head and Neck .	22
Grand total of Skeleton .	248

INTRODUCTION

August Rudolf Friedrich Hoernle was born on 19.10.1841 in Sekundra near Agra, where his father Rev. T.C. Hoernle was a missionary. He was sent to Germany when he was seven years old and attended school in Stuttgart. He began his university studies in Basel and went to London in 1860 to study Sanskrit with T. Goldstuecker. He returned to India in 1865 and remained there till 1899. He became professor of philosophy in Jai Narain's College in Benares and was appointed principal of the Cathedral Mission College in Calcutta in 1877. From 1881-99 he was principal of the Madrasa in Calcutta. Hoernle continued his Indological studies after his return to England in 1900. He had been a member of the Royal Asiatic Society of Bengal in Calcutta and was its vice-president for some years. He died on 12.11.1918 in Oxford.

Hoernle took keen interest in the study of many Indological subjects. His work on the Bower manuscript was of great importance. This manuscript was named after its finder, Lieutenant H. Bower, who had found it in 1890 in an old stupa near Kaschgar in Central Asia. For palaeographical reasons this manuscript is ascribed to the 4th century A.D. and it comprises several medical texts. One of the texts describes different medicines and their ingredients, ointments for the eyes, and discusses garlic, which is said to increase man's life-span by one hundred years. The second text has prescriptions for 14 recipes to be used externally and internally. The longest text is called *Nāvanītaka* and has extracts from older medical text-books. All texts are metrical, the language is a mixture of Prakrit and Sanskrit. Hoernle published these texts under the title *The Bower Manuscript*, *Facsimile Leaves*, *Nagari Transcription*, *Romanised Transliteration* and *English translation with notes*, Calcutta 1893-1912.

In the course of working on this manuscript, Hoernle had

the opportunity to acquire knowledge of Indian medical literature and he composed the present work in 1907. Several other articles on Indian medicine appeared in the "Journal of the Royal Asiatic Society" and in "Archiv fuer die Geschichte der Medizin" I, 1908.

According to Indian mythology, Ayurveda was first perceived (not composed) by Brahmā, and he taught this science to Dakṣa-Prajāpati, who taught it to the Aśvinīkumāras, and they taught it to Indra. About the further hierarchy of Ayurvedic propounders, there are different views in Ayurvedic texts. According to *Suśruta saṃhitā*, Lord Dhanvantari learned it from Indra and he taught to Divodāsa who in turn taught it to Suśruta, Aupadhenava, Aurabhra, Pauṣkalāvata, Gopurarakṣita and Bhoja. According to *Caraka saṃhitā*, Bhardvāja learnt it from Indra and he taught to Ātreya Punarvasu. The latter in turn taught it to Agniveśa, Bheḍa, Jatukarṇa, Parāśara, Hārita, Kṣārapāṇi etc. According to *Kāśyapa saṃhitā*, Indra taught ayurveda to Kāśyapa, Vaśiṣṭha, Ātreya and Bhṛgu. Many different medical works were composed by these sages of the past. However, all of them are grouped under two schools. The *Ātreya* school primarily deals with medicine and the *Dhanvantari* school mainly deals with surgery. Many of these texts are no more extant.

The following are the eight important branches of Ayurveda :

(1) *Kāyacikitsā* or Internal Medicine;
(2) *Śalya tantra* or Surgery;
(3) *Śālakya tantra* or the Treatment of diseases of head and the neck;
(4) *Agada tantra* or Toxicology;
(5) *Bhūta vaidyā* or the management of seizures by evil spirits and other mental disorders;
(6) *Bāla tantra* or Paediatrics;
(7) *Rasāyana tantra* or Geriatrics including rejuvenation Therapy; and
(8) *Vājikaraṇa tantra* or Science of aphrodisiacs.

Some scholars hold that *Pañcakarma cikitsā* (Five elimination therapies) in an additional branch of Ayurveda.

The *vedas* are the oldest repository of human knowledge

and they are replete with information about the theory and practice of ayurveda. Suśruta has attributed ayurveda to be a *upaveda* or subsidiary subject of the *Atharva veda.* According to *Caraṇa vyūha*, Ayurveda is the *upaveda* of the *Ṛg veda.* According to another view, Ayurveda is the fifth *veda* and independent of the four *vedas.*

Prior to the birth of Lord Buddha, Ayurveda flourished in this part of the world and was in practice in all its eight specialised branches. Lord Buddha himself was born by a Ceaserean operation. During this period, surgery including treatment of diseases of eye, ear, nose and throat (*Śalya tantra* and *Śālākya tantra*) was at the appogic of its development. During the life-time of Buddha, there was a famous physician by the name Jīvaka. Because of his proficiency in the art of healing including surgery, he was thrice crowned as the king of the physicians and surgeons. He was an expert in paediatrics and even excelled in brain surgery. He successfully performed major abdominal and cranial operations. He was a disciple of Ātreya, the renowned professor of Taxila University who was a pioneer of the Indian system of medicine.

Ātreya was very much impressed by the intelligence, far-sightedness, power of keen observation and surgical acumen of Jivaka. There are many interesting stories about Jīvaka in Tibetan and Pali scriptures.

Ātreya used to ask Jīvaka, his disciple, to accompany him to the patient's house for assisting him in the treatment. One day, Ātreya prescribed a medicine for a patient which, according to Jīvaka, was not correct. He came back with his perceptor and again returned to the patient's house and changed the recipe. By this change of medicine, the patient became alright and this, when Atreya came to know, impressed him very much.

Ātreya's admiration and affection for Jīvaka was not liked by the latter's class-mates and they used to doubt about the impartiality to the teacher Ātreya. One day, the teacher asked all his students to take an examination to test their wisdom and asked all of them including Jīvaka to go to the market and enquire about the prices of certain medicinal commodities. After enquiring, all of them came back. Ātreya enquired from all students including Jīvaka, the prices of medicinal commodities other than those he mentioned to the students. It was none other than Jīvaka who could successfully reply to all the queries. This showed the power of imagination and foresight of Jīvaka which are considered to be the attribute of a good physician.

The third story goes like this. One day, Ātreya asked all his students to go to the hill nearby and fetch the things which have no medicinal value. All students except Jīvaka, returned with many items, which, according to them, had no medicinal value. Jīvaka came back empty handed and replied to his teacher that he did not find anything which does not have medicinal value. This showed the thoroughness of the study of Jīvaka.

The fourth story is about an elephant. One Jīvaka and his class-mates were returning from the river after taking a bath. His friends were amusingly talking about the foot-prints of an elephant. When Jīvaka was asked about the foot-prints of the elephant, he replied that they were of a female elephant who was blind of the right eye, was pregnant, was about to give birth to a calf the same day and it would be a male calf. Jīvaka further continued that on the back of the elephant was riding a lady, who was also blind of the right eye and she would give birth to a son the same day. This was reported amidst laughter as an example of Jīvaka's madness to their teacher Ātreya. The facts were thereafter got verified and they were all found to be correct. Jīvaka was asked to explain as to how he came to know of all this. He said, "The foot-prints of a male elephant are round and those of a female elephant are slightly oblong. Because she had eaten grass which grew on the left side of the foot-path, he inferred that she was blind of the right eye. Because the impressions of her hind feet were deeper, this made him to infer that she was pregnant. Of the two, the impressions of the right foot was deeper. Thus, he inferred that she was going to give birth to a male calf. From the urine she had passed, he inferred that the delivery was imminent". In the same way, he explained his statements regarding the lady who was riding the elephant.

In addition to the above, there are many interesting

anecdotes in the Tibetan and Pali scriptures about the performance of abdominal and cranial surgery by Jīvaka.

The *Bhoja prabanda* gives an account of the cranial operation performed by two physicians on King Bhoja who reigned from 1010-1056 A.D. He was suffering from a serious type of headache and the physicians opened his cranial bone and corrected the malady. The significant description of this operation is that they used an anaesthetic powder called *mohacūrṇa*, which made the king unconscious. After the operation was over, the king was administered another powder called *sañjīvanī* by which he regained his consciousness. Unfortunately, the details of these two types of drugs are not available now.

These anecdotes have been narrated here with a view to showing that during the post-vedic period, especially between 500 B.C. to A.D.1000 surgery in Ayurveda reached the apogee of its development.

Perfection in surgery obviously depends upon a sound knowledge of human anatomy. Therefore, it can be safely assumed that up to tenth century A.D, physicians and surgeons of Ayurveda had mastered the subject anatomy and were successfully performing craniotomy etc., which are considered to-day as major surgical manoeuvres.

Unfortunately, Lord Buddha succumbed to death after an operation by an Ayurvedic surgeon, and thereafter, surgery was considered as a form of violence against which his followers stood very firm and prohibited the practice of various surgical measures by people, including surgeons of the country. The knowledge of surgery including anatomy gradually declined and looks on these subjects subsequently disappeared. This process of decline, of course, took centuries. The loss, to some extent, was compensated by the development of Iatro-chemistry or *rasa śāstra* mainly by Buddhist scholars. Metallic and mineral preparations helped people to overcome some ailments which were earlier treated by surgery. None the less, some other ailments which badly needed surgical operations, remained untreated and surgery went in the later medieval period into the hands of barbers and people of low intectual quotient. There is description of dissection of dead bodies for acquiring knowledge of anatomy, but subsequently, touching a dead body, what to speak of dissecting it, was considered as a sinful act.

Even at present, books on surgery, namely, *Suśruta saṃhitā* and on medicine, namely, *Caraka saṃhitā* and *Aṣṭāṅga hṛdaya*, provide anatomical descriptions. Originally, *Caraka saṃhitā* and *Suśruta saṃhitā* were written prior to seventh century B.C., but they were subsequently redacted and there were many misinterpretations and unauthorised interpollations. At certain stage, some of these books were not available, and subsequent authors and redactors composed different books by compiling material from several other sources. Such books were later known by their original titles. For example, *Agniveśa tantra* which was redacted by Caraka and is at present known as *Caraka saṃhitā*, went extinct atleast partly during the medieval period and the present *Caraka saṃhitā* is actually composed by Dṛḍhabala. Therefore, quotations taken from this book by the subsequent commentators whose works are available even now, are not found in the existing texts. *Nāḍi parīkṣā* or pulse examination, is considered even now synonymous with Ayurvedic practice, but the description of pulse examination is not available in any of the available Ayurvedic classics. But the detailed description of pulse examination was available in *Caraka saṃhitā* which is evident from the references quoted in the *Āyurved Saukhya of Ṭoḍarānanda* which was compiled by the famous minister of Akbar, Mahārājā Todarmalla during 16th century A.D. In Tibetan medical works many passages of *Caraka saṃhitā* are translated, but those are not available in the existing editions of *Caraka saṃhitā*. Vāgbhaṭa has written an auto-commentory and a *vārtika* (explanatory notes) on his famous work *Aṣṭāṅga hṛdaya*. These two works along with *Aṣṭāṅga hṛdaya* are now available in translated form in Tibetan language, but the original Sanskrit texts of the auto-commentary and *vārtika* have gone extinct. They provide detailed anatonomical description of human body. *Rgyud bzi* which literally means *Catus-tantra* and which was originally known in Sanskrit as *Amṛta aṣṭāṅga gyūhopadeśa tantra*, was available in Sanskrit in India. A Tibetan scholar, Vairocana, the disciple of Padma saṁbhava came to India in 8th century A.D. and studied this book from an Ayurvedic physician called Candra-nandana. In this work which has of course undergone some changes after its original Tibetan translation, there is detailed description about the pule examination and anatomy of the human body. The original *Amṛta aṣṭāṅga gyūhopadeśa tantra* is no more available in Sanskrit. This work gives detailed description, among others, of kidneys, lungs, pancreas, liver, spleen and heart. Description of these organs in the extant Ayurvedic classics are either not available, or available only in brief.

On surgery and treatment of diseases of eye, ear, nose and throat (*Śālya tantra* and *Śālākya tantra*) the following classical works were composed :

(1) *Aupadhenava tantra*
(2) *Aurabhra tantra*
(3) *Vṛdha Suśruta tantra*
(4) *Pauṣkalāvata tantra*
(5) *Vaitaraṇa tantra*
(6) *Bhoja tantra*
(7) *Kāravīrya tantra*
(8) *Gopurarakṣita tantra*
(9) *Bhāluki tantra*
(10) *Kāpila tantra*
(11) *Videha tantra*
(12) *Nimi tantra*
(13) *Gautama tantra*
(14) *Kāṅkāyana tantra*
(15) *Gārgya tantra*
(16) *Gālava tantra*
(17) *Sātyaki tantra*
(18) *Śaunaka tantra*
(19) *Karāla tantra*
(20) *Cakṣuṣya tantra* and
(21) *Kṛṣṇātreya tantra.*

Unfortunately, none of these texts are available at present. Only quotations from these texts are available in some of the extant commentaries on Ayurvedic classics. All these works provided detailed anatomical description of the human body.

To sum up : our knowledge of human anatomy from ayurvedic texts at present is imperfect not because they were not available, but because we have lost many books providing anatomical description of human body and some others which are available now do not provide the correct information because during the course of history, they were either redacted, recomposed and wrongfully interpollated.

Dr. Hoernle's "Critical study of Osteology or the Bones of the Human Body" should be studied while keeping the above mentioned facts in view. Information on this aspect of anatomy has been provided and critically scrutinised by him only from such classics which are unfortunately mutilated and from such commentaries the authors of which lived in a period when dissection of dead human body to achieve first hand knowledge of anatomy was considered sinful. None the less, the wealth of knowledge from human anatomy—its extent and accuracy has impressed the author as would be evident from the Preface to this work. The scholarship of the author and the seriousness of his studies can be appreciated by the reader from each paragraph of this monumental work.

Bhagwan Dash

CONTENTS

LIST OF ILLUSTRATIONS

STUDIES IN THE MEDICINE OF ANCIENT INDIA

PART I

THE BONES OF THE HUMAN BODY

SECTION I

INTRODUCTION: MEDICAL SCHOOLS, CHRONOLOGY

§ 1. *Explanation of Terms: Medical Authors, and their Works*

1. The theory of the Ancient Indians regarding the skeleton, or the bony frame of the human body, has been transmitted to us in three different systems. These are the systems of Ātreya, Suśruta, and Vāgbhaṭa.

2. *Ātreya, the Physician.* Ātreya was not so much a surgeon as a physician. He is said to have had six pupils; and his teaching of medicine is said to have been committed to writing by all six in the form of a *Saṁhitā*, or Compendium. It may, therefore, antecedently, be expected that we shall find their six medical compendia to agree in all essential points. At present, however, no more than two of them are known to us. These are the Compendia of Agniveśa and Bheḍa (or Bheḷa).

3. *Charaka and Dṛiḍhabala.* As to the latter, the *Bheḍa Saṁhitā*, we know, at present, of the existence of but a single manuscript (§ 12). The former, the *Agniveśa Saṁhitā*, has had a changeful history. In its original form it has not survived, though it appears to have still existed in the eleventh century when the commentator Chakrapāṇi-

datta (§ 2, cl. 11) quotes it.[1] At present it exists only in a redaction undertaken, at a much later date, by a Kashmir physician, called Charaka. He, however, appears never to have completed it. Possibly death may have intervened. In any case, the concluding portion of the redaction, about one-third of the whole work, was supplied, several centuries afterwards, by another Kashmir physician Dṛiḍhabala, the son of the physician Kapilabala. The entire compendium consists of eight sections (*sthāna*). The portion contributed by Dṛiḍhabala comprises, as we know from the same Chakrapāṇidatta,[2] the last seventeen chapters of the sixth, and the whole of the seventh and eighth sections. In the preparation of this portion, Dṛiḍhabala, as he himself informs us,[3] utilized a large number of existing treatises. Among these may have been Agniveśa's original Compendium, but his main sources, as a comparison of their respective works shows, appear to have been the *Aṣṭāṅga Saṁgraha,* or Summary of Medicine, of Vāgbhaṭa I, and the *Nidāna,* or Pathology, of Mādhava. But Dṛiḍhabala did not limit himself to his complementary task: he also revised the portion written by Charaka himself. He was, as he himself informs us in a passage at the end of the eighth section,[4] a native of a settlement (*pura*), called Panchanada, i. e. five-stream-land. In India the confluence of streams is apt to be treated as a sacred place of pilgrimage (*tīrtha*); and there are there several such places called Panchanada. Anciently one of them appears to have existed in Kashmir, near the confluence of the rivers Jhelam (*Vitastā*) and Sindhu. Its place is indicated by the modern village of Paṇtzinōr (lit. five channels), which lies close to what was the original site of that confluence, before its removal to its present site, in the latter half of the ninth

[1] e.g. in his glosses on the Treatment of Fever (*Jvara-cikitsita*), Tübingen MS., No. 463, fol. 356 *a*, l. 1.

[2] *Ibid.*, fol. 534 *b*.

[3] See *Caraka Saṁhitā*, ed. Jīvānanda Vidyāsagara (1896), p. 827.

[4] The passage is omitted in Jīvānanda's edition of 1877, apparently by some accident. It is given in the edition of 1896, p. 930, ver. 78; also in the edition of Gangādhar, p. 90, as well as in the edition of the two Sen, p. 1055. Its genuineness is attested by Chakrapāṇidatta's commentary, Tübingen MS., No. 463, fol. 639 *a*, l. 2.

century, in the reign of King Avantivarman. It is this Kashmirian Panchanada, which probably was the home of Dṛiḍhabala.[1] The early commentators of the eleventh and thirteenth centuries (e. g. Chakrapāṇidatta and Vijaya Rakshita) often refer to a Kashmirian Recension (*Kāśmīra pāṭha*) when commenting on passages of the earlier portion of the Compendium, i. e. the portion written by Charaka himself.[2] The probability is that in all these cases the reference is to Dṛiḍhabala's Revision of Charaka's work; for in references to the concluding portion of the Compendium, Dṛiḍhabala, as a rule, is quoted by name as its author.[3] It seems clear from their method of quotation that the medical writers of that period were fully aware of the exact share which Dṛiḍhabala had in Charaka's redaction of Agniveśa's original Compendium. At a still earlier period, Mādhava, when he quotes Charaka's redaction in his *Nidāna*, or Pathology, shows no acquaintance with the revised version of it made by Dṛiḍhabala. At the present day the latter's share

[1] See Dr. Stein's Translation of the *Rājataraṅgiṇī*, ch. iv, 248, v, 66 ff.; also his account of the removal of the confluence, vol. ii, pp. 239 ff., 419 ff. The usual identification of Panchanada with the Panjab is untenable; for Dṛiḍhabala clearly indicates a locality (*pura*), not a country, as his home. Dr. Cordier, in his *Récentes Découvertes*, identifies it with 'Panjpur au nord d'Attock, Pañjab', on the authority, as he has informed me privately (letter of January 13, 1905), of 'an Indian Nāgri map lithographed in Benares' and of 'the Indian Post-Office Guide'. I am afraid he has been misled by his authorities. Dr. Stein, whom I asked to verify on the spot, writes to me (letter of March 1, 1905) that there is no Panjpur in the region of Attock, nor in 'the latest edition of the Indian Postal Guide'. There is, however, an isolated ridge known as Panjpīr, or 'Hill of the Five Pīrs', in the Yusufzai Plain, NNW. of Attock, a Muhammadan place of pilgrimage. This appears to have caused the confusion; but between Panjpīr and Panchanadapur there can obviously be no connexion. See also my article on 'the Authorship of the Charaka Saṁhitā' in the *Archiv für die Geschichte der Medizin*, 1907.

[2] e.g. Chakrapāṇidatta, on *Jvara-cikitsita*, in Jīv. ed. (1896), pp. 455, 456; or Tübingen MS., No. 463, fol. 348 *a*, l. 7 and fol. 348 *b*, l. 2. Also Vijaya Rakshita, on *idem*, Jīv. ed., pp. 453–4, in *Madhukoṣa*, Jīv. ed., p. 29; also on *Arśaś-cikitsita*, Jīv. ed., p. 549 (or ed. 1877, p. 574), in *Madhukoṣa*, p. 71; again on *Yakṣma-cikitsita*, Jīv. ed., p. 522, in *Madhukoṣa*, p. 95.

[3] e.g. by Chakrapāṇidatta, in *Sūtra Sthāna*, ed. Harinath Viśarad, p. 123. Also by Vijaya Rakshita, in *Madhukoṣa*, Jīv. ed., pp. 84, 120, 124, 147, 152, 162, 179, 180.

in the redaction of Charaka is practically forgotten in India, and the whole work is there known simply as Charaka's Compendium (*Caraka Saṁhitā*). In the present dissertation it will always (unless otherwise specified) be referred to under that name. For all practical purposes it may be understood that Charaka's Compendium represents Ātreya's system of medicine, as handed down by his pupil Agniveśa. At all events, this is certain in respect of the passages relating to the bones of the human body. For these passages are contained within that portion of the Compendium which is the production of Charaka himself; and the existence as early as the sixth century B.C., of the osteological system contained in them, is guaranteed by references to it in the *Śatapatha Brāhmaṇa*, a Vedic work of that age (§ 42).

4. *Versions of Ātreya's System.* Of Ātreya's theory of the skeleton, then, we possess two versions: one by Agniveśa, contained in Charaka's Compendium, the other by Bheḍa (or Bheḷa), contained in Bheḍa's Compendium. In the present dissertations these two versions will be spoken of as the 'Medical Version' of Ātreya's theory. There exists, however, also another version of that theory, which has been handed down in the ancient Law-book of Yājnavalkya (*Yājñavalkya Dharmaśāstra*), and three other non-medical works (§ 14). This version, in the following pages, will be referred to as the 'Non-medical Version'. By this term, unless otherwise specified, Yājnavalkya's Law-book must always be understood, as being the most reliable source of that version. It will be shown subsequently (§ 24) that there is some good reason for believing that this Non-medical Version really represents a third medical version of Ātreya's theory, going back to another pupil of Ātreya, different from Agniveśa and Bheḍa, but whose name is no longer known.

5. *Suśruta, the Surgeon.* In contrast with Ātreya, the physician, Suśruta was a surgeon. While the former professed general medicine (*Āyurveda*, or the Science of life), the latter made surgery (*Śalya*) his special study. Suśruta, likewise, wrote a Compendium (*Saṁhitā*) of General Medicine (*Āyurveda*), but, agreeably with his profession, its main concern was with surgical matters. It thus treats of some subjects, such as surgical instruments, which are

not noticed at all in the Compendium of Charaka.[1] Moreover, it omits all mention of some diseases in the treatment of which surgery, at that time, did not enter. For this reason, from the point of view of general medicine, Suśruta's Compendium, of course, had the appearance of incompleteness. Hence after some time (§ 2, cl. 5), an anonymous writer composed a Supplement (*Uttara-tantra*) which treated of all the subjects unnoticed by Suśruta. Among the latter were even subjects belonging to minor surgery (*Sālākya*), which circumstance shows that, for example, the surgical treatment of some eye-diseases (as cataract, &c.) was still unknown in the time of Suśruta. At the present day the whole work, inclusive of the Supplement, is known simply as Suśruta's Compendium (*Suśruta Saṁhitā*), and in the present dissertation (unless otherwise specified) it will be quoted under that name. In order to distinguish, however, Suśruta the Supplementor, or Suśruta II, from the original Suśruta, the latter is sometimes designated by Indian commentators 'Suśruta the elder' (*vṛddha Suśruta*). For our present purpose it is important to notice that the passages relating to the bones of the human body occur in the original work of Suśruta the elder. At the same time, it is quite possible that the Supplementor, in addition to his proper task, may have subjected the original portion of the compendium to some amount of revision. But from indications in the before-mentioned *Śatapatha Brāhmaṇa* (§ 42), it is not probable that this occurred in the case of the passages in question.

[1] Suśruta devotes two whole chapters (the seventh and eighth of the *Sūtra Sthāna*) to the description of surgical instruments, and one whole chapter (the twenty-fifth) to the principles of surgical operation. Charaka appears to speak of surgical operations in two places of his Compendium. The operation of laparotomy is described in the *Cikitsita Sthāna*, ch. xviii, verses 179 ff. (Jīv. ed., p. 653); and an operation for the extraction of a dead foetus is briefly mentioned in a clause of the *Śārīra Sthāna*, ch. viii, § 64 (p. 364). In neither of these cases, however, is any surgical instrument named. Moreover, chapter xviii (on *Udara*) was not written by Charaka at all, but by Dṛiḍhabala, who extracted his information from Suśruta's Compendium (*Cik. Sth.*, xiv, pp. 454–5), where the appropriate instrument (*vrīhimukha*, a kind of trocar) is named; and the clause in chapter viii is probably a similar interpolation of the same Dṛiḍhabala.

6. *Vāgbhaṭa I.* Vāgbhaṭa knew both Compendia, of Charaka and of Suśruta. He refers to both these medical writers by name, and quotes, or at least utilizes, their works. In his time Charaka's Compendium was still incomplete, but Suśruta's Compendium had already received its Supplement. This is particularly shown by Vāgbhaṭa's treatment of the diseases of the eye, which are dealt with in Suśruta's Supplement, while in Charaka's incomplete work they are not described at all. Vāgbhaṭa wrote a Compendium on General Medicine, which, on the model of the Supplemented Compendium of Suśruta, he divided into six sections (*sthāna*),[1] and to which he gave the name of Summary of the Octopartite Science (*Aṣṭāṅga Saṁgraha*).[2] The name indicates Vāgbhaṭa's object. It was to gather up into a harmonious whole the more or less conflicting medical systems current in his time, especially those contained in the Compendia of Charaka and Suśruta. In pursuance of this object he introduced, especially with reference to the diseases of the eye, many modifications in the classification and nomenclature which had hitherto been accepted in medicine. It also led him to the adoption of compromises—by no means always successful—of which, as the present dissertation will show, his exposition of the skeleton presents a conspicuous example.

7. *Vāgbhaṭa II.* On the basis of Vāgbhaṭa's Summary a much later namesake of his, whom I shall designate Vāgbhaṭa II, wrote a new work, in the name of which a return is made to the

[1] The concluding section is called *Uttara Sthāna* in Vāgbhaṭa's Summary, but *Uttara Tantra* in Suśruta's Compendium. The latter consists of five *Sthāna* and an *Uttara-tantra*, while the former is made up of six *Sthāna*. The difference in the nomenclature is significant. Suśruta's original work consisted of only five sections (*sthāna*), to which, at a later date, a supplementary treatise (*tantra*) was added. On the other hand, the division into six sections (*sthāna*), inclusive of the supplementary treatise, was first devised by Vāgbhaṭa for his own work.

[2] Indian Medicine is divided into eight branches: (1) Internal Medicine (*Kāya Cikitsā*); (2) Major Surgery (*Śalya*); (3) Minor Surgery (*Śālākya*); (4) Daemonology (*Bhūta-vidyā*); (5) Toxicology (*Viṣa*); (6) Tonics (*Rasāyana*); (7) Aphrodisiacs (*Vṛṣa*); (8) Paedotrophy (*Kumāra-bhṛtya*).

older usage, by calling it the Compendium of the Essence of the Octopartite Science (*Aṣṭāṅga Hṛdaya Saṁhitā*). With reference to him the author of the Summary (*Saṁgraha*) is sometimes called, by Indian commentators, Vāgbhaṭa the elder (*vṛddha Vāgbhaṭa*).

§ 2. *Chronology*

1. It will naturally be expected that some information should be given regarding the chronology of the works and their authors mentioned in the preceding paragraph. Unfortunately there still exists very great incertitude with respect to their absolute, and to some extent even to their relative, dates. On a future occasion I hope to enter more fully into the discussion of the chronological question: for our present purpose the following statement will suffice.

2. *Origin of Medicine.* According to the Indian medical tradition the knowledge of medicine had a twofold origin. On the one hand, it was delivered by the god Indra to the sage Bhāradvāja, and by him to Ātreya: on the other, it descended from Indra to Dhanvantari (also called Divodāsa, and Kāśirāja), and from him to Suśruta. This tradition traces medicine from a mythical, through a semi-mythical, to an historical beginning. It may be taken to mean that Ātreya, the physician, and Suśruta, the surgeon, were understood to be the first founders, in their respective departments, of medicine as a science. Before them there existed only what may be called medicine men, who practised medicine as a witchcraft, and the source of whose knowledge was claimed to be supernatural.

3. *Ātreya and Suśruta.* According to another, non-medical, line of Indian tradition, preserved in the Buddhist *Jātakas*, or Folklore, there existed in India in the age of Buddha two great universities, or seats of learning, in which 'all sciences' (*sabba-sippāni*, or *sarva-śilpāni*), including medicine, were taught by 'professors of world-wide renown' (*disā-pāmokkha ācariya*, or *diśā-prāmukhya ācārya*). These two universities were *Kāśī*, or Benares, in the East, and the still more famous *Takṣaśilā*, or Taxila (on the Jhelam river) in the West. In the latter university, in the time of Buddha or shortly before it, the leading Professor of Medicine

was Ātreya.[1] He, accordingly, should have flourished at some time in the sixth century B. C. As one of the names of Suśruta's teacher is Kāśīrāja, which literally means King of Kāśī, he may not unreasonably be referred to the university of Kāśī, or Benares. This would place the origin of surgery, as a science, in the East of India. As a matter of fact, the origin, at least of ophthalmic surgery, is uniformly placed by Indian tradition in the eastern province of Bihar, being credited to Nemi, the 'lord of Videha' (or Tirhut). Regarding the date of Suśruta we have the following indications. He must have been acquainted with the doctrines of Ātreya. With reference, for example, to the bones of the human body, he introduces his own exposition with a remark pointing out the difference between Ātreya's system and his own in respect of the total number of the bones (see § 27). This proves that Suśruta cannot have been anterior to Ātreya. On the other hand, there are indications in the *Śatapatha Brāhmaṇa*, a secondary Vedic work, that the author of it was acquainted with the doctrines of Suśruta (see §§ 42, 56, 60, 61). The exact date of that work is not known, but it is with good reason referred to the sixth century B.C. (see § 42). The probability, therefore, appears to be that Suśruta was a rather younger contemporary of Ātreya, or, let us say, a contemporary of Ātreya's pupil Agniveśa.

4. *The Atharva Veda.* As bearing on the very early date of both Ātreya and Suśruta, we have a rather significant piece of evidence in the *Atharva Veda*. That work, in its tenth book, contains a hymn on the creation of man (see § 43), in which the several parts of the skeleton are carefully and orderly enumerated in striking agreement more especially with the system of Ātreya as contained in Charaka's Compendium.[2] The date of the *Atharva Veda* is not exactly known, but it belongs to the most ancient, or primary Vedic, literature of India. It cannot be placed later

[1] The famous physician Jīvaka, a contemporary of Buddha, is stated to have studied medicine in the Taxila University, under Ātreya (see Rockhill's *Life of Buddha*, pp. 65, 96).

[2] There are numerous other passages of a similar character in the *Atharva Veda*. The whole evidence is reviewed by me in the *Journal of the Royal Asiatic Society* for 1906, p. 915 ff., and for 1907, p. 1 ff.

than the sixth century B.C., because references to it are found in secondary Vedic works, such as the *Śatapatha Brāhmaṇa* above referred to. The larger portion of it (Books I–XVIII), indeed, admittedly belongs to a much earlier period, possibly as early as about 1000 B.C.; and the hymn in question is included in this older portion. Moreover, within that portion it belongs to a division (Books VIII–XII) which bears a distinctly hieratic character. It thus takes us back to that prehistoric, or semi-mythical age of the 'medicine men' who combined the functions of priest and physician. This period, as already stated (clause 2), Indian tradition represents by the name of Bhāradvāja, and to him it actually ascribes the authorship of one of the hymns (the twelfth of the tenth book) of that hieratic division.[1]

5. *Charaka and Nāgārjuna.* According to a Buddhist tradition [2] Charaka was the trusted physician of the celebrated 'Indo-scythian' King Kanishka. Unfortunately the date of Kanishka himself is still in dispute, opinions varying from the first century B.C. to the third century A.D.[3] The preponderance of evidence appears to me in favour of Kanishka's reigning in the middle of the second century, *circa* 125–150 A.D. There exists an Indian medical tradition which assigns the revised and supplemented edition of Suśruta's original work to Nāgārjuna.[4] If he should be the well-known Buddhist patriarch of that name who is said to have been a contemporary of King Kanishka, his date would practically coincide with that of Charaka. Accordingly the original Compendia of Agniveśa and Suśruta would have been revised and re-edited at much the same time.

[1] On the date of the *Atharva Veda*, see pp. cxl–clxi in Professor Lanman's edition of Whitney's Translation of the *Atharva Veda Saṁhitā*; also Professor Macdonell's *Sanskrit Literature*, pp. 185–201.

[2] Discovered by Professor Sylvain Levi, *Indian Antiquary*, vol. xxxii, p. 382; *Vienna Oriental Journal*, vol. xi, p. 164.

[3] See V. A. Smith, *Early History of India*, pp. 225–6; Dr. Fleet, in *Journal of the Royal Asiatic Society*, 1906, p. 979 ff.; Mr. D. R. Bhandarkar, in *Journal of the Bombay Branch of the Royal Asiatic Society*, vol. xx, p. 269 ff.

[4] See Ḍallana's Commentary to Suśruta's Compendium (ed. Jīvānanda), p. 2; also Dr. Cordier's *Récentes Découvertes*, pp. 12, 13.

6. *Vāgbhaṭa the Elder.* Regarding the relation of Vāgbhaṭa I to Charaka and Suśruta the elder, his posteriority is proved by his referring to both these writers by name, and sometimes even quoting their actual words.[1] His relation to Suśruta II, the Supplementor, is less certain. So far as known to me, he never actually quotes from him; still his Summary (*Saṁgraha*) presents numerous indications of a decided posteriority. His treatment, e. g. of the diseases of the eye, though in its general lines agreeing with that of the Supplementor, yet in its more artificial and scholastic method of classification—Vāgbhaṭa I counting ninety-four diseases against the seventy-six in the Supplementor's more natural system—suggests his posteriority to Suśruta II The place assigned to Vāgbhaṭa I by later Indian Medicine, in its traditional series of the three men, Charaka, Suśruta, Vāgbhaṭa, makes in the same direction; for there can be no doubt that, in that series, the term Suśruta refers to the Supplemented Compendium which is now known under Suśruta's name. If Suśruta II is rightly placed in the second century A. D., as a contemporary of Charaka, Vāgbhaṭa I is, of course, also posterior to him. Indeed, there is good reason for placing Vāgbhaṭa I as late as the early seventh century A. D. The Buddhist pilgrim, Itsing, who resided ten years in the Nalanda monastery (in Bihar), from about 675–685 A. D., states in his *Record of Buddhist Practices* that the 'eight arts (i. e. branches of medicine, *ante*, footnote 2, p. 6) formerly existed in eight books, but lately a man epitomized them, and made them into one bundle (or book)', and he adds that 'all physicians in the five parts of India (i. e. the whole of India) practise according to his book'.[2] Seeing that Vāgbhaṭa I's Compendium bears that precise name of 'Epitome (or Summary, *Saṁgraha*) of the Octopartite Science', the conclusion seems warranted that Itsing was referring to that Summary. If so, Vāgbhaṭa I cannot have preceded Itsing by any very long interval of time; nor may the interval be

[1] By name, e. g. in *Saṁgraha*, Bombay ed., vol. i, p. 246; vol. ii, p. 421. Again quoted from Charaka, *ibid.*, vol. i, pp. 20, 93; vol. ii, pp. 212, 213, *et passim*; from Suśruta I, *ibid.*, vol. i, pp. 109, 121, 177, 247; vol. ii, p. 303, *et passim.*

[2] See Professor Takakusu's Translation, p. 128; also *Journal Royal Asiatic Soc.*, 1907, p. 413 ff.

made too short, because time was necessary for the diffusion of the Summary as a standard work 'throughout India'. Accordingly Vāgbhaṭa I may be placed early in the seventh century, or about 625 A. D. This estimate of his date is supported by certain structural features of his Summary, which are explained in §§ 38–40. It is, further, in agreement with the progressive decadence in the knowledge and practice of anatomy and surgery, which is apparent in the medical writings subsequent to the time of Suśruta II. One of the results of the present dissertation is to bring out the contrast between the treatment of the bones of the human body in the hands of Suśruta and Vāgbhaṭa I. While that of the former exhibits a remarkable familiarity with the structure of the skeleton, the latter's treatment of the subject is so replete with inconsistencies and incongruities as to show that in the time of Vāgbhaṭa I practical anatomy had fallen into disuse. At a still later time, in the Compendium of Vāgbhaṭa II, the information about the skeleton is limited to the bare statement that the total number of bones is 360.[1] Again, the surgical treatment of certain diseases of the eye, such as cataract, which occupies a considerable space in the Supplement (*Uttara Tantra*) of Suśruta II, is much less prominent in the Summary (*Saṁgraha*) of Vāgbhaṭa I, while in the subsequent writings of Mādhava, Dṛiḍhabala, and Vāgbhaṭa II it is altogether ignored. The dates of the latter three authors fall somewhere, at no great intervals, in the period from the 7th–9th centuries A. D.; and facts, such as those just mentioned, indicate the place of Vāgbhaṭa I to be intermediate, yet much nearer to them than to Suśruta II, and thus tend to confirm the assignment of the former to the early seventh century A. D.

7. *Mādhava, Dṛiḍhabala, and Vāgbhaṭa II.* With regard to the chronological position of the three authors, Mādhava, Dṛiḍhabala, and Vāgbhaṭa II, two points are quite certain. In the first place, all three are posterior to Vāgbhaṭa I. This, to start with, is a necessary inference from their attitude, as above explained (clause 6), towards anatomy. But

[1] Contained in half a verse, *Aṣṭāṅga Hṛdaya, Śārīra Sthāna*, ch. iii, ver. 16 *a* (1st ed., vol. i, p. 548).

there is positive proof. Mādhava cites Vāgbhaṭa I by name, and also quotes from him anonymously.[1] Dṛiḍhabala, though he does not name Vāgbhaṭa I as his authority, quotes from him very frequently.[2] Also his total of ninety-six diseases of the eye is based on Vāgbhaṭa I's total of ninety-four (see p. 13). As to Vāgbhaṭa II, according to his own statement,[3] his Compendium (*Aṣṭāṅga Hṛdaya Saṁhitā*) is based on the Summary (*Aṣṭāṅga Saṁgraha*) of Vāgbhaṭa I, and reproduces it copiously. In the second place, all three are anterior to Chakrapāṇidatta, whose date is about 1060 A.D. The latter names Dṛiḍhabala, and expressly specifies the extent of his contribution to Charaka's Compendium.[4] He also frequently quotes Dṛiḍhabala as the author of the last section (*Siddhi Sthāna*) of that Compendium.[5] As to Vāgbhaṭa II, quotations from him, by name, are very numerous in Chakrapāṇidatta's Commentary on Charaka's Compendium.[6] Mādhava's anteriority to Chakrapāṇidatta necessarily follows from the fact of his preceding (see p. 13) both Dṛiḍhabala

[1] By name, in *Siddhayoga*, i, 27, cf. *Saṁgraha*, vol. ii, p. 1, l. 8. Quoted, in *Nidāna* (ed. Jīv.), ii, 22, 23, cf. *Saṁgraha*, vol. i, p. 266, ll. 2–5.

[2] *Caraka Saṁhitā* (ed. Jīv., 1896), *Cikitsita Sthāna*, xvi, ver. 31, p. 624, cf. *Saṁgraha*, vol. ii, p. 26, ll. 7, 8; *ibid.*, xvi, verses 53 ff., p. 626, cf. *Saṁgraha*, vol. ii, p. 27, ll. 8 ff.; *ibid.*, xvi, ver. 64 *b*, p. 627, cf. *Saṁgraha*, vol. ii, p. 27, l. 19; *ibid.*, xvi, verses 76 ff., p. 628, cf. *Saṁgraha*, vol. ii, p. 28, ll. 20 ff.; *ibid.*, xvi, ver. 97, p. 638, cf. *Saṁgraha*, vol. ii, p. 108, ll. 15 ff.; *et passim.*

[3] See *Aṣṭāṅga Hṛdaya*, *Uttara Sthāna*, ch. 40, ver. 82 (1st ed., vol. ii, p. 826).

[4] See Chakrapāṇidatta's Commentary, in Tübingen MS., no. 463, fol. 534 *b*.

[5] e.g. Chakrapāṇidatta's Commentary (ed. Visarad), p. 123, ll. 18, 19, cf. *Caraka Saṁhitā* (ed. Jīv., 1896), *Siddhi Sthāna*, vi, ver. 3, p. 887; *ibid.*, p. 238, ll. 15, 16, cf. *Siddhi Sthāna*, vi, ver. 19, p. 888.

[6] e.g. in Visarad's edition, p. 15, ll. 17, 18, cf. *Aṣṭāṅga Hṛdaya*, *Sūtra Sthāna*, ch. i, ver. 3 (1st ed., vol. i, p. 6); *ibid.*, p. 124, ll. 12, 13, cf. *Aṣṭ. Hṛd.*, *ibid.*, ch. xiii, ver. 33 (vol. i, p. 282); *ibid.*, p. 250, ll. 22, 23, cf. *Aṣṭ. Hṛd.*, *Nidāna Sthāna*, ch. x, ver. 21 (vol. i, p. 772).—As Vāgbhaṭa II so extensively reproduces the text of Vāgbhaṭa I, it is important to note that in this, as well as in the preceding footnotes concerning Mādhava and Dṛiḍhabala, only such passages have been selected as evidence as are found only in the *Saṁgraha* of Vāgbhaṭa I, or in the *Saṁhitā* of Vāgbhaṭa II, according as the case in hand required.

and Vāgbhaṭa II. These three medical authors, accordingly, must have their place somewhere between the seventh and eleventh centuries A. D.

8. *Mādhava.* Coming now to the chronological place of Mādhava, Dṛiḍhabala, and Vāgbhaṭa II, relatively to one another—a point still involved in much obscurity—the trend of the available evidence appears to make for the following positions. In the first place: Mādhava is anterior to Dṛiḍhabala. There are two facts which seem to be conclusive on this point. One concerns the enumeration of the diseases of the eye. Suśruta II, giving a detailed list, counts seventy-six such diseases, while Vāgbhaṭa I, recasting the list of Suśruta II, makes out a total of ninety-four. Mādhava, who elects to abide by Suśruta II's method of counting, nevertheless increases the total to seventy-eight,[1] by adding two diseases of the eyelashes. Vāgbhaṭa II simply adopts the list of Vāgbhaṭa I. Dṛiḍhabala, attempting a compromise, states the total to be ninety-six.[2] He does not explain how he arrived at that total, nor, indeed, does he give any details at all, but simply refers the curious on the subject to other medical authorities. In these circumstances it may be

[1] The memorial verses, as commonly printed in Mādhava's *Nidāna*, giving a total of seventy-six, are spurious and false. Jīvānanda's edition gives them at the end (p. 347), but Udoy Chand Dutt's edition at the beginning (p. 220) of the chapters on the diseases of the eye. Moreover, they do not agree with Mādhava's own text; for they omit the two diseases of the eyelashes (*pakṣma-kopa* and *pakṣma-śāta*), mentioned by Mādhava at the end of the last of those chapters (Jīv., p. 347, verses 22, 23; U.C. Dutt, p. 236). Adding these two diseases, the total becomes seventy-eight. The various systems of enumerating the diseases of the eye adopted by Suśruta II, Vāgbhaṭa I, Mādhava, and Dṛiḍhabala respectively, are very complicated. It is impossible, in the present case, to state more than the simple facts. In a subsequent dissertation on the diseases of the eye I hope to have an opportunity of explaining the details.

[2] In *Caraka Saṃhitā, Cikitsita Sthāna*, ch. xxvi, ver. 222 (Jīv., p. 761). The edition published by the two Sens reads seventy-six (p. 884, l. 4); but this is a mere reprint from Gangādhar's Berhampore edition (p. 575), for which there is no known manuscript authority. It appears to be an 'emendation' of Gangādhar himself. All existing MSS. read ninety-six; e.g. Tübingen MSS., No. 458, fol. 632 *a*, l. 2; and No. 459, fol. 216 *b*, l. 5; India Office MSS., No. 335, fol. 419 *b*, l. 1, and No. 359, fol. 153 *a*, l. 7; Deccan College MS., No. 925, fol. 334 *a*, l. 6.

concluded that Dṛiḍhabala obtained his total of ninety-six by adopting Vāgbhaṭa I's total of ninety-four (which corresponds to Suśruta II's total of seventy-six) and adding to it the two new diseases set up by Mādhava. It thus follows that Mādhava is anterior to Dṛiḍhabala. The second fact concerns the so-called Kashmir Recension (*Kāśmīra-pāṭha*) of Charaka's Compendium. Vijaya Rakshita, in his commentary (called *Madhukoṣa*) on Mādhava's Pathology (*Nidāna*), notices several passages, cited by Mādhava from Charaka's Compendium, where the Kashmir Recension differs from the Recension quoted by Mādhava. The inference is that Mādhava cites the passages as written by Charaka himself; that the Kashmir Recension was not known to him, and that, in fact, that Recension was not yet in existence. Seeing that the Kashmir Recension was the work of the Kashmir physician Dṛiḍhabala (§ 1), it follows that Dṛiḍhabala is posterior to Mādhava. No doubt every link in this chain of inference possesses no more than probable force; still, the cumulative effect of the two arguments is to raise the presumption that, as a fact, Mādhava is anterior to Dṛiḍhabala.[1]

9. *Dṛiḍhabala.* In the second place, Dṛiḍhabala is anterior to Vāgbhaṭa II. The latter, in one of the concluding verses of his Compendium,[2] refers to the very insufficient character of the information on the diseases of the eye to be found in Charaka's Compendium as compared with that given in Suśruta's Compendium. Seeing that that information is contained in one of Dṛiḍhabala's complementary chapters,[3] Vāgbhaṭa's remark proves that he was

[1] It is true that the commentator Vijaya Rakshita (*c.* 1240 A. D.), in an explanatory statement on *Nidāna* (ed. Jīv., p. 147), xxii, 5, ll. 1, 2 = *Caraka Saṁhitā, Cikitsita Sthāna*, xxviii, ver. 24 (Jīv., p. 773), apparently implies the posteriority of Mādhava to Dṛiḍhabala. But it should be observed that the object of Vijaya Rakshita is not to make a chronological, but an exegetical statement. The chronological implication may not have been intended by him, even assuming that in the thirteenth century the exact chronological relation of Mādhava to Dṛiḍhabala was still within the knowledge of medical writers.

[2] See *Aṣṭāṅga Hṛdaya, Uttara Sthāna*, ch. xl, ver. 83; in the 1st ed., vol. ii, p. 826.

[3] Viz. the twenty-sixth chapter on *Trimarmīya*, in the *Caraka Saṁhitā, Cikitsita Sthāna*, verses 221–56 (Jīv. ed., 1896, pp. 761–4). The fact that Vāgbhaṭa II simply speaks of Charaka's Compendium

acquainted with Dṛiḍhabala's completion of Charaka's Compendium. Moreover, Vāgbhaṭa II not infrequently revises the versified form in which prose passages had been quoted by Dṛiḍhabala from the Summary (*Saṁgraha*) of Vāgbhaṭa I.[1] Lastly, it may be noted that Aruṇadatta, in his commentary on Vāgbhaṭa II's Compendium, expressly refers to Dṛiḍhabala's edition of the Compendium of Charaka as the source of one of the verses of Vāgbhaṭa II.[2] This last point is particularly effective. The verse in question occurs in the introductory portion of the nineteenth chapter of Charaka's Compendium on the Treatment of Chronic Diarrhoea[3] (§ 99, cl. 2). In that portion Dṛiḍhabala summarizes in versified form the prose account of the subject in the Anatomical Section of the Summary of Vāgbhaṭa I.[4] That it is really a summary of Vāgbhaṭa I's account is obvious from the fact that his terms and phrases are as far as possible retained by Dṛiḍhabala. Vāgbhaṭa II still further summarizes the summary of Dṛiḍhabala; and that his doubly summarized account is really based on the latter, but not on Vāgbhaṭa I, is shown by the fact that it contains none of the terms and phrases of the latter, but retains intact three of the verses (among them the

without any reference to Dṛiḍhabala's authorship of the chapter in question creates no difficulty. As observed in § 1, the whole work, inclusive of Dṛiḍhabala's complement, came to be known simply as Charaka's Compendium; and it is not at all uncommon to find Dṛiḍhabala quoted as 'Charaka'; e.g. by Vijaya Rakshita in his *Madhukoṣa* (Jīv., 1901), pp. 159, 161, 163.

[1] e.g. the prose direction in *Saṁgraha, Cikitsita Sthāna*, ch. xvii (vol. ii, p. 99, l. 23), is expressed by Dṛiḍhabala in a single verse (*Caraka Saṁhitā, Cik.*, xviii, ver. 85 *a*; Jīv., p. 646), while Vāgbhaṭa II gives it in two verses (*Aṣṭāṅga Hṛdaya, Cik.*, xv, verses 96 *b*, 97 *a*, in 1st ed., vol. ii, p. 285). Other examples are: Vāgbhaṭa II in *Cikitsita*, xv, verses 61 *b*–63 (vol. ii, p. 279) and verses 91 *b*, 92 (vol. ii, p. 284), compared with Dṛiḍhabala, in *Cik.*, xviii, verses 67 *b*–69 (Jīv., pp. 644–5) and verses 80, 81 (Jīv., p. 645), and with Vāgbhaṭa I's prose in *Cik.*, xvii (vol. ii, p. 98, ll. 9–12, and p. 99, ll. 21–23).

[2] See *Aṣṭāṅga Hṛdaya* (1st ed.), vol. i, p. 571, l. 19. The verse in question is 62 *b*, 63 *a*, in the third chapter of the *S'ārīra Sthāna*.

[3] See *Cikitsita Sthāna, Grahaṇī-roga*, xix, ver. 14, in Jīv. ed., 1896, p. 656.

[4] See *Aṣṭāṅga Saṁgraha, Sārīra Sthāna*, ch. vi, in the Bombay ed., vol. i, pp. 230 ff.

verse in question) of Dṛiḍhabala.[1] This state of things was evidently realized by Aruṇadatta, for, as already stated, he expressly mentions Dṛiḍhabala as the source of Vāgbhaṭa II.

10. *Their Dates.* The evidence of Arabic sources points to the seventh or eighth century for Mādhava, and that of Tibetan and other sources to the eighth or ninth century for Vāgbhaṭa II.[2] According to the evidence, already explained, Dṛiḍhabala takes his place intermediately between Mādhava and Vāgbhaṭa II. Accordingly it is probable that all these three medical writers come in the period from the seventh to the ninth century, at no very great interval from one another. In any case none of them can be later than *c.* 1060 A. D., the date of Chakrapāṇidatta.

11. *Commentators and their Dates.* Of early commentators on the Compendia of Charaka and Suśruta, and on the Summary of Vāgbhaṭa I, whose works have come down to us, the following may be mentioned.

On Charaka's Compendium we have Chakrapāṇidatta's Commentary, called *Caraka Tātparya Ṭīkā* (i. e. Explanation of Charaka's Meaning) or *Ayurveda Dīpikā* (i. e. Light on General Medicine). Its author is known to have lived about 1060 A. D.

On Suśruta's Compendium we have Ḍallana's commentary, called *Nibandha Saṁgraha*, or Summary of Commentaries. The earliest known quotations of this work are by Hemādri and Vāchaspati,[3] who lived about 1260 A. D.; and as Ḍallana himself quotes Chakrapāṇidatta, he should be placed in the twelfth century. He frequently quotes also a commentary (*pañjikā* or *candrikā*) by Gayadāsa (or simply Gayin), called *Nyāya Candrikā*, or Reasoned Elucidation. Gayadāsa, therefore, cannot be placed later than the eleventh century, and he may have been a contemporary of Chakrapāṇidatta, seeing that neither appears to quote from the other.[4]

[1] Namely, verses 59, 60, 62 in *Aṣṭāṅga Hṛdaya, Śārīra Sthāna* ch. iii (1st ed., vol. i, pp. 566, 567, 569).

[2] For details and authorities see Professor Jolly's *Indian Medicine*, §§ 5, 6, pp. 7–9.

[3] According to information by letter (October 30, 1904) from Dr. P. Cordier.

[4] See Professor Jolly in the *Journal of the German Oriental Society*, vol. lviii, p. 114 ff.; and Dr. P. Cordier's *Récentes Découvertes*, p. 15.

On the Compendium of Vāgbhaṭa II we have a commentary by Aruṇadatta, called *Sarvāṅga Sundarī* (i. e. Excellent in all Branches of Medicine).[1] On the Pathology (*Nidāna*) of Mādhava there exists a commentary, called *Madhukoṣa* (i. e. Receptacle of Honey), the joint work of Vijaya Rakshita and his pupil Śrīkaṇṭhadatta, and another by Vāchaspati, called *Āṭaṅka Darpaṇa* (i. e. Mirror of Diseases). The latter, as he himself states (in verse 4 of his Introduction), consulted the *Madhukoṣa* for the purpose of writing his own commentary, and Vijaya Rakshita controverts a certain doctrine of Aruṇadatta regarding the structure of the eye.[2] Vāchaspati further states (in verse 5 of his Introduction) that his father Pramoda was chief physician at the court of 'Mahamada Hammīra', that is, of the Amīr Muizzuddīn Muhammad (the celebrated Muhamed Ghori) who reigned in Delhi from 1193 to 1205 A. D. Moreover, Vijaya Rakshita quotes Guṇākara who wrote the *Yogaratnamālā* in 1239 A. D.[3] Accordingly we obtain the following approximate dates:

Aruṇadatta, about 1220 A. D.
Vijaya Rakshita, about 1240 A. D.
Vāchaspati, about 1260 A. D.

12. *Bhāskara Bhaṭṭa and Bhava Miśra.* To a slightly earlier date than that of Chakrapāṇidatta belongs a medical author, Bhāskara Bhaṭṭa. He appears to have lived about 1000 A. D.[4] He wrote a tract on Anatomy, called *Śārīra Padminī* (i. e. Lotus among Works on Anatomy). The state-

For further information on the commentaries on Suśruta's Compendium, see my Article in the *Journal of the Royal Asiatic Society of London* for 1906, p. 283.

[1] The title makes a pun: it also means 'a woman beautiful in all her limbs'.

[2] It concerns the true position of the so-called *bāhya paṭala* or outer cover of the eyeball, i. e. the cornea *plus* aqueous humour. See *Aṣṭāṅga Hṛdaya, Uttara Sthāna*, ch. xii, ver. 1 (in 1st ed., vol. ii, p. 516).

[3] Information by letter (October 30, 1904) from Dr. P. Cordier. The quotation occurs in the *Madhukoṣa* on *Nidāna*, v, 7 (Jīv., p. 68). On the date of Guṇākara, see Peterson's *Report*, 1886–92, p. xxvi.

[4] See *Epigraphia Indica*, vol. i, p. 340. The *Śārīra Padminī* was brought to notice by Dr. P. Cordier in his *Récentes Découvertes*, p. 30.

ments on the skeleton, contained in this treatise, reproduce the doctrine of Suśruta, as modified by Vāgbhaṭa I (see § 36).

A very much later author, who also reproduces Suśruta's doctrine on the skeleton, and who will be mentioned occasionally in the following pages, is Bhāva Miśra. He lived in the sixteenth century, and wrote a voluminous compilation, of no originality, from previous medical writings, under the name of *Bhāva Prakāśa* (i. e. Manifestation of the Truth).

SECTION II

TEXT-CRITICAL. THE RECORDS

A. The System of Ātreya-Charaka

§ 3. *Charaka's Statement, and its Recensions*

The Medical Version of Ātreya's system of the bones of the human body, as handed down by Charaka, is contained in the beginning of the seventh chapter (*adhyāya*) of the fourth or Anatomical Section (*Śārīra Sthāna*) of his Compendium.

There exist two recensions of Charaka's statement. One is contained in the edition of the Compendium which was printed by Jīvānanda Vidyāsagara in Calcutta in 1877, where it is found on page 370, lines 5–19. The other occurs in Gangādhar's edition, page 186, lines 11–22, printed in Berhampore, 1879 (*Bahrampura. saṁvat* 1936). These two recensions differ so widely from each other that it is necessary to inquire into their respective authorities.

The recension of Jīvānanda has the following witnesses in its favour. In the first place, it has the support of all accessible manuscripts. I have been able to examine the following nine:

1. The two Tübingen University MSS., M. a. I. 458 and 459 (Cat., Nos. 141, 142). They come from Benares, whence they were procured by myself for the late Professor von Roth in 1873. The original MS. from which No. 142 was copied is dated in *saṁvat* 1778, i. e. 1721 A. D.

2. The two India Office MSS., Nos. 335 and 881 (Cat., Nos. 2637 and 2640), originally belonging to the Colebrooke Collection, and therefore probably from Calcutta. No. 2640 is dated 1806 A. D.

3. The two Deccan College MSS., No. 368 (Bhandarkar's Report of 1882–3) and No. 925 (Kathavate's Report of 1891–5); from Western India; dates unknown.[1]

4. Two Kashmir MSS., in Śāradā characters. One, No. 3266 (p. 182 of Dr. Stein's Catalogue), belongs to the Jammu Library, and was excerpted for me through Dr. Stein's kind intermediation. The excerpt from the other I owe to the kindness of Dr. P. Cordier (see his *Récentes Découvertes*, p. 9). The dates of these two MSS. are unknown; but as both are written on paper they must be comparatively modern.

5. The Alwar Palace Library MS., No. 1624, an excerpt from which was transmitted to me by the kindness of Major P. T. A. Spence, the British Political Agent.

It should be observed that these nine MSS. come from widely separated Indian localities. They are, therefore, independent witnesses—a fact which enhances their testimony.

In the second place, the recension of Jīvānanda has the support of the oldest existing commentary of Chakrapāṇidatta (*c.* 1060 A. D.). A considerable number of names of more or less ancient glossators or commentators is known, for a list of which Dr. P. Cordier's *Récentes Découvertes*, pp. 10, 11, may be consulted. But the commentary of Chakrapāṇidatta is the only one that now survives, and even of it, manuscripts are extremely rare, and all are incomplete. I was able to consult the Tübingen University MS., M. a. I. 463 (Cat., No. 146). It fortunately contains Chakrapāṇidatta's glosses on Charaka's statement in question. These glosses are based entirely on the recension which is printed in Jīvānanda's edition, and while they refer to various interpretations of it, they give no indication whatsoever of the existence of a recension even faintly resembling that of Gangādhar's edition.

In the third place, the recension of Jīvānanda has the support of the Medical Version of Ātreya's system as handed down by Bheḍa (or Bheḷa), as well as of the Non-medical Version of that system as preserved in Yājnavalkya's Law-book and other non-medical works (see § 14). Seeing that all three versions—the

[1] The loan of these two MSS. I owe to the kindness of Professor K. P. Pathak, of the Deccan College.

Medical Versions of Charaka and Bheḍa, and the Non-medical Version—equally profess to present the teaching of Ātreya, their almost verbal agreement affords the strongest testimony in favour of Jīvānanda's recension of the Version of Charaka.

On the other hand, the recension of Gangādhar—so far as I have been able to ascertain—is absolutely destitute of all support. It first appears in the Berhampore edition of 1879, published by Dharanidhar Ray. Neither Gangādhar nor Dharanidhar refers to any MSS., nor does either mention any *variae lectiones*. The same recension next appears in the Calcutta edition of Avinās Chandra Kaviratna (1884). He does not state his sources; but, to all appearance, he simply reprints from the Berhampore edition. The same recension once more appears in the Calcutta edition of Debendranath Sen and Upendranath Sen (1897). In their preface the joint editors profess not only to have collected, with much trouble and expense, 'many manuscripts from Kāsī [Benares], Kashmir, Bombay, Draviḍa [Madras?], Poona, and other places,' but also to have consulted some very old (*pracīna-tama*) and correct (*viśuddha*) MSS. in their own possession. It will be well to receive this statement with considerable reserve; for it is well known that MSS. of Charaka's Compendium are neither so common, nor so old, nor so correct as the joint editors suggest. They very rarely quote any *variae lectiones*, and in the few cases in which they do so they never refer to any particular MS. authority. Thus in the whole Anatomical Section, comprising eight chapters (seventy-six pages in print), they mention only two unimportant, and unidentified variants (in the eighth chapter, p. 429). In the seventh chapter of that section which contains the statement on the skeleton, they mention no variants at all, nor give any indication whatsoever of their being aware of the existence of an entirely discrepant recension. Under these circumstances, despite the claim made in the preface, the conclusion is unavoidable that the joint edition is essentially nothing more than a reprint from Avinās Chandra's, and ultimately from Gangādhar's editions. The three aforesaid editions are prints produced in Calcutta, or at least in Bengal. Recently the same recension has been published in Bombay, by Sankara Shastri, in a cheap edition.

This fact, at first sight, might be thought to suggest the existence of some MS. source in Bombay, but cheap editions do not go to the trouble and expense of collating MSS., but usually reprint already existing editions; and there can be no reasonable doubt that the Bombay edition is but a reprint from its Calcutta predecessors.

So far it has been impossible to trace Gangādhar's recension back any farther than his own Berhampore edition. When we add—what will be shown in detail in subsequent paragraphs (§§ 9, 10)—that that recension is not only full of incongruities and inconsistencies, but that it also presupposes a knowledge of the system of Suśruta, some of whose peculiar terms (e. g. *kūrca*, or cluster of bones) it adopts, the conclusion is irresistible that, in all probability, it reproduces no genuine text of any Charaka MS., but is an ill-considered attempt of Gangādhar himself to reconstruct or (as he thought) improve the text of the, perhaps grossly incorrect, MS., or MSS. of Charaka's Compendium, which he may have had at his disposal in the preparation of his edition. The spurious recension, thus originated, was afterwards unquestioningly and thoughtlessly adopted by Gangādhar's Bengal successors. All the more credit is due to Jīvānanda for preserving, in his earlier edition of 1877, the genuine recension of the text of Charaka's Compendium; and it is much to be regretted that in his recent re-edition of 1896 (p. 351, clause 5) he should have been misled into substituting the spurious recension of Gangādhar.

§ 4. *The genuine Recension of Charaka*

The genuine traditional recension of the statement of Charaka on the bones of the human body runs as follows (Original Text in § 71):

'The body consists of the following parts (*aṅga*): the two arms (*bāhu*), the two legs (*sakthi*), the head and neck (*śiro-grīva*), and the trunk (*antarādhi*). These make up the sexipartite (*ṣaḍaṅga*) body. Inclusive of the teeth and nails, it has three hundred and sixty bones. These are

1. 32 teeth (*danta*).
2. 32 sockets (*ulūkhala*) of the teeth.
3. 20 nails (*nakha*).

4. 60 phalanges (*aṅguli*) in the hands and feet.
5. 20 long bones (*śalākā*) of the hands and feet.
6. 4 bases of the long bones (*śalāk-ādhiṣṭhāna*).
7. 2 heels (*pārṣṇi*).
8. 4 ankle-bones (*gulpha*) of the two feet.[1]
9. 2 wrist-bones (*maṇika*) of the two hands.[1]
10. 4 bones of the two forearms (*aratni*).
11. 4 bones of the two legs (*jaṅgha*).
12. 2 knee-caps (*jānu*).
13. 2 elbow-pans (*jānu-kapālikā*).[1]
14. 2 hollow bones (*nalaka*) of the two thighs (*ūru*).
15. 2 hollow bones (*nalaka*) of the two arms (*bāhu*).
16 *a*. 2 shoulders (*aṁsa*).
16 *b*. 2 shoulder-blades (*aṁsa-phalaka*).
17. 2 collar-bones (*akṣaka*).
18. 1 windpipe (*jatru*).
19. 2 palatal cavities (*tāl-ūṣaka*).
20. 2 hip-blades (*śroṇi-phalaka*).
21. 1 pubic bone (*bhag-āsthi*).
22. 45 back-bones (*pṛṣṭha-gat-āsthi*).
23. 15 bones of the neck (*grīvā*).
24. 14 bones of the breast (*uras*).
25 *a*. 24 ribs (*pārśvaka*) in the two sides.
25 *b*. 24 sockets (*sthālaka*) of the ribs.
25 *c*. 24 tubercles (*arbuda*) fitting into the sockets.
26. 1 (lower) jaw-bone (*hanv-asthi*), or chin.
27. 2 basal tie-bones of the (lower) jaw (*hanu-mūla-bandhana*).
28. 1 bone constituting the nose, prominences of the cheeks, and brows (*nāsikā-gaṇḍakūṭa-lalāṭa*).
29. 2 temples (*śaṅkha*).
30. 4 cranial pan-shaped bones (*śiraḥ-kapāla*).

These are the three hundred and sixty bones, inclusive of the teeth and nails.'

§ 5. *Ancient Inconsistency*

There is a slight inconsistency in the statement of Charaka which it may be well to point out at once. In the introductory clause which enumerates the six *aṅga*, or constitutive parts of the body, Charaka places these parts into three divisions,

[1] The terms 'ankle-bone' and 'wrist-bone', here and throughout this dissertation, signify the malleoli and styloid processes respectively; also, 'elbow-pan' signifies the olecranon process.

viz. (1) the extremities (two arms and two legs), (2) the head and neck, and (3) the trunk. That Charaka looked upon the head and neck as constituting but one division, apart from the extremities and the trunk, is shown by his using a peculiar compound word *śiro-grīva*, made up from *śiras*, head, and *grīvā*, neck, to indicate that division—a circumstance which the commentator Chakrapāṇidatta is careful to point out (§ 11). Now, though Charaka does not (as Suśruta and Vāgbhaṭa I do, §§ 28, 37) expressly state that his enumeration of the bones follows the three divisions, yet certain divisions are clearly discernible in it: only they are not quite consistent with his introductory clause. First, we have a small preliminary division, comprising Nos. 1–3, the teeth, their sockets, and the nails, altogether eighty-four bones. That these form a kind of supplemental division is, indeed, indicated by Charaka himself in the introductory clause. Next, there comes the first proper division, comprising Nos. 4–15. It refers to the four extremities, and includes 108 bones. Thirdly, we have the second division, referring to the trunk. It comprises Nos. 16–25, and includes 158 bones. Lastly, there is the third division, comprising Nos. 26–30. It refers to the head alone, and includes ten bones. The bones belonging to the neck are found classed in the second division, which deals with the trunk. They form Nos. 18 and 23, and include sixteen bones. There is also No. 19, two palatal cavities, which properly belongs to the head. Agreeably with Charaka's own introductory clause one would expect these eighteen bones to be classed with those of the head in the third division, and to stand immediately before No. 26, jaw-bone. The probability is that they did stand so in the text as it left Charaka's hands, and that the misplacement is due to unintelligent copying in later times. This surmise receives considerable support from the fact that in the parallel Non-medical Version of Ātreya's system (§ 16) we find that the bones of the neck, Nos. 18 and 23 (Nos. 19, 20 in § 16), actually take their proper place immediately before the bones of the head (see § 17, cl. 1 *a*). It is true that in this Version, too, No. 19, the palatal cavities, is similarly misplaced, and that the Medical Version of Bheḍa (§ 12) shows exactly the same misplacements as the

Medical Version of Charaka. But this circumstance only proves that the misplacements must be of very ancient date.

§ 6. *Ancient Corruptions*

There is a further point in which the traditionally transmitted form of the Medical Version of Charaka is almost certainly corrupted. No. 16 *a*, two shoulders (*aṁsa*), is evidently superfluous. By the side of No. 16 *b*, two shoulder-blades (*aṁsa-phalaka*), and No. 17, two collar-bones (*akṣaka*), there is no room left for any 'shoulders' (see § 56). The repetition of a word is not at all an uncommon clerical error. Thus the Tübingen MS., No. 458, reads *bāhu*, arms, and *ūru*, thighs, in addition to No. 15, *bāhu-nalaka*, hollow bones of the arms, and No. 14, *ūru-nalaka*, hollow bones of the thighs. Similarly the Deccan College MS., No. 368, and the Bheḍa MS. repeat *ūru* by the side of *ūru-nalaka ;* likewise the Alwar Palace MS. and one of the Śāradā MSS. repeat *bāhu* by the side of *bāhu-nalaka* ; see the critical notes in § 72. In these cases, there cannot be the smallest doubt that we are simply confronted by clerical errors. But by parity of reasoning, it is as good as certain that in No. 16 *a*, *aṁsa*, shoulder, we have a very ancient false repetition, due to the immediately following No. 16 *b*, *aṁsa-phalaka*, shoulder-blade, which, probably owing to its adoption in the system of Vāgbhaṭa I (§ 38, cl. 2), succeeded in establishing itself permanently in all MSS. In confirmation it may be noted that in the parallel Non-medical Version of the Law-book of Yājnavalkya, the item *aṁsa* is actually omitted (§§ 16 and 17).[1] The omission of No. 16 *a*, *aṁsa*, shoulder, of course, renders the total of 360 short by 2 (viz. 358); but, on the other hand, the probability is that in No. 9 the correct reading should be four wrist-bones (*maṇika*) instead of two. For, as a matter of fact, as will be shown in the sequel (§ 52, cf. pp. 30, 49, 50, 63), there are four wrist-bones, homologous to the four ankle-bones.

Another instance of a similar ancient false repetition we have in No. 13, *kapālikā*, elbow-pan, where now all MSS. read *jānu-kapālikā*, falsely duplicating the preceding No. 12, *jānu*, knee-

[1] The omission, here suggested, is also confirmed by the osteological summary which is given in the hymn of the Atharva Veda, see § 43, cl. 6.

cap. Here, again, it may be noted that the parallel Non-medical Version does not exhibit the duplication of *jānu*. It has simply No. 12, *jānu*, knee-cap, and No. 13, *kapola*, elbow-pan, the latter being really a false reading for *kapāla* (§ 53).

§ 7. *Restoration of the Statement of Charaka*

Admitting the emendations indicated in the two preceding paragraphs, the correct form of Charaka's statement of the Medical Version may be restored as follows (Original Text in § 73):

1. 32 teeth (*danta*).
2. 32 sockets (*ulūkhala*) of the teeth.
3. 20 nails (*nakha*).
4. 60 phalanges (*aṅgulī*).
5. 20 long bones (*śalākā*).
6. 4 bases of the long bones (*śalāk-ādhiṣṭhāna*).
7. 2 heels (*pārṣṇi*).
8. 4 ankle-bones (*gulpha*).
9. 4 wrist-bones (*maṇika*).
10. 4 bones of the forearms (*aratni*).
11. 4 bones of the legs (*jaṅgha*).
12. 2 knee-caps (*jānu*).
13. 2 elbow-pans (*kapālikā*).
14. 2 hollow bones (*nalaka*) of the thighs (*ūru*).
15. 2 hollow bones (*nalaka*) of the arms (*bāhu*).
16. 2 shoulder-blades (*aṁsa-phalaka*).
17. 2 collar-bones (*akṣaka*).
18. 2 hip-blades (*śroṇi-phalaka*).
19. 1 pubic bone (*bhag-āsthi*).
20. 45 back-bones (*pṛṣṭha-gat-āsthi*).
21. 14 bones of the breast (*uras*).

22 *a*. 24 ribs (*pārśvaka*).
22 *b*. 24 sockets (*sthālaka*) of the ribs.
22 *c*. 24 tubercles (*arbuda*) fitting into the sockets.

23. 15 bones of the neck (*grīvā*).
24. 1 windpipe (*jatru*).
25. 2 palatal cavities (*tāl-ūṣaka*).
26. 1 (lower) jaw-bone (*hanv-āsthi*) or chin.
27. 2 basal tie-bones of the jaw (*hanu-mūla-bandhana*).
28. 1 bone constituting nose, prominences of the cheeks and brows (*nāsikā-gaṇḍakūṭa-lalāṭa*).
29. 2 temples (*śaṅkha*).
30. 4 cranial pan-shaped bones (*śiraḥ-kapāla*).

Total 360.

§ 8. *Gangādhar's Recension*

Gangādhar's recension of the statement of Charaka on the bones of the human body runs as follows (Original Text in § 74):

'The body consists of the following parts: two arms (*bāhu*), two legs (*sakthi*), the head and neck (*śiro-grīva*), and the trunk (*antarādhi*). These make up the sexipartite body (*ṣaḍaṅga*). Inclusive of the teeth, their sockets, and the nails, it has three hundred and sixty bones. These are

1. 32 sockets (*ulūkhala*) of the teeth.
2. 32 teeth (*danta*).
3. 20 nails (*nakha*).
4. 20 long bones (*śalākā*).

5 *a*. 4 bases (*adhiṣṭhāna*) of the long bones.
5 *b*. 4 backs (*pṛṣṭha*) of the hands and feet.
6. 60 phalanges (*aṅguli*).
7 *a*. 2 heels (*pārṣṇi*).
7 *b*. 2 clusters (*kūrca*) of bones below (the long bones).
8. 4 wrist-bones (*maṇika*).
9. 4 ankle-bones (*gulpha*).
10. 4 bones of the forearms (*aratni*).
11. 4 bones of the legs (*jaṅgha*).
12. 2 knee-caps (*jānu*).
13. 2 elbow-pans (*kūrpara*).
14. 2 thighs (*ūru*).
15. 2 arms (*bāhu*) together with (16) the shoulders (*aṁsa*).
17. 2 collar-bones (*akṣaka*).
18. 2 palates (*tālu*).
19. 2 hip-blades (*śroṇi-phalaka*).
20 *a*. 1 vulval bone (*bhag-āsthi*) in women, or penis-bone (*meḍhr-āsthi*) in men.
20 *b*. 1 sacral bone (*trika*).
20 *c*. 1 anal bone (*gud-āsthi*).
21. 35 back-bones (*pṛṣṭha-gata*).
22. 15 bones of the neck (*grīvā*).
23. 2 collar-bones (*jatru*).
24. 1 (lower) jaw-bone (*hanv-asthi*), or chin.
25. 2 basal tie-bones of the jaw (*hanu-mūla-bandhana*).
26 *a*. 2 brows (*lalāṭa*).
26 *b*. 2 eyes (*akṣi*).
26 *c*. 2 cheeks (*gaṇḍa*).
26 *d*. 3 nasal bones (*nāsikā*) called *ghoṇa*.
27 *a*. 24 bones of the two sides (*pārśva*).
27 *b*. 24 ribs (*pārśvaka*) forming a cage (*pañjara*).

27 *c*. 24 sockets of them (*sthālaka*) resembling tubercles (*arbuda*), the whole (27 *a–c*) amounting to 72.
28. 2 temporal bones (*śaṅkhaka*).
29. 4 cranial pan-shaped bones (*śiraḥ-kapāla*).
30. 17 bones of the breast (*vakṣas*).

These are the three hundred and sixty bones.'

§ 9. *Inconsistencies and Incongruities of Gangādhar's Recension*

1. Gangādhar's recension of the statement of Charaka is full of inconsistencies and incongruities. To begin with, the sum of the several items of the list does not agree with the total stated at its conclusion. The latter is 360, while the former is either 370 or 368, according as No. 16 is counted separately, or together with No. 15, though the wording of the clause in the original seems to imply that Nos. 15 and 16 are to be taken as a single item. The attempt of Gangādhar to remove this inconsistency will be explained in the next paragraph. In the meantime, other inconsistencies are now enumerated in the order of their occurrence in the list of Gangādhar.

(*a*) Nos. 4 and 5 *b* are obviously the very same bones, that is to say, the long bones of the metacarpus and metatarsus. It makes no difference whether they are considered from the inner side (palm, or sole, No. 4) or from the outer side (back, *pṛṣṭha*, No. 5 *b*) of the hand or foot.

(*b*) Similarly Nos. 5 *a* and 7 *b* are the identical bones of the carpus and tarsus. This will be fully explained in the sequel (§ 49). Here it may be noted that *kūrca*, or cluster, is the term for these bones which was introduced by Suśruta in substitution of Charaka's term *adhiṣṭhāna* (or *sthāna*), base (§ 28). Its appearance in the recension of Gangādhar proves that that recension cannot possibly represent the genuine text of Charaka, but that it was prepared subsequently with a knowledge of the terminology of Suśruta. This remark also applies to Gangādhar's use of the term *kūrpara* for elbow-pan (olecranon, No. 13); see §§ 21, 28.

(*c*) In No. 20 *a*, the distinction between the so-called 'vulval bone' (*bhagāsthi*) and the 'penis-bone' (*meḍhrāsthi*) involves an obvious anatomical absurdity. Neither the vulva nor the penis is a bony structure. It has arisen from a misunderstanding of Charaka's term *bhagāsthi*, which refers to the pubic bone, i.e. the pubic arch (§ 60). The word *bhaga*, by itself (but not in conjunction with *asthi*, bone) denotes also the vulva, &c., or the external female sexual organs; and the term *bhagāsthi*, having been erroneously identified with the term *bhaga*, led further to the erroneous fabrication, and introduction, of a term *meḍhrāsthi*, or 'penis-bone', for the male sexual organ (§ 60). The anatomical misconception involved in this procedure alone must be fatal to any claim of Gangādhar's recension to represent the genuine text of Charaka.

(*d*) The principle of enumeration involved in Nos. 20 *b*, 20 *c*, and 21, differs entirely from that of Charaka's genuine No. 22 (§ 4) which counts forty-five back-bones. It will be shown in the sequel (§ 59; see also § 19) not only that the principle of counting which underlies the system of Gangādhar's recension presupposes a knowledge of Suśruta's principle of counting the back-bones, but that it applies that principle in an unintelligent way.

(*e*) No. 23 is affected by a double incongruity. The recension of Gangādhar counts two *jatru*. From this circumstance it is clear that he understands the word *jatru* to refer to the two collar-bones. Now this is a comparatively late meaning of the word which is not traçeable farther back than the *Amarakoṣa*, a Sanskrit vocabulary of uncertain date, but probably written in the early part of the sixth century A. D. At all events, as will be shown in the sequel (§ 62), in the early medical works, *jatru* uniformly refers to the neck, or the windpipe in the neck. Its use, therefore, in the sense of collar-bone proves that the recension of Gangādhar cannot represent the genuine text of Charaka. Moreover, its use in that sense involves the further incongruity of counting the collar-bones twice; for No. 17, *akṣaka*, also refers to the collar-bones.

(*f*) No. 26 *a*, *b*, *c*, *d*, as will be shown in the sequel (§ 66, see also pp. 37 and 40), imply a view of the bones of the skull utterly at variance with that indicated in the genuine text of Charaka—a view, moreover, which presupposes a knowledge of Suśruta's views, imperfectly understood.

(*g*) No. 27 *a*, *b*, *c*, likewise, is affected by a double incongruity. One is of the formal kind: the ribs are pitchforked into the midst of the bones of the head, standing as they do between No. 26, brows, eyes, cheeks and nose, and No. 28, temporal bones. Moreover, as will be shown in the sequel (§ 58), the terms of the three parts of No. 27, which, as given in the genuine text of Charaka, are perfectly intelligible and correct, convey no consistent or intelligible meaning in the recension of Gangādhar.

(*h*) No. 30 is open to several objections. It counts 17 breast-bones against 14 of Charaka's genuine text (§ 4, No. 24); and its larger count presupposes a knowledge of the system of Suśruta. The position of the breast-bones, too, at the very end of the list, after the bones of the head, is very curious. It is to be noted, however, that on this point the recension of Gangādhar follows the arrangement of the list as given in the Non-medical Version of Yājnavalkya's Law-book and the Agni Purāna (§ 16, No. 27). This circumstance, combined with the fact that in his commentary Gangādhar refers to those two non-medical works by name, supports the surmise that the recension of Gangādhar is not based on any manuscript authority, but is an ill-judged construction of his own.

2. On three points, however, Gangādhar is undoubtedly right in his reconstruction. One of these refers to No. 16, *aṁsa*, shoulder. The traditional text of the statement of Charaka had erroneously duplicated that item (§ 6). The recension of Gangādhar corrects that error; though, curiously enough, it does so by omitting the more accurate term *aṁsa-phalaka*, shoulder-blade. This curious circumstance clearly points to the use, by Gangādhar, of the existing traditional text of Suśruta's Compendium in the preparation of his recension of the statement of Charaka. For in that traditional text the term *aṁsa* is employed (though erroneously, as shown in §§ 30, 55, 56) in the sense of *aṁsa-phalaka* to denote the shoulder-blade. The second point refers to No. 8, where the recension of Gangādhar reads 'four wrist-bones' instead of the 'two wrist-bones' of the traditional recension. Here, too, in all probability, his emendation is right (see § 52). The third point refers to the position of No. 23, *jatru*. As

pointed out in § 5, this item is misplaced in the traditional list. The recension of Gangādhar, though it misinterprets the term, assigns to the item its correct place immediately after No. 22, *grīvā*, neck-bones. In doing so—it may be noted again—Gangādhar simply follows the guidance of Yājnavalkya's Law-book and the Agni Purāna (§ 16, No. 20).

§ 10. *Harmonization of Gangādhar's Recension*

In his commentary, Gangādhar makes a strenuous attempt to harmonize the actual total, 368 or 370, of the several items of his list with the required total 360. It involves a very forced manipulation of the list, which will now be explained. His procedure is as follows. It divides itself into five steps. The first step refers to the extremities. Excluding Nos. 1 and 2 as well as Nos. 5 *a* and 5 *b*, the remaining numbers down to No. 16, give us 128 bones, that is to say, thirty-two bones for each of the upper and lower extremities. Next, adding Nos. 1 and 2, that is, sixty-four bones, the total is raised to 192. The third step refers to the posterior part of the trunk. Transferring No. 18 (*tālu*, palate) to a subsequent step, and counting No. 20 *a* (the vulval and penis-bones) as a single item (for woman and man respectively), we obtain, from No. 17 to No. 21, a total of forty-two, which added to the previous total 192, raises it to 234. The fourth step refers to the head and neck. Transferring Nos. 23 (*jatru*) and 27 *a*, *b*, *c* (ribs, &c.) to the next step, but adding the previously omitted No. 18 (palate), and counting from No. 22 to No. 29, we obtain a total of thirty-five, which added to the previous total 234, makes up 269. The fifth step refers to the anterior portion of the trunk. Here come in the previously omitted Nos. 23 (*jatru*) and 27 *a*, *b*, *c* (ribs, &c.), to which is added No. 30 (breast-bones). These give a total of ninety-one, which, added to the previous total 269, finally results in the required total 360.

This scheme of harmonization is open to several serious objections:

1. It throws out of the count the two items No. 5 *a*, bases of the long bones, and No. 5 *b*, backs of the hands and feet.

Gangādhar would appear to have realized (what has been already pointed out in § 9) that these two numbers merely duplicate the items enumerated as Nos. 7 *b* and 4 respectively. For the bones of the back of the hands and feet (No. 5 *b*) are precisely the long bones (No. 4), and the bases (No. 5 *a*) are the clusters (*kūrca*, No. 7 *b*). So far Gangādhar, undoubtedly, is right; but his error is that he counts only two clusters. The subjoined tabular statement makes this perfectly plain:

	Extremities.	*Upper.*	*Lower.*
No. 3.	Nails (*nakha*) . .	10	10
„ 4.	Long bones (*śalākā*) .	10	10
„ 5.	Phalanges (*aṅguli*) .	30	30
„ 7 *a*.	Heels (*pārṣṇi*) . .	—	2
„ 7 *b*.	Clusters (*kūrca*) . .	2	—
„ 8.	Wrist-bones (*maṇika*) .	4	—
„ 9.	Ankle-bones (*gulpha*) .	—	4
„ 10.	Forearms (*aratni*) . .	4	—
„ 11.	Legs (*jaṅgha*) . .	—	4
„ 12.	Knee-caps (*jānu*) . .	—	2
„ 13.	Elbow-pans (*kūrpara*) .	2	—
„ 14.	Thighs (*ūru*) . .	—	2
„ 15.	Arms (*bāhu*) . .	2	—
	Totals .	64	64

This gives, as Gangādhar explains, a total of thirty-two bones for each of the four extremities, and a grand total of 128. But it will be noticed that he counts only the clusters (*kūrca*) of the hands, that is, as we should call them, the carpal bones. He omits the other two *kūrca*, that is, the clusters or tarsal bones of the feet. In their place, he counts two *pārṣṇi*, that is, the heel-bones of the feet; for, as will be seen from the table, Gangādhar's arrangement of the bones of the extremities proceeds on the principle of homology. Now the heel-bones do belong to the tarsal cluster of bones, but, though they are its prominent constituents, they do not exhaust the cluster. The truth is that Gangādhar's recension of the statement of Charaka is a faulty adaptation to the scheme of Suśruta, which, as will be shown in the sequel (§ 49), consistently counts four *kūrca*, or clusters of small bones. The genuine schemes of both, Suśruta and Charaka, are consistent, each in its own way; but the recension of Gangādhar is inconsistent, and proves itself thereby not to be the genuine recension of the scheme of Charaka.

2. With regard to the term *kūrca*, as used in the recension of Gangādhar, there is a special grammatical difficulty. The clause in question, *dve kūrcādhas*, is very difficult to construe. The only construction grammatically legitimate is to supply *asthīni*, that is, *dve asthīni kūrc-ādhas*, or 'two bones below the *kūrca*'. This, however, yields no intelligible sense. In order to give the sense which Gangādhar wishes to extract from it, the clause should read *dve kūrce adhas*, i.e. 'two *kūrca* below (*scl.* the long bones)'; and this form of the clause could become *dve kūrcādhas* only through a very anomalous double *sandhi*, or contraction; viz. *kūrce adhas* = *kūrca[y]adhas* = *kūrcādhas*. Even so, the difficulty remains that *kūrca*—a word apparently first used by Suśruta in its anatomical application—is not neuter (*dve kūrce*), but masculine (*dvau kūrcau*); see Suśruta's Compendium, *Śārīra Sthāna*, chap. vi, clause 29 (Jīv. ed., p. 340). Avināsa Chandra, in his glosses to Gangādhar's recension which he adopts in his edition of Charaka's Compendium, apparently takes *kūrcādha* to be a single noun, synonymous with *kūrca*, but there exists no such noun in Sanskrit, and even if it did, the clause should read *dve kūrcādhe*.

3. A further difficulty in Gangādhar's scheme of harmonization is that it takes no account of the term *aṁsa*, shoulder, which his recension couples with the fifteenth item. The clause of that item reads *dve* (*scl. asthīni*) *bāhvoḥ s-āṁsayoḥ*, i.e. 'two bones in the arms together with the shoulders'. It seems obvious that arm and shoulder could not well be considered as constituting a single bone. Gangādhar avoids the difficulty by calmly ignoring the presence of *aṁsa*, shoulder, and explaining the clause to mean that 'there is one bone in each arm'. On the other hand, Avināsa Chandra, in his glosses, counts *aṁsa*, shoulder, separately. Consequently, with his counting two bones in the arms, and two in the shoulders, the list works out a total of even 370 bones. Seeing that the recension of Gangādhar nowhere mentions the shoulder-blades (*aṁsa phalaka*), it does seem not impossible that by the term *aṁsa* it intended to indicate those bones. If so, the dilemma presents itself: did

Gangādhar intend shoulder-blade (*aṁsa*) to be counted separately from arm (*bāhu*), or to be taken as constituting with it but a single bone. In the former case, retaining in other respects Gangādhar's scheme of harmonization, the total works out at 362 bones (that is, Gangādhar's 360 *plus* the two *aṁsa*). In the latter case, we have the incongruity of treating arm *plus* shoulder-blade as a single bone. In either case, the recension of Gangādhar stands self-condemned as an incongruous and inconsistent compilation.

4. While, as we have just seen, the shoulder-blade, though such a prominent bone of the human body, is not given any distinct recognition in the recension of Gangādhar, the collar-bone, on the other hand, is counted twice over, under the denominations *akṣaka* and *jatru* in Nos. 17 and 23. The pair of *akṣaka* Gangādhar explicitly defines in his commentary as being *kaṇṭhādho 'ṁsakau*, that is, 'the two shoulder-bones below the throat.' This definition only fits the collar-bones. Anyhow, it fits them better than the shoulder-blades. It is also the usual interpretation of the term *akṣaka*, given by other commentators who refer it to the collar-bones. As to the term *jatru*, Gangādhar gives no definition of it; but it is to be noted that, while the genuine recension of the statement of Charaka treats it as denoting a single bone, the recension of Gangādhar uses it as the name of a pair of bones. It will be shown in the sequel (§ 62) that when used in the latter way the term always refers to the collar-bones. The duplication of the collar-bones in the recension of Gangādhar is obviously fatal to its claim of being a genuine presentation of the text of Charaka.

§ 11. *The Glosses of Chakrapāṇidatta*

1. It has been stated in § 3 that the genuineness of Jīvānanda's Recension of Charaka's statement on the bones of the human body is confirmed by the commentary of Chakrapāṇidatta written some time in the middle of the eleventh century A. D. Manuscripts of this work are very rare, and in a more or less incomplete state. The subjoined translation has been made from the Tübingen University Library MS., M. a. I. 463

(Cat. No. 146),[1] where the original passage occurs in vol. iii, fols. 284 *b* and 285 *a*. It runs as follows (Original Text in § 75):

2. 'With reference to the list of bones, the words "head and neck" (*śiro-grīvam*) must be taken together, and signify but one part, viz. the head. The word "trunk" (*antarādhi*) refers to the middle part of the body. The words "and sixty" (*ṣaṣṭa*) mean sixty additional to three hundred. The term "dental socket" (*dant-olūkhala*) signifies the place where the tooth is fixed. Though in the chapter on the various kinds of food and drink, the nails (*nakha*) are relegated to the waste products of the body on account of their being developed from the waste portion of what is taken as food, nevertheless, in the present case, on account of their resemblance to the bones, they are counted among the latter.[2] In each finger and toe there are

[1] The original of this MS. was in Benares in 1873, where a copy of it was procured by me for the late Professor von Roth. It is rather inaccurate, but fairly complete, there being only a very large lacuna in the sixth section (*Cikitsita Sthāna*). Through the kind intermediation of Professor R. Garbe I have the loan of it. Tübingen, No. 145, is another incomplete copy of the same Benares MS. A second MS. of the same commentary is recorded as No. 2160 in the *Notices of Sanskrit MSS.* It is described as 'incomplete, containing only the first five books'. A third MS. is being used by Kaviraj Harinath Viśarada in his edition of Charaka's Compendium with Chakrapāṇidatta's Commentary (Calcutta, śaka 1817 = A.D. 1895). A fourth MS., 'complet et bien conservé' is announced by Dr. P. Cordier in his *Récentes Découvertes*, p. 10, and (according to a private letter from him, October 30, 1904) is being copied for him. From a few passages, kindly collated by him for me it appears to agree closely with the Benares MS. referred to above. A copy, from it, of the osteological statement was kindly supplied by him to me (§ 75). Further, two MSS., Nos. 2503 and 2855, are stated in *Notices*, vol. xi, p. 39, to exist in the Government of India Collection in Calcutta, but on inquiry I am informed that No. 2855 is lost; and No. 2503, which I obtained on loan, I find on examination to be not a MS. of Chakrapāṇidatta's Commentary, but a fragment of the text of Charaka's Compendium, viz. the 30th chapter of the *Sūtra Sthāna* and the *Vimāna Sthāna*.

[2] The reference is to the 28th chapter of the Introductory Section (*Sūtra Sthāna*) of Charaka's Compendium. It is there explained that the food taken by man contains a good part (*prasāda*) and a waste part (*kiṭṭa*). The former is assimilated by the system and turned into chyle (*rasa*), which, in its turn, serves to build up the various parts of the body (blood, muscles, bones, &c.). The latter is secreted by the body as its waste products (*mala*), the nails, in particular, being secreted by the bones.

three joints (*parvan*). Hence, as there are twenty fingers and toes, there are sixty bones in the joints. As to the third joint of the thumb and great toe, it must be understood to be contained within the respective hand or foot. The long bones (*śalākā*), too, of the thumb and great toe, must be understood to be of small size. The place where the long bones of the fingers and the toes meet, there is their base (*adhiṣṭhāna*). The word "knee" (*jānu*) signifies the knee-cap (*jānuka*), marking the articulation of leg and thigh. The "two collar-bones" (*akṣaka*) are the two pegs that run athwart the anterior part of the trunk between the articulations of the shoulder and the throat.[1] The two "palatal cavities" (*tālūṣaka*) signify the two palatal bones. The "pubic bone" (*bhagāsthi*) is the cross (*tiryag*) bone that serves to compact the two hip-bones in front. By the term "sockets" (*sthālaka*) are meant the shallow (*nimna*) bases for the ends of the ribs; and by the words "tubercles fitting into the sockets" (*sthālak-ārbudāni*) are meant the tubercle-like bones which occur in the middle between the ribs and the shallows. The "nose" (*nāsikā*), the "prominences of the cheeks" (*gaṇḍakūṭa*), and the "brows" (*lalāṭa*) must be taken together, and counted as a single bone. According to those who read the three items separately, the nose, the prominences of the cheeks, and the brows constitute three distinct bones; but in this way the total [360] does not work out.'

3. The main interest of this commentary lies not so much in the explanations which it gives of the several items of the list of bones, as in the evidence it affords of the state of the text of Charaka in the eleventh century. The value of the explanation is much impaired by its apparently fragmentary character. Out of the thirty items in the list of Charaka (§ 4), it comments only on twelve (viz. Nos. 1–6, 12, 17, 19, 21, 25 *a*, *b*, *c*, 28). For no less than eighteen items (Nos. 7–11, 13–16, 18, 20, 22–4, 26, 27, 29, 30) we have no comment; and as there are among them some not quite transparent terms (e.g. Nos. 9, 13, 18, 27), it is difficult to avoid the suspicion that the text of the commentary has not been preserved intact.

[1] The original of this clause is very corrupt: it has been conjecturally restored; its general purport seems clear enough.—*Koṣṭha* signifies the whole of the anterior part of the trunk, as opposed to *pṛṣṭha*, or the whole of the 'back', or posterior part. The articulations referred to are the scapulo-clavicular (*aṁsa*) and the sterno-clavicular (*jatru*, see § 62).

4. Regarding the evidence on the condition of the text of Charaka's statement, the fortunate preservation of Chakrapāṇidatta's gloss on No. 19, *tālūṣake*, shows the misplacement of that item as already extant in his time. The extreme antiquity, indeed, of this particular misplacement, as has already been pointed out in § 5, is guaranteed by its occurrence in the Non-medical Version, as well as in the Medical Version of Bheḍa (§ 12). In default of any gloss on No. 18, *jatru*, and No. 23, *grīvā*, it must remain uncertain, whether they were misplaced in Charaka's text as Chakrapāṇidatta saw it, or whether he read them in their right position as shown in the Non-medical Version (§ 16). Again the commentary's silence on No. 9, *maṇika*, No. 13, *jānu-kapālika*, and No. 16, *aṁsa*, leaves it also uncertain how far Chakrapāṇidatta's text may have supported the emendations suggested in § 6.

5. Of great importance is the remark of Chakrapāṇidatta on No. 28, the complex bone of nose, cheeks, and brows. For, first, it shows that he must have read Charaka's text as given in Jīvānanda's recension, and that, accordingly, Gangādhar's recension is not genuine. For the latter breaks up the complex into three parts, and makes each part to consist of two bones. Its procedure, therefore, results in producing a total of six bones, where the genuine recension has only a single bone, and where even the rival text, which Chakrapāṇidatta mentions, has no more than three bones. Secondly it renders it very probable, that when speaking of this rival text, Chakrapāṇidatta was referring to the Medical Version as traditionally presented in the Compendium of Bheḍa. For that Version (§§ 12, 13) makes No. 28 to consist of three bones, and consequently works out a wrong total (362).

§ 12. *The Medical Version according to Bheḍa*

1. As stated in § 1, Ātreya's theory of the skeleton is found also in Bheḍa's Compendium (*Bheḍa Saṁhitā*). Of this compendium, at present, no more than a single manuscript is known to exist, dated about 1650 A. D., and preserved in the Palace Library

in Tanjore (Burnell's Catalogue, No. 10773).[1] The arrangement of the Compendium of Bheḍa agrees with that of the Compendium of Charaka. Accordingly his statement on the bones of the human body is also found in the seventh chapter of the Anatomical Section (*Śārīra Sthāna*). It runs as follows (Original Text in § 76):

2. 'There are three hundred and sixty bones. These are the following:

1. 32 teeth (*danta*).
2. 32 sockets (*ulūkhala*) of the teeth.
3. 20 nails (*nakha*).
4. 60 phalanges (*aṅguli*).
5. 20 long bones (*śalākā*) of the hands and feet.
6. 4 bases (*adhiṣṭhāna*) of the long bones.
7. 2 heels (*pārṣṇi*).
8. 4 ankle-bones (*gulpha*) of the two feet.
9. 2 wrist-bones (*maṇika*) of the two hands.
10. 4 bones of the two forearms (*aratni*).
11. 4 bones of the two legs (*jaṅgha*).
12. 2 knee-caps (*jānu*).
13. 2 elbow-pans (*jānu-kapālikā*).
14. 2 hollow bones (*nalaka*) of the two thighs (*ūru*).
15. [2 hollow bones (*nalaka*) of the two arms (*bāhu*).]

16 *a*. 2 shoulders (*aṁsa*).
16 *b*. 2 shoulder-blades (*aṁsa-phalaka*).

17. 2 collar-bones (*akṣaka*).
18. 1 windpipe (*jatru*).
19. 2 palatal cavities (*tāl-ūṣaka*).
20. 2 hip-blades (*śroṇi-phalaka*).
21. 1 pubic bone (*bhag-āsthi*).
22. 45 back-bones (*pṛṣṭha-gat-āsthi*).
23. 15 neck-bones (*grīvā*).
24. 14 breast-bones (*uras*).

[1] Of this MS. I possess an excellent copy in Telugu, which I owe to the munificence of the Government of Madras, by whose orders it has been prepared for me (November, 1905). Dr. P. Cordier also possesses two copies, one in Telugu, the other in Devanagari, the latter being a transcript from his Telugu copy (information by letter of September 10, 1904; see also *Récentes Découvertes*, pp. 4, 5). Professor Aufrecht's *Catalogus Catalogorum*, vol. i, p. 416, notices another MS., 'Radh. 32,' in a native library in Lahore; but the existence of it at present lacks verification.

25 *a*. 24 ribs (*pārśvaka*).
25 *b*. 24 sockets (*sthālaka*) in the two sides.
25 *c*. 24 tubercles (*arbuda*) fitting into the sockets.
26. 1 (lower) jaw-bone (*hanv-asthi*), or chin.
27. 2 basal tie-bones of the jaw (*hanu-mūla-bandhana*).
28 *a*. 1 nasal bone (*nās-āsthi*).
28 *b*. 1 bone in the prominences of the jaw (*hanu-kūṭa*)
28 *c*. 1 bone in the brows (*lalāṭa*).
29. [2 temples (*śaṅkha*).]
30. 4 cranial pan-shaped bones (*śīrṣa-kapāla*).'

§ 13. *Peculiarities and Defects of Bheḍa's Statement*

With reference to the condition of the text of the statement of Bheḍa the following points deserve notice:

1. Nos. 15 and 29, which are enclosed in angular brackets, are missing in the original Sanskrit text (§ 76). That these omissions are due to clerical lapses in the existing MS. is obvious from the fact that otherwise the required total (360) does not work out. Accordingly in the list (§ 12) they have been supplied.

2. In No. 28 *b*, Bheḍa's text has the peculiar reading *hanu-kūṭa*, prominence of the jaw, where Charaka's text (§ 4) has *gaṇḍa-kūṭa*, prominence of the cheek. It will be shown in § 65 that though both terms may well be synonymous, the term *hanu-kūṭa* is really inconsistent with the system of Ātreya. It is not improbably, therefore, a false reading for *gaṇḍa-kūṭa*.

3. In the original text (§ 76) the statement appears to contain two additional items, which have been omitted in the translation (§ 12). In reality these additions are merely explanatory (marginal) glosses which have become wrongly incorporated into the text. First, No. 9, in the original text, runs as follows: 'two *maṇika*, two *pāṇika*, of the two hands.' Here the two words *maṇika* and *pāṇika*, are simply synonyms, explanatory of each other; and either *maṇika* or *pāṇika* is the intrusive gloss, more probably, to judge from its secondary position, the latter. In the India Office MS., No. 881 (Cat. No. 2640), the word *pāṇike* is actually substituted for *maṇike*. Secondly, in No. 19, the original text has 'two *tālūṣaka*, two *cubuka*'. Here, probably,

there has occurred a misplaced insertion of the gloss *cubuka*. That word means 'chin', and probably served as a marginal gloss to explain the term *hanv-asthi* (No. 26). By some mischance or misunderstanding it got misplaced, and was then wrongly inserted into the text after *tālūṣaka* (No. 19). Both *hanvasthi* and *tālūṣaka* are very unusual terms, and the transfer of the gloss *cubuka* from one to the other is readily intelligible in the hands of an ignorant scribe.

4. There is a difficulty with respect to the total of the listed bones. According to the introductory clause of the list, its total should be 360, but the addition of its items actually works out a total of 362. It is obvious that there must be a defect somewhere in the list. The probability, as will be shown in the sequel (§ 66), is that the defect lies in No. 28 *a, b, c*. The real text of the clause expressing that item must have run similarly to that in the list of Charaka (§ 4); and instead of a nasal bone, and a bone for the prominences of the jaw and of the brows respectively (i. e. three bones altogether), it must have spoken of but one bone, that is, a single complex bone, including all three organs: nose, prominences, and brows. With this correction we obtain the correct total 360.

5. It is probable, however, that a further correction should be made. It will be noted that all the inconsistencies and corruptions, noticed in the case of the list of Charaka (§§ 5, 6), occur also in the list of Bheḍa. Accordingly, just as in the list of Charaka, No. 16 *a*, *aṁsa*, shoulders, should be omitted, and on the other hand, in No. 9, 'four wrist-bones' should be read instead of 'two wrist-bones'. The total 360 thus remains untouched.

§ 14. *Non-medical Version of Ātreya's System*

1. The existence of a Version of the theory of Ātreya on the skeleton in some works of a non-medical character has been referred to in § 1. This Non-medical Version is found in two legal and two religious text-books. The former are the Law-book of Yājnavalkya (*Yājñavalkya Dharma-śāstra*) and the Institutes of Vishnu (*Viṣṇu Smṛti*). The latter are the Vishnu

Dharmottara (*Viṣṇu-dharmottara*) and the Agni Purāna (*Agni Purāṇa*).

2. The Law-book of Yājnavalkya is a versified treatise of Hindu law, the approximate date of which is about the middle of the fourth century A. D.[1]

3. The Institutes of Vishnu, on account of its being partly written in prose, is supposed to belong, at least in its original form, to a considerably earlier date; but in its final redaction, it is placed (by Professor Macdonell) 'not earlier than 200 A. D.', or (by Professor Jolly) 'in the third or fourth century A. D.'[2] But it is probable that isolated portions have been interpolated into the work at much later dates. In any case, in respect of the passage containing the Non-medical Version of the skeleton, there is sufficient evidence (§ 22) proving that it cannot have existed in the Institutes of Vishnu before the twelfth century A. D. Indeed, the very fact that the passage is in no way required by its context, suggests its being a much later otiose amplification, interpolated into the text from some other work. The surmise is confirmed by the fact that the passage in question is not found in all MSS. of the Institutes. On this point I have been able to test the following seventeen MSS.:[3]

1. India Office, No. 915 (Cat. 1342 = Jolly V^1).[4]
2. " " No. 1545 (Cat. 1345 = Jolly V^2).[4]
3. " " No. 1247 (Cat. 1347 = Jolly V^3).
4. " " No. 540 (Cat. 1341 = Jolly V).
5. " " No. 200 (Coll. Bühler = Jolly V^4).[4]

[1] See Professor Jolly's *Recht und Sitte*, p. 21, in the Cyclopaedia of Indo-Aryan Research; and Professor Macdonell's *Sanskrit Literature*, p. 429.

[2] Professor Macdonell, *ibid.*, p. 428; Professor Jolly, *ibid.*, p. 7; also in *Sacred Books of the East*, vol. vii, Introduction, p. xxxii.

[3] The first five MSS. were used by Professor Jolly in his edition in the Bibliotheca Indica. The first six MSS. have been examined by myself; so also extracts from Nos. 13–17, kindly supplied to me by Mahāmahopadhyāya Hara Prasāda Shastri. For the examination of No. 7 I am indebted to the kindness of Rao Bahadur M. Rangacharya; of Nos. 8 and 9 to that of Professor S. K. Bhandarkar; of Nos. 10–12 to that of Professor K. B. Pathak.

[4] Nos. 1, 2 and 5 are provided with Nanda Paṇḍita's Commentary.

6. India Office, No. 913 (Cat. 1340).
7. Government Oriental Library, Madras, No. 87.
8. Elphinstone College, Bombay, No. 162 (Coll. Bühler).
9. " " " No. 174 (Coll. Bühler).[1]
10. Deccan College, No. 19 (Bhandarkar's Report, 1880).
11. " " No. 20 (Bhandarkar's Report, 1882).
12. " " No. 155 (Peterson's Report, III).
13. Calcutta, Sanskrit College, No. 5.
14. " " " No. 62.[1]
15. Asiatic Society of Bengal, No. II A. 10.
16. " " " No. II A. 11.
17. " " " No. II B. 25.[1]

From among these MSS., twelve (Nos. 1, 2, 4–9, 13–15, 17) contain the passage in question, while five (Nos. 3, 10–12, 16) do not contain it. It appears to be generally assumed, on the authority of Max Müller,[2] that the Law-book of Yājnavalkya borrowed the passage from the Institutes of Vishnu. The evidence which will be adduced in § 22, goes to show that the truth is rather the reverse. The passage, most probably, was inserted into the Institutes by some one who was familiar with the Mitaksharā commentary on the Law-book. This must have happened at a comparatively late date, though at least some time before 1622 A. D. For Nanda Paṇḍita, who wrote his *Vaijayantī* commentary on the Institutes in that year,[3] comments on the passage.

4. The Vishnu Dharmottara is held to be a part of the Garuḍa Purāna. Its existence as early as about 1100 A. D. is guaranteed by a quotation in the *Dānasāgara*, a work ascribed to King Ballāla Sena of Bengal, who reigned about that time. Numerous detached portions of the work are known to exist. Among these there is one called 'the Chapter on Anatomy' (*Śārīrādhyāya*), of which the Tübingen University Library possesses a unique MS., M. a. I. 483 (Cat. No. 167).[4] The treatise, thus called, professes to be a versified compilation from

[1] Nos. 9, 14 and 17 are provided with Nanda Paṇḍita's Commentary.
[2] *Sacred Books of the East*, vol. vii, Introduction, p. xx.
[3] Professor Jolly's edition, Pref., p. 1, and his translation, Introd., p. xxxiii.
[4] Through the liberality of the authorities of the Library who loaned it to me, I was enabled carefully to examine it.

the Compendia of Charaka and Suśruta. Its statement on the skeleton, however, is a literal extract from the Law book of Yājnavalkya.

5. The date of the Agni Purāna is not known, but the point is of small interest; for there can be no doubt that the 369th chapter, entitled 'the Parts of the Human Body' (*Śārīrāvāyavāḥ*), in which the statement on the skeleton occurs, is not a portion of the original work. A comparison of it with the 'Chapter on Anatomy' in the Vishnu Dharmottara Purāna shows that about two-thirds of its contents (i. e. twenty-nine out of a total of forty-three verses) are literally plagiarized from it. Moreover, it betrays itself as a later interpolation by its very position in the book, occurring as it does after chapters 367 and 368 which treat of the Dissolution of the World (*pralaya*), and before chapter 370 which treats of the various hells (*naraka*), while its proper place would have been with chapters 278–85 which treat of Medicine.[1] A further corroborative evidence is the fact that it is wanting in many MSS. The Bibliotheca Indica edition (as stated in its Preface, p. ii, and Introd., p. xxxvii) is based on ten MSS.[2] Out of these, eight MSS. appear to have contained the chapter in question, while it was wanting in two. To these two must be added the India Office MS., No. xxv (W. 4), and the Bodleian Library MS., No. 42, which I have examined myself, and neither of which contains the chapter. Neither is it contained in the two MSS. of the Asiatic Society of Bengal, No. III H. 38 and No. III G. 31, which have been collated for me in Calcutta. This gives eight MSS. for, and six against the originality of the chapter. As one of those

[1] These chapters profess to give Suśruta's system of medicine. But there is very little distinctly Suśrutiyan to be found in them; nor, for that matter, anything more distinctly Charakiyan. A good test case is the half-verse 8, on p. 29, in chapter 278, which agrees with neither Charaka (ed. 1896, p. 479) nor Suśruta (p. 824) nor Vāgbhaṭa. On the other hand, two verses (13 and 14 on p. 35 in chapter 279) of an incantation are found also in Suśruta (*Sūtra Sthāna*, 44th *adhyāya*, p. 160).

[2] The editor had eleven MSS., but he discarded one at an early stage. One of his MSS. is now in the India Office, No. 5 (7) of the Saurendra Mohun Tagore Collection. The statement on the skeleton is found on fol. 115 *b*, ll. 2 ff.

eight MSS. is dated in śaka 1595, i.e. A. D. 1673 (Ed., pref., p. ii), it follows that the interpolation of the chapter goes back, at least, to the middle of the seventeenth century.

§ 15. *The Recensions of the Non-medical Version*

1. The evidence given in the preceding paragraph renders it practically certain that the Law-book of Yājnavalkya is the original source of the Non-medical Version, from which it passed into the Institutes of Vishnu, and into the two Purānas. With regard to the two latter, there can be no doubt on this point, seeing that their versified statements of the Non-medical Version (original Texts and Translations, in § 86) are mere copies of the versified statement in the Law-book of Yājnavalkya. The case of the Institutes of Vishnu might at first seem doubtful because of its statement of the Non-medical Version being in prose, while that in the Law-book is in verse. But it will be shown in § 22 that, while in essentials the two statements are identical, their points of difference indicate that the author of the statement in the Institutes of Vishnu must have been familiar with the statement in the Law-book of Yājnavalkya. The fact, therefore, of his making his statement in prose and in very concise terms must be explained by his desire to write it in conformity with the general character of the diction of the Institutes.

2. On account of their essential identity, the four examples may be considered to represent a single recension of the Non-medical Version, of which the example contained in the Law-book of Yājnavalkya forms the representative type. As such the latter will be treated in the sequel of the present dissertation. There exists, however, a rather different recension of the Non-medical Version—differing in essential points regarding terminology as well as numeration—in the commentary of Gangādhar which accompanies his edition of Charaka's Compendium (*Śārīra Sthāna*, pp. 187, 188). It becomes necessary, therefore, again to inquire into the evidence of the genuineness of the two recensions. Briefly stated the case is similar to that of the two recensions of the Medical Version in Charaka's Compendium.

For the recension of Gangādhar there exists—so far as my knowledge goes—not a single MS. authority, while all MSS. that I have been able to examine, and all old commentaries, at present known, support the recension as given in the published editions of the two legal treatises and the Agni Purāna.[1] These are: Professor Stenzler's edition of the *Yājñavalkya Dharmaśāstra* (London, 1849), verses 84–90 of the third chapter (*adhyāya*), on pp. 89, 90 (translated on pp. 98, 99); Professor Jolly's edition of the *Viṣṇu Smṛti* in the Bibliotheca Indica (Calcutta, 1881), clauses 55–79 of the 96th section, on pp. 196, 197 (translated in the *Sacred Books of the East*, vol. vii, pp. 283–5); Dr. Rajendralal Mitra's edition of the *Agni Purāṇa*, in the Bibliotheca Indica (Calcutta, 1879), verses 27 *b*–33 of the 369th chapter, on pp. 308–9 of the third volume. The MSS. (twelve and eight respectively) which support the published recensions contained in the Institutes of Vishnu and the Agni Purāna have been already enumerated in the preceding paragraph. It remains to enumerate the MSS. of the Law-book of Yājnavalkya which I have examined. There are fifteen of these, and they all support the published recension. They are the following:

1. India Office, No. 1079 } with the Mitaksharā commentary.
2. „ No. 2035 }
3. „ No. 2060 }
4. „ No. 3022, with Aparārka's commentary.
5. „ No. 1278, with Śūlapāṇi's „
6. „ No. 1176, with Mitra Miśra's „
7–10. „ Nos. 1786, 2074, 2167, 2823.
11. „ No. 23 (50), S. M. Tagore Collection.
12. Bodleian Library, No. 55.
13. Asiatic Society of Bengal, No. I B. 51.
14, 15. „ „ „ No. II A. 10, 11.

3. Of old commentaries on the Law-book of Yājnavalkya we have four.[2] The oldest is the Mitaksharā (*Mitākṣarā*) written

[1] The statement in the Vishnu Dharmottara Purāna has not yet been published.

[2] There exists a fifth commentary by Viśvarūpa, which is still older than the Mitaksharā, and has been described by Professor Jolly in the *Nachrichten der K. Gesellschaft der Wissenschaften zu Göttingen*, 1904, Heft 4. Only one MS. of it appears to be known, which, however, is not accessible to me.

by Vijnāneśvara (*Vijñāneśvara*), who lived about 1100 A. D. A near contemporary of his is Aparārka or Aparāditya, who wrote his commentary about 1150 A. D. Rather later comes Śūlapāṇi in the fifteenth, and Mitra Miśra in the seventeenth century A. D.[1] The latter two commentators follow the lead of the Mitaksharā, while Aparārka, in many points, takes a line of his own; but all four comment on a text which was identical with the published recension.

4. On the Institutes of Vishnu we have the commentary of Nanda Paṇḍita, called *Vaijayantī*, which was written in 1622 A. D.,[2] and which supports the published recension of the text.

§ 16. *The Genuine Recension of the Non-medical Version*

The genuine Non-medical Version, as it is found in the Law-book of Yājnavalkya, in its third chapter, verses 84–90, runs as follows (Original Text in § 77):

'(In the body) there are six parts (*aṅga*); and of bones there are in it three hundred and sixty; namely:

[Verse 85] 1. 64 teeth (*danta*) with their sockets (*sthāla*).
2. 20 nails (*nakha*).
3. 20 long bones (*śalākā*) of the hands and feet.
4. 4 bases (*sthāna*) of the long bones.

[Verse 86] 5. 60 phalanges (*aṅguli*).
6. 2 heels (*pārṣṇi*).
7. 4 ankle-bones (*gulpha*).
8. 4 bones of the forearms (*aratni*).
9. 4 bones of the legs (*jaṅgha*).

[Verse 87] 10. 2 knee-caps (*jānu*).
11. 2 elbow-pans (*kapola*).
12. 2 thighs (*ūru-phalaka*).
13. 2 shoulder-blades (*aṁsa-samudbhava*).
14. 2 collar-bones (*akṣa*).
15. 2 palatal cavities (*tālūṣaka*).
16. 2 hip-blades (*śroṇi-phalaka*).

[1] See Professor Jolly's *Recht und Sitte*, p. 33, in the Cyclopaedia of Indo-Aryan Research.

[2] For the date, see Professor Jolly's edition, Preface, p. i; also his Translation, in the *Sacred Books of the East*, volume vii, Introduction, p. xxxiii.

[Verse 88] 17. 1 pubic bone (*bhag-ästhi*).
18. 45 back-bones (*pṛṣṭha*).
19. 15 neck-bones (*grīvā*).
20. 1 windpipe (*jatru*).
21. 1 (lower) jaw-bone (*hanu*), or chin.
[Verse 89] 22. 2 basal bones of the jaw-bone (*hanu-mūla*).
23 *a*. 3 bones constituting brows, eyes, and cheeks, (*lalāṭ-ākṣi-gaṇḍa*).
23 *b*. 1 nasal bone (*nāsā*) called *ghana*.
24. 72 ribs (*pārśvaka*) with their sockets (*sthālaka*) and tubercles (*arbuda*).
[Verse 90] 25. 2 temporal bones (*śaṅkhaka*).
26. 4 cranial pan-shaped bones (*śiraḥ-kapāla*).
27. 17 breast-bones (*uras*).

These bones make up the skeleton of man.'

This list works out the correct total 360.

§ 17. *Merits, Defects, and Peculiarities of the Non-medical Version*

1. As has already been pointed out in §§ 5, 6, the advantage of the Non-medical Version for text-critical purposes is that it confirms the corrections suggested in those paragraphs. For

(*a*) It places the organs of the neck, that is, No. 19, neck-bones (*grīvā*), and No. 20, windpipe (*jatru*), in their proper place in connexion with, and immediately before, the bones of the head.

(*b*) It avoids the reduplication of the words *aṁsa* in connexion with No. 13, and *jānu*, in connexion with No. 11.

2. On the other hand, the Non-medical Version has three defects; namely:

(*a*) It places No. 24, the ribs together with their sockets and tubercles, in the midst of the bones which belong to the head.

(*b*) It also places No. 27, breast-bones (*uras*), at the end of the whole list, that is, practically along with the bones of the head.

(*c*) The preceding two defects are mere misplacements, but the most serious defect of the Non-medical Version is that it entirely ignores the two bones of the arms (*bāhu*) and the four bones of the wrists (*maṇika*). These bones, as a reference to the lists of the Medical Versions of Charaka (§§ 4, 7) and Bheḍa (§ 12) shows, should have been enumerated between Nos. 7 and 8, and Nos. 12 and 13 respectively.

3. Further, the Non-medical Version has three peculiarities; namely:

(*a*) It uses the peculiar term *aṁsa-samudbhava*, sprung from the shoulder, to denote the shoulder-blade, instead of the term *aṁsa-phalaka* of the Medical Version (No. 16 *b* in §§ 4, 12).

Of far greater importance than this verbal difference are the following two:

(*b*) In No. 27 it counts seventeen breast-bones, instead of the fourteen of the Medical Version (No. 24 in §§ 4, 12).

(*c*) In No. 23 *a* it adds the eyes to the brows and cheeks, which alone are named in the Medical Version (No. 28 in §§ 4, 12).

4. With regard to the third peculiarity the following point is to be noted. The Medical Version, as preserved by Charaka, counts a single bone for the complex of nose, cheeks, and brows (No. 28 in § 4). But there existed, as Chakrapāṇidatta tells us (§ 11), another view, presented in Bheḍa's Compendium (§ 12), according to which the Medical Version is interpreted as counting three bones, that is, one for each of the three items: nose, cheeks, brows. By adopting this rival view, and adding the eyes as a fourth item, the author of the Yājnavalkyan Law-book obtained four bones (Nos. 23 *a*, *b*) against the single bone of the Medical Version, that is, he obtained three extra bones. Similarly by his counting seventeen breast-bones against the fourteen of the Medical Version, he obtained another three extra bones. Thus both operations together gave him six extra bones. The rationale of his procedure is now obvious: its intention is to correct the shortage of six bones caused by the omission of the arms and wrists, as thus:

Required total	360
Omitted: 2 arms, 4 wrist-bones . . .	6
Balance	354
Add 3 breast-bones and 3 facial bones . .	6
Total	360

It may be particularly noted that this corrective result affords a strong confirmation of the suggestion, put forward in § 6, that the true number of the bones of the wrists is four, not two, as the traditional list of Charaka (§ 4) now has it.

5. With regard to the source from which the Non-medical Version derived its peculiarities, it will be shown in the sequel (§§ 29, 30, 33) that it was, in all probability, the statement of Suśruta on the bones of the human body.

§ 18. *Gangādhar's Recension of the Non-medical Version*

In his commentary on Charaka's Compendium, in illustration of the statement of Suśruta (§ 27) that the professors of General Medicine hold the number of bones to be 360, Gangādhar quotes the Non-medical Version, as he states himself, from the Law-book of Yājnavalkya and the Agni Purāna. As given by him, that Version is not quite easy to follow, but it would seem to yield the following list, which works out the required total of 360 (Original Text in § 78):

[Verse 85] 1. 64 teeth (*daśana*) with their sockets (*sthāla*).
2. 20 nails (*nakha*).
3. 20 long bones (*śalākā*).
4. 4 bases (*sthāna*) of the long bones.
[Verse 86] 5. 60 phalanges (*anguli*).
6. 4 heels (*pārṣṇi*).
7 *a*. 4 wrist-bones (*maṇika*). } [1]
7 *b*. 4 ankle-bones (*gulpha*). }
8. 4 bones of the forearm (*aratni*).
9. 4 bones of the legs (*jangha*).
[Verse 87] 10. 2 knee-caps (*jānu*).
11. 2 elbow-pans (*kūrpara*).
12. 2 thighs (*ūru-phalaka*).
13. 2 shoulder-blades (*aṁsa-samudbhava*).
14. 2 collar-bones (*akṣaka*).
15. 2 palatal cavities (*tālūṣaka*).
16. 2 hip-blades (*śroṇi-phalaka*).
[Verse 88] 17. 1 pubic bone (*bhag-āsthi*).
18 *a*. 1 sacral bone (*trika*).
18 *b*. 1 anal bone (*pāyu*).
18 *c*. 35 back-bones (*pṛṣṭha*).

[1] These two items of bones are stated in Gangādhar's list to be situated 'below the clusters' (*kūrca*).

19. 15 neck-bones (*grīvā*).
20. 2 collar-bones (*jatru*).
21. 1 (lower) jaw-bone (*hanu*) or chin.
[Verse 89] 22. 2 basal bones of the jaw (*hanu-mūla*).
23 *a*. 6 bones constituting brows, eyes, and cheeks (*lalāṭ-ākṣi-gaṇḍa*).
23 *b*. 1 nasal bone (*nāsā*) called *ghana*.
24. 72 ribs (*pārśvaka*) with their shallow sockets (*sthālaka*) and tubercles (*arbuda*).
[Verse 90] 25. 2 temporal bones (*śaṅkhaka*).
26. 4 cranial pan-shaped bones (*śiraḥ-kapāla*).
27. 15 breast-bones (*uras*).

§ 19. *Criticism of Gangādhar's Recension*

1. At the end of the Non-medical Version, as given by him, Gangādhar adds the remark: 'this is the statement found in the *Agneya Purāṇa* and in the *Yājñavalkya Saṁhitā* Law-book.' As a fact, however, it is not a real quotation that he gives, but an 'edited' recension of the statement. For his recension differs considerably in several points from the traditional recension in the Law-book.

(*a*) In No. 6 Gangādhar counts four heels instead of two.

(*b*) In No. 18 *c* he counts thirty-five back-bones instead of forty-five.

(*c*) In No. 20 he counts two *jatru* (collar-bones) instead of one (windpipe).

(*d*) In No. 23 *a* he counts six bones instead of three.

(*e*) In No. 27 he counts fifteen breast-bones instead of seventeen.

(*f*) In No. 7 *a* he inserts four wrist-bones.

(*g*) In Nos. 18 *a*, *b* he inserts a sacral and an anal bone.

2. Among these differences, the items *c*, *d*, and *f* enable us to see the reason which led Gangādhar to elaborate his emended recension of the Non-medical Version. We have seen (§ 17) that the traditional Non-medical Version entirely neglects to count the two arms and four wrist-bones. From the fact of Gangādhar counting the four wrist-bones, it is evident that he had noticed the defect of the traditional recension. But it may be asked why he did not also count the two arms. The answer is indicated

by the differences noted in the items *c* and *d*. They show that Gangādhar was acquainted with the interpretation of Vijnāneśvara in his Mitaksharā Commentary (§§ 20, 21). He followed that commentator in including the arms under the term 'forearm' (No. 8, *aratni*); also, in taking *jatru* to refer to the two collar-bones, as well as in allotting two bones to each of the three items: brows, eyes, cheeks. As Vijnāneśvara, however, failed to realize the omission of the four wrist-bones, Gangādhar supplied the deficiency. Moreover, he did not follow Vijnāneśvara in discounting the four bases (No. 4, *sthāna*). There is, however, still another circumstance that influenced Gangādhar's emended recension; namely, his acquaintance with Suśruta's statement on the skeleton. From the traditional recension of that statement (§ 27), he obtained his count of four heels, as well as of the sacral and anal bones.

3. The combined result of the two modifying influences was the augmentation of Gangādhar's list by twelve bones. And it was to counterbalance this excess that Gangādhar reduced the back-bones by ten, and the breast-bones by two; as thus:

Grand total of the Non-medical Version (§ 20, col. iv)		360
Add, Two extra heels in No. 6	2	
Four wrist-bones in No. 7 *a*	4	
One extra *jatru* in No. 20	1	
Three extra bones in No. 23 *a*	3	
One sacral bone in No. 18 *a*	1	
One anal bone in No. 18 *b*	1	
	—	12
Total		372
Deduct, Ten back-bones in No. 18 *c*	10	
Two breast-bones in No. 27	2	
	—	12
Balance		360

It seems hardly necessary to point out, and it will be shown in the Third Section, that all this manipulation of the numbers of the list is performed without any reference to, and has no warrant in, the actual state of the skeletal structure.

4. Regarding the influence of the statement of Suśruta on the recension of Gangādhar, another indication of it may be

noted in the latter's employment of the terms *kūrca*, cluster (§ 18, footnote), and *kūrpara*, elbow-pan (No. 11). Both terms are peculiar to the system of Suśruta (§§ 27, 28). The genuine recension of the Non-medical Version does not use the term *kūrca* at all, and instead of *kūrpara* it uses the term *kapola* (No. 11 in § 16). The reason, no doubt, why Gangādhar preferred the Suśrutiyan term *kūrpara* was that he saw that the term *kapola* was misleading. It properly signifies the cheek, and is here out of place, because the cheeks are enumerated afterwards under the name *gaṇḍa* (No. 23 *a*). The fact is (§ 21, cl. 3) that *kapola* is an ancient false reading for *kapāla*, a pan, which signifies the pan-like olecranon process of the elbow (§ 53), and which is used in the Medical Versions of Charaka (§ 4) and Bheḍa (§ 12) in the slightly modified form of *kapālikā*, a small pan.[1]

§ 20. *The Commentaries on the Non-medical Version*

1. The commentaries on the Non-medical Version contained in the Law-book of Yājnavalkya throw not a little light on the subject of the defects and peculiarities of that Version. The subjoined table exhibits a conspectus of their theories of interpretation. Columns I to IV refer to the Law-book itself, and columns V to VIII to the commentaries of Aparārka (V), Vijnāneśvara (Mitaksharā, VI), Śūlapāṇi (VII), Mitramiśra (VIII). Column III gives the number of bones of each item of the list, and column IV the totals of the bones named in each verse. For the original texts and translations of the commentaries, see §§ 79–82.

[1] As a fact, the India Office MS., No. 540, of the *Viṣṇu Smṛti*, reads *kapāla*; see § 84.

I. VERSE.	II. ITEMS OF LIST.	III. YĀJN.	IV. YĀJN.	V. AP.	VI. VIJN.	VII. ŚŪL.	VIII. MIT.
85	1. Teeth and sockets	64					
	2. Nails (*nakha*)	20	108	108	104	104	104
	3. Long bones (*śalākā*)	20					
	4. Bases (*sthāna*)	4					
86	5. Phalanges (*aṅguli*)	60					
	6. Heels (*pārṣṇi*)	2					
	7. Ankle-bones (*gulpha*)	4	74	74	74	74	74
	8. Forearms (*aratni*)	4					
	9. Legs (*jaṅgha*)	4					
87	10. Knee-caps (*jānu*)	2					
	11. Elbow-pans (*kapola*)	2					
	12. Thighs (*ūru-phalaka*)	2					
	13. Shoulder-blades	2	14	12	14	14	14
	14. Collar-bones (*akṣa*)	2	}				
	15. Palatal cavities (*tālūṣaka*)	2	}	2			
	16. Hip-blades (*śroṇi-phalaka*)	2					
88	17. Pubes (*bhaga*)	1					
	18. Back-bones (*pṛṣṭha*)	45					
	19. Neck-bones (*grīvā*)	15	63	63	64	64	64
	20. Windpipe (*jatru*)	1			2	2	2
	21. Chin (*hanu*)	1					
89	22. Basal tie-bones	2					
	23 *a*. Bones of brows (*lalāṭa*)	1		1	2	2	2
	" eyes (*akṣi*)	1	78	2 80	2 81	2 81	2 81
	" cheeks (*gaṇḍa*)	1		2	2	2	2
	23 *b*. Nasal bone (*nāsā*)	1					
	24. Ribs, &c. (*pārśvaka*)	72					
90	25. Temporal bones (*śaṅkha*)	2					
	26. Cranial pan-shaped	4	23	23	23	23	23
	27. Breast-bones (*uras*)	17					
	Grand totals		360	360	360	360	360

2. It will be noticed at once that the totals of Aparārka (col. V) differ from those of the three other commentators (cols. VI, VII, VIII). The latter agree among themselves; and a comparison of their comments shows that the views of Vijnāneśvara, who is the oldest among them, have been simply adopted by the two others. Aparārka, who was a near contemporary of Vijnāneśvara, holds an independent view, which differs in respect of four of the six totals; viz. the first, third, fourth, and fifth. These differences will now be considered *seriatim*.

3. In verse 85, Vijnāneśvara (in his commentary called *Mitākshara*) makes the total of the bones to be 104. He arrives at this total by discounting the bases (*sthāna*). According to him the terms *sthāna* (base) and *śalākā* (long bone) refer to the same organ (hand or foot, as the case may be), but describing it from two different points of view: *śalākā* describes the two hands and feet with reference to the total number of their individual bones, which is twenty, while *sthāna* describes them with regard to the four sets into which those twenty bones are divided. Of course, in a mere enumeration of the bones, both terms are not required; and as we are not primarily concerned with any sets they may form among themselves, but only with their number as individual bones, the four *sthāna* (or sets of *śalākā*) are rejected from the count. On the other hand, according to Aparārka, the two terms *śalākā* and *sthāna* refer to quite different organs, *śalākā* denoting the long bones (metacarpal and metatarsal), and *sthāna*, the bases of the long bones, that is, the carpus and tarsus, or what Suśruta calls *kūrca* or cluster of small bones. The reason—a textual one—that led the two commentators to this difference of interpretation, will be found fully explained in an Exegetical Note, § 83. Here it is only necessary to point out that Aparārka is correct; for the interpretation of Vijnāneśvara entirely omits from the count two such important organs as the carpus and tarsus. The total of the bones in verse 85, therefore, must be 108, as stated by Aparārka.

4. In verse 87, Vijnāneśvara makes the total of the bones to be fourteen, while Aparārka counts only twelve. The difference arises from Aparārka's taking *akṣa-tālūṣaka* (Nos. 14, 15)

to be but a single term, and to denote a single bone, that is, a bone situated, as he supposes, 'on the edge of the eye' (*netra-prānta*), there being, of course, two such bones, one on the edge of either eye.[1] On the other hand, Vijnāneśvara takes that term to be double, and to denote two distinct bones; namely, *akṣa* to signify 'the bone between the eye and the ear' (*karṇa-netrayor-madhye*),[2] and *tālūṣaka* to denote the hard palate (*kākuda*). In this case, so far as the counting is concerned, Vijnāneśvara, no doubt, is correct. Aparārka was probably led to his fanciful interpretation of the single term by the necessity of working out the required grand total of 360 bones. But with regard to the meaning of the term *akṣa*, both of them are wrong. That term is merely a shorter form of the word *akṣaka*, and denotes the collar-bone (§ 55).[3]

5. In verse 88, Vijnāneśvara makes the total of the bones to be sixty-four, while Aparārka counts sixty-three. The difference arises from the fact that Vijnāneśvara counts two *jatru* (No. 20), while Aparārka counts but one. In this case Aparārka again is right, for Vijnāneśvara commits the mistake of taking *jatru* to mean collar-bone. The subject will be fully discussed in the Third Section (§ 62); here it must suffice to point out that Vijnāneśvara's interpretation is in the teeth of the text which he interprets, and which distinctly says that there is but one *jatru*.

6. In verse 89, Vijnāneśvara makes the bones amount to eighty-one, while Aparārka counts eighty. The difference arises from their counting the bones referred to in the complex term *lalāṭ-ākṣi-gaṇḍa*, brow-eye-cheek (No. 23 *a*), in two different ways. Aparārka takes the term to denote one brow, two eyes, and two cheeks, or altogether five bones, while Vijnāneśvara counts two brows, two eyes, and two cheeks, or a total of six bones. In this case, both are wrong. In the text, that complex term

[1] He evidently takes *akṣa* to be synonymous with *akṣi*, eye.

[2] In fact, Vijnāneśvara's *akṣa* is identical with Aparārka's *akṣa-tālūṣaka*.

[3] Both Professors Stenzler and Jolly have been misled by the commentaries in their translations 'Schläfen' (*Yajnavalkya's Gesetzbuch*, p. 98) and 'lower part of the temples' (*Sacred Books of the East*, vol. vii, p. 284); so also Mandlik, p. 253, has 'temples'.

is not qualified by any numeral—a circumstance which indicates that but one bone is reckoned for each of the three items.[1] Hence there are no more than three bones in No. 23 *a*, and the total of the bones included in verse 89 is really seventy-eight. That this is the true interpretation of the text is proved by the fact that it works out the correct grand total 360, as shown in col. IV (also § 16).

§ 21. *Continuation*

1. Regarding the principal defect of the Non-medical Version—its total neglect of the bones of the arms and wrists—it is instructive to note the shifts to which the commentators are put to explain it.

2. As to the omission of all mention of the wrist-bones, the commentators do not seem to have realized it at all, for none of them makes any reference to it. Gangādhar, as we have seen (§ 19), did realize it; and he, therefore, introduced the wrist-bones (*maṇika*) in his reconstruction of the Non-medical Version. But the early commentators noticed only the omission of the arms—a circumstance, indeed, which cannot surprise us, seeing that the arms form such a conspicuous part of the body. But the way in which they deal with the omission is characteristic. The only solution of the difficulty which they are able to suggest, consistently with their respect for the integrity of their sacred text, is to declare that the arms (*bāhu*) are virtually included in the term forearm (*aratni*, No. 8). Thus Vijnāneśvara says (see § 80), 'the bones of the arms, being implied in the term forearm, number four'; and his explanation is unquestioningly adopted by the later commentators, Śūlapāṇi and Mitra-

[1] That is to say, *ekaikam*, 'one in each,' is to be understood with the clause *lalāṭ-ākṣi-gaṇḍe*, but not *dve dve*, 'two in each,' as Vijnāneśvara understands. His erroneous interpretation has gained such credence that it has actually modified the text of the list in the Institutes of Vishnu (§ 22), and that it has been unquestioningly accepted by the translators of the two legal treatises: Professor Stenzler, p. 98, 'an deren Wurzel zwei; ebenso an Stirne, Augen, Wangen,' and Professor Jolly (*Sacred Books of the East*, vol. vii, p. 284), 'there are two (bones) to the forehead, (two) to the eyes, and (two) to the cheeks.'

miśra (§§ 81, 82).[1] The total inappropriateness of such an interpretation is obvious; for the entire arm (or upper extremity) consists of three bones, two in the forearm and one in the arm. The total, accordingly, of the bones of the two upper extremities amounts to six. But Vijnāneśvara and his followers do not seem to have been aware of the fact that the forearm contained two bones. This is pretty clear from their comments (see §§ 80–82). Their idea was that each extremity consisted of two bones, arm and forearm, and similarly leg and thigh, each containing a single bone. Anyhow, Aparārka, while giving the same explanation (§ 79), candidly says, 'though the term forearm (*aratni*) does not really include the arm (*bāhu*), yet here, for the sake of securing the number four of the bones, it is so employed' (i. e. as inclusive of the arm). This shift of interpretation necessarily led to another incongruity. If the term forearm (*aratni*) included the arm (*bāhu*), by parity of reason the term leg (*jaṅgha*) must include the thigh (*ūru*). As a matter of fact the commentators do draw that conclusion. Thus Aparārka expressly says (§ 79), 'similarly the word leg (*jaṅgha*) here signifies the whole lower extremity, and hence the bones of the two legs number four.' But he fails to notice that the bones of the thighs are expressly and separately enumerated in verse 87, where accordingly he counts them a second time.

3. The true explanation of the difficulty, of course, must be of a very different kind; and it is one which the text of the Non-medical Version itself suggests with some degree of probability. The place where the mention of the bones of the arms and wrist-bones would come in is verse 87. Now the wording of that verse is marked by some peculiarities. It runs as follows:

dve dve jānu-kapol-oruphalak-āṁsa-samudbhave ।
akṣa-tālūṣake śroṇiphalake ca vinirdiśet ॥

Literally this means: 'two (bones) each in the knees, cheeks, thigh-blades, and in what springs from the shoulder; also, (as) one

[1] Also Nanda Paṇḍita adopts it in his commentary on the *Viṣṇu Smṛti* (§ 85).

should declare, in the collar-bones, palatal cavities, and hip-blades.' Here the item 'cheeks' is utterly out of place, occurring as it does between the knees and thighs. To any one conversant with the skeletal structure it must be obvious that words meaning elbow and arm should have their place there; and there can be no doubt whatever that *kapola* is simply an ancient misreading for *kapāla*, elbow-pan.[1] Gangādhar recognized the truth, and hence in his reconstruction of the Non-medical Version (§ 19, cl. 4) he substituted the correct synonym *kūrpara*. There is another ancient misreading in the term *ūru-phalaka*, thigh-blade; for *phalaka* denotes a broad, flat bone, and is quite inappropriate as a descriptive of the thigh-bone. The true reading, of course, must be *nalaka*, which signifies a cylindrical, hollow bone, and which occurs, in this connexion, in the Medical Versions of Charaka and Bheḍa (§§ 4, 12). Very striking is the use of the otiose phrase 'one should declare' in the midst of a statement packed as concisely as possible with the details of a long enumeration. It clearly suggests that it is inserted as mere padding to fill up an awkward lacuna. Yājnavalkya, or whoever was the author of the Non-medical Version, must have had a defective MS. copy of the Medical Version to work with. There were false readings in it (*kapola*, *ūru-phalaka*) as well as lacunae (arms and wrist-bones). As he was unable to supply the lacunae, he had recourse to padding. The use of the curious term *aṁsa-samudbhava*, springing from the shoulder, to denote the shoulder-blade, is perhaps due to the same need of padding. For though it is not a false descriptive, it is a needlessly long substitute for the shorter terms *aṁsa-ja* or *aṁsa-phalaka*. In addition to padding, however, the author had also to make good the shortage of six bones caused by the omission of the arms and wrist-bones. This he did, as shown in § 17 (p. 48), by augmenting the number of the breast-bones and facial bones by three bones each, or a total of six bones. We have here a case of ill-instructed 'editing' of a medical text similar to

[1] Accordingly, the translation 'Backen' by Professor Stenzler (p. 98) and 'cheek' by Professor Jolly (*Sacred Books of the East*, vol. vii, p. 284) should be replaced by 'Elbogenknochen', and 'funny-bone' or 'crazy-bone' respectively.

that from which the texts of Charaka and Suśruta suffered recently at the hands of Gangādhar (§§ 9, 35), and anciently at the hands of Vāgbhaṭa I (§ 40).

§ 22. *The Non-medical Version of the Institutes of Vishnu*

1. The essential identity of the Non-medical Version, as it is found in the Institutes of Vishnu, with the same Version as it occurs in the Law-book of Yājnavalkya, is shown by the fact that it also omits all mention of the arms and wrist-bones, and that it also corrects the resulting shortage of six bones by a corresponding increase in the number of bones of the breast and face, as explained in § 17 (p. 48).

2. On the other hand, there are significant points of difference. These will be enumerated with reference to the table given in § 20.

(*a*) The list in the Institutes omits No. 4, bases (*sthāna*), altogether.

(*b*) In No. 20 it counts two *jatru* or collar-bones.

(*c*) In No. 23 *a* it counts two bones for each of the three items: brows, eyes, cheeks; that is a total of six bones.

Referring to column VI of that table, it will be seen that these three points of difference exactly reflect the interpretation which Vijnāneśvara, in his Mitaksharā Commentary, places on the statements of the Law-book of Yājnavalkya. According to him, the item 'bases' (*sthāna*) is practically superfluous; accordingly the Institutes of Vishnu omits that item altogether. Again, Vijnāneśvara takes *jatru* to mean collar-bone, and counts two of them, in spite of the plain statement of the text that there is only one *jatru*: the Institutes, as interpreted by Nanda Paṇḍita, follows suit. Once more Vijnāneśvara counts two brows, two eyes, and two cheeks: the Institutes does the same, and in fact actually introduces the number two (*dve*) into the text (p. 56, footnote). The conclusion from this remarkable agreement is unavoidable that whoever drew up the list as we find it in the Institutes, did so on the basis of Vijnāneśvara's interpretation, and that accordingly the introduction of that list in the Institutes cannot be placed earlier than the date of Vijnāneśvara, that is after 1100 A. D. (§ 14). Seeing that the Institutes of Vishnu appears to be often quoted in the Mitaksharā,[1] it does not seem impossible that the appearance of the list in the Institutes is due to Vijnāneśvara himself.

3. In connexion with the late date of the introduction of the Non-medical Version into the Institutes of Vishnu, it is instructive to note the attempts that have been made, in some manuscripts of that work, to amend the text so as to remedy the great defect of the omission of the arms. As to the omission of the wrist-bones it appears never to have been realized by any one, copyist or commentator. Among the seventeen MSS. enumerated in § 14, there are four, Nos. 4, 12, 13, 17 (see § 84), which offer a curiously emended text. They omit the clause referring to the thighs and shoulder-blades (*ūro-'ṁsayoḥ*, No. 66 in Professor Jolly's edition, and Nos. 12, 13 in the table in § 20), and instead of the clause referring to the long bones (*pāṇi-pāda-śalākāś-ca*, No. 59 in the edition, and No. 3 in the table) they substitute the clause: 'two arms, two forearms, two thighs' (*dve bāhū, dve prabāhū, ūru-dvayam*). But this emendation is no real improvement; for though it introduces the arms (*bāhu*), and retains the thighs (*ūru*), it eliminates the shoulder-blades (*aṁsa*), and reduplicates the forearms (*prabāhu*) which had already been mentioned under the term *aratni* (No. 63 in the edition, and No. 8 in the table).[2] But though the emendation is not a success, it at all events proves that the text of the Institutes, so far as the list of the bones is concerned, was not considered too sacred to be altered. In the case of the Law-book of Yājnavalkya, as shown in § 21, though the commentators recognized the omission

[1] See Professor Jolly's Introduction, p. xxxii, in *Sacred Books of the East*, vol. vii. It would be interesting to examine (what I have not been able to do) all early quotations of the list from the Institutes. If no quotation earlier than Nanda Paṇḍita can be found, the introduction of the list into the Institutes may be due to that commentator who adopts all the views of Vijnāneśvara.

[2] With regard to the repetition of the forearms, it may be noted that it only occurs in two MSS., viz. Nos. 12 and 17. In the critical footnotes in the *Bibliotheca Indica* edition, p. 197, the reading in question, which occurs in No. 12 (Professor Jolly's MS. V), is not recorded.

of the arms, they were unwilling to meddle with the time-honoured text, and accordingly had recourse to shifts of interpretation. The fact that there was no reluctance to meddle with the text of the Institutes of Vishnu, would seem to show that in that work the list enjoyed no right of inviolability, but was known to be of recent introduction.

4. It only remains to note two lesser points of difference and of agreement between the Institutes of Vishnu and the Law-book of Yājnavalkya. The two points of difference are the following:

(*a*) In No. 1 the Institutes substitutes the curious term *sūkṣma*, or minute (*scl.* bone), for *sthāla*, to denote the sockets of the teeth.

(*b*) It places No. 27, breast-bones (*uras*), not at the very end of the list, but between No. 24, ribs, and No. 25, temples—a location which is no less incongruous (see § 17).

The two points of agreement are the following:

(*a*) In No. 23 *b* the Institutes of Vishnu also uses the curious term *ghanāsthikā*, or *ghana*-bone, to denote the nose.

(*b*) It also places the phalanges (No. 5) after the long bones (No. 3), whereas in the Medical Version of Charaka and Bheḍa the phalanges occupy their natural and logical position in advance of the long bones (§§ 4, 12).

§ 23. *The Non-medical Version in the 'Anatomy'*

1. It remains to notice a work which also contains a version of Ātreya's system of the skeleton. Into the preceding discussion it has not been introduced, because its author and age are at present unknown. Nevertheless its testimony[1] on some of the points which have been discussed is sufficiently striking to deserve to be taken into consideration. Its name is simply *Śārīra*, or 'Anatomy', and so far as I know, it is not otherwise known. It is contained in the same MS. volume No. M. a. I. 483 (Cat. No. 167) of the Tübingen University Library which contains also the 'Chapter on Anatomy' of the Vishnu Dharmottara Purāna, already mentioned in § 14.[2] Its

[1] This curiously corroborative testimony was discovered by me only after the preceding paragraphs had been written.

[2] The MSS. of both works are written by the same 'hand' of

versified contents are compiled from many different sources, some of which are quoted by name.[1] Its statement on the skeleton, in particular, is taken from the Law-book of Yājnavalkya, and accordingly gives the Non-medical Version. Though in this case the source is not named, there can be no hesitation as to its identity, seeing that in most of the verses there is a literal agreement (see § 87). But the interesting point is that the agreement fails mainly in verse 87, where, as shown in § 21, the great defect of the Non-medical Version comes in. This verse is entirely rewritten in the 'Anatomy', so as to admit the insertion of the two arms and four wrist-bones.

2. The statement on the skeleton in the 'Anatomy' runs as follows (Original Text and literal translation in § 87):

'The body has six parts (*aṅga*), and of bones it has three hundred and sixty; namely,

[Verse 85] 1. 64 teeth (*danta*) with their sockets (*ulūka*).
2. 20 nails (*nakha*).
3. 20 long bones (*śalākā*).
4. 4 bases (*sthāna*) of the long bones.

[Verse 86] 5. 60 phalanges (*aṅguli*).
6. 2 heels (*pārṣṇi*).
7. 4 ankle-bones (*gulpha*).
8. 4 bones of the forearms (*aratni*).
9. 4 bones of the legs (*jaṅgha*).

[Verse 87] 10. 2 collar-bones (*aṁsa*).
11. 2 shoulder-blades (*aṁsa-phalaka*).

a Bengali writer, and their leaves are numbered consecutively on the left-hand reverse margin. It was probably for this reason that in the Catalogue they are described as being a single work called *Viṣṇudharmottara.* But that they are really two separate works is proved by the following facts: (1) There is an alternative numbering of the folios on their right-hand reverse margins, which is separate for either of the two works; (2) The end of the first work is indicated on the obverse of the fifth folio (or the eighth of the total consecutive count) by the colophon *iti Viṣṇudharmottar-oktaṁ Śārīraṁ samāptam*, i.e. here ends the 'Anatomy' declared in the Vishnudharmottara; while the end of the second work is on the obverse of the thirteenth folio (twentieth of the total) as *iti Śārīraṁ samāptam*, i.e. here ends the 'Anatomy'; (3) The subject of the two works is identical, and to a large extent they go over the same ground; witness, e.g. the occurrence of the list of bones in both works.

[1] e.g. Charaka, *Yoga-muktāvalī*, *Kaulāvali Nirṇaya*, *Lauha-pradīpa.*

12. 4 wrist-bones (*hasta-maṇika*).
13. 2 hollow bones (*nalaka*) of the arms (*bāhu*).
14. 2 hollow bones (*nalaka*) of the thighs (*ūru*).
15. 2 palates (*tālu*).
16. 2 eyes (*netra*).
17. 2 knee-caps (*jānu*).
18. 2 elbow-pans (*jānu-kapālikā*).
19. 2 hip-blades (*śroṇi-phalaka*).
20. 2 basal tie-bones of the (lower) jaw (*hanu-mūla bandhana*).

[Verse 88] 21. 1 pubic bone (*bhaga*).
22. 45 back-bones (*pṛṣṭha*).
23. 10 neck-bones (*grīvā*).
24. 1 windpipe (*jatru*).
25. 1 (lower) jaw (*hanu*), or chin.

[Verse 89] 26. 1 facial bone constituting nose, cheeks, and brows (*nāsa-gaṇḍakūṭa-lalāṭaka mukhe*).
27. 72 ribs (*pārśvaka*) with their sockets (*kaulaka*) and tubercles (*arbuda*).

[Verse 90] 28. 2 temporal bones (*śaṅkhaka*).
29. 4 cranial pan-shaped bones (*śiraḥ-kapāla*).
30. 17 breast-bones (*uras*).

These make up the skeleton of man.'

3. Comparing the foregoing statement with what has been explained in §§ 17 and 21 regarding the construction of the Non-medical Version in the Law-book of Yājnavalkya, the following points may be observed:

(*a*) The author of the 'Anatomy' noticed the omission of the arms and wrist-bones, and the consequent padding of verse 87 with otiose elements. Hence he entirely rewrote that verse, eliminating all padding, and thus making room for the inclusion of the four wrist-bones (No. 12) and two arms (No. 13).

(*b*) He further noticed the difference in the way of counting the facial bones; viz. that Charaka counted a single bone for the complex of nose, cheeks, and brows, while the Non-medical Version counted four bones, one for each of the four items: nose, cheeks, brows, and eyes. Accordingly[1] he restored Charaka's count (No. 26), which process involved the exclusion of the eyes.

(*c*) On the other hand, probably accepting the authority of the system of Suśruta as against that of Charaka, he retained

[1] Probably on the authority of Chakrapāṇidatta's Commentary (§ 11).

the eyes, but assigned to them a special place in No. 16, in the reconstructed verse 87.

(*d*) For the same reason, he appears also to have retained the count of seventeen breast-bones (No. 30).

The result of all this manipulation of the statements of the Non-medical Version was that there were now five bones in excess of the required total 360. Hence

(*e*) He reduced the number of neck-bones by five, counting ten (No. 23) against Charaka's fifteen (No. 23 in § 4).

4. The whole operation, as above explained, may be exhibited thus:

Grand total of the Non-medical Version .		360
Add, Two arms (No. 13)	2	
Four wrist-bones (No. 12)	4	
Two eyes (No. 16)	2	
	—	8
Total		368
Deduct, Three facial bones (No. 26) . .	3	
Five neck-bones (No. 23) . .	5	
	—	8
Balance		360

The objection to this operation is twofold. First, the inclusion of the two eyes is not warranted by the Medical Version of either Charaka or Bheḍa. The eyes, in fact, form no item of the skeletal structure in the system of Ātreya, but belong to the system of Suśruta (§ 30). Secondly, the reduction in the number of neck-bones is not warranted by any true view of the skeletal system. The correct procedure for the author of the 'Anatomy' would have been to restore Charaka's count of the breast-bones, that is, to count fourteen breast-bones (No. 24 in § 4) instead of seventeen. This reduction of three bones in the breast, together with the exclusion of the two eyes, would have given him the five bones which he required to redress the excess resulting from his operation.

5. On the other hand a distinct improvement made by the author of the 'Anatomy' is his correction of the two ancient false readings *kapola* and *ūru-phalaka* (Nos. 11 and 12 in § 16,

and see § 21, cl. 3), for which he substitutes the true readings *ūru-nalaka* and *kapālikā*.

§ 24. *Relation of the Medical Version to the Non-medical*

1. We are now in possession of all the evidence to enable us to sum up the case concerning the relation of the two Medical Versions (§§ 4, 12) to the Non-medical.

2. When the needful corrections are made in the Non-medical Version, which have been indicated in §§ 17–23, that is, when the omitted six bones of the arms and wrists are inserted, and on the other hand, the alterations, made for the purpose of correcting those omissions, are cancelled, the Non-medical Version reveals itself in all essentials to be exactly the same as the Medical Version of Charaka in the restored form given in § 7.

3. But in two striking points of terminology, the Non-medical Version differs from the Medical Version, whether of Charaka or of Bheḍa. These are: first, the use of the term *sthāla* (No. 1 in § 16) or *sūkṣma* (§ 22, cl. 4 *a*) to signify the sockets of the teeth, where the two Medical Versions have the term *ulūkhala*. Secondly, its use of the term *ghanāsthikā* to denote the nose, which is not found in the two Medical Versions. The latter term has been a puzzle to all commentators. They simply refer to it as 'the so-called *ghana* bone' (*ghana-saṁjñam-asthi*), but do not attempt to explain it. But seeing that there exists a Sanskrit word *ghrāṇa*, or Prākrit *ghāṇa*, meaning 'smelling' or 'nose', it may be suggested that *ghanāsthikā* represents the Sanskrit word *ghrāṇ-āsthikā*, lit. smelling bone, which in the ordinary Prākrit would take the form *ghāṇatthikā*, but in the North-Western Prākrit, or the well-known Vernacular Sanskrit of those parts, which were the home of the school of Ātreya, might very well have been *ghanāsthikā*.

4. Also, in a formal point of arrangement, the Non-medical Version differs from the two Medical Versions. In the former the phalanges are placed after the long bones (§ 22, cl. 4 *b*). In the Medical Versions of Charaka (§ 4) and Bheḍa (§ 12), on the other hand, they precede the long bones. The latter arrangement, it is hardly necessary to say, observes the natural and logical order of the bones.

5. These differences, comparatively trifling as they are, seem to warrant the inference that the Non-medical Version is based neither on the Compendium of Charaka (i.e. ultimately of Agniveśa) nor on that of Bheḍa, but that, as suggested in § 1 (p. 4), it represents a third Medical Version which may have stood in the Compendium of another of the six pupils of Atreya, whose identity at present is unknown.

6. A coincidence may be worth noting. In the existing MS. of the *Bheḍa Saṁhitā* the clause referring to the arms is missing (§ 13, cl. 1). Exactly the same omission is found in the Non-medical Version (§ 17, cl. 2 *c*). The author of that version, as has been suggested in § 21 (p. 58), must have had a defective MS. of the Medical Version to work with. The actual existence of such defective manuscripts is curiously corroborated by the MS. of the *Bheḍa Saṁhitā*.

§ 25. *General Conclusions*

The principal results of the investigation in the preceding paragraphs may now be summarized as follows:

1. In the Medical and Non-medical Versions we possess three independent presentments of the doctrine of Ātreya concerning the skeleton, transmitted, probably, by three members of his school. To two of these members, Agniveśa and Bheḍa, the two Medical Versions professedly are due. Agniveśa's Version we possess only as contained in the Compendium of Charaka, but that Charaka introduced no material change into it, is proved by its close agreement with the Version of Bheḍa. The name of the third member, on whose presentment of Ātreya's system the Non-medical Version probably is based, is not known, neither its reputed author Yājnavalkya, nor any of the old commentators recording any tradition on the subject.

2. The text of the statement on the skeleton has not been preserved in a quite perfect condition in any of the three Versions. Several of the corruptions now found in them, e.g. the misplacement of No. 19, palatal cavities (*tālūṣaka* in §§ 4, 12, or No. 15 in § 16), are of a very ancient date, going back at least to the fourth century A. D., seeing that they appear in

the Law-book of Yājnavalkya which belongs to that century (§ 14). Fortunately (as may be seen by comparing § 4 with § 7), with the exception of one, none of these corruptions is of any great importance. Being clerical errors of misplacement or duplication they merely affect the external form of the statement. The single exception which affects the substance of the statement is the error concerning the number of the wrist-bones (*maṇika*), which is said to be two instead of four (No. 9 in §§ 4, 12). That there existed in the medical manuscripts, in this particular place, a more or less serious corruption of the text from a very early date, is shown by the fact that in the fourth century A. D. Yājnavalkya, in preparing his Law-book, apparently was unable to make anything of the medical text which was available to him, and thus came to omit from his Non-medical Version all mention of the wrist-bones. Nevertheless, as will be shown in § 52, with a little attention to the actual structure of the skeleton, it is easy enough to detect and remedy the error. As has been shown in § 23 (p. 63), the error was detected and corrected by the unknown author of the 'Anatomy'; and it is one of the merits of Gangādhar's edition of the Compendium of Charaka, that in his otherwise much misconceived reconstruction of Charaka's Medical Version (§ 8), he made the number of the wrist-bones to be four.[1]

NOTE.—It may be useful briefly to put together the various indications which go to prove that, in the osteological summary of Charaka, the true number of the wrist-bones was not two but four:

(1) As shown in paragraph 6, the exclusion of the two *aṁsa* as an otiose repetition necessitates a corresponding increase in the number of wrist-bones.

(2) As shown in § 52, the system of Charaka, consistently construed, requires the count of four wrist-bones.

(3) As shown in § 17, that count is a necessary factor of a correct appreciation of the confusion in the Non-medical Version.

(4) As shown in §§ 19 and 23, both Gangādhar and the anonymous author of the 'Anatomy', in their attempted reconstructions,

[1] Possibly Gangādhar may have been acquainted with the anonymous 'Anatomy'. See also the remarks in § 78 on Gangādhar's doctrine of four wrist-bones, in his reconstruction of the Non-medical Version.

find it necessary to admit that count; and in fact, without it no intelligent and consistent reconstruction appears to be possible.

Regarding the exclusion of the item *aṁsa*, as an otiose duplication, it is supported by the following circumstances:

(1) The actual occurrence of the similar duplication of *jānu* (§ 6).

(2) The actual omission, in the Non-medical Version, of both reduplicated words *aṁsa* and *jānu* (§§ 16, 17).

(3) The exclusion of *aṁsa* in the attempted reconstruction of Gangādhar (§ 9, p. 30).

(4) The mention of only two bones in the shoulder, in the osteological system of the Atharva Veda (§ 43, cl. 6).

B. The System of Suśruta

§ 26. *Suśruta's Statement and its Recensions*

1. Suśruta's system of the bones of the human body is stated in the beginning of the fifth chapter of the third or Anatomical Section (*Śārīra Sthāna*) of his Compendium.

2. There exist two recensions of this statement. One is printed in Jīvānanda's edition of the Compendium, p. 331, paragraphs 15 and 16 (Calcutta, 1889), as well as in all other editions with which I am acquainted; e. g. in the editions of Madhusūdana Gupta, p. 339 (Calcutta, 1834), of Prabhuram Jīvanaram, p. 481, paragraphs 18–21 (Bombay, 1901), Vīrasvāmi (Madras). The other occurs in Gangādhar's Commentary (called *Jalpa-kalpataru*) on the Compendium of Charaka, p. 188, lines 5–14 (Berhampore, 1879, see § 3). These two recensions differ so widely from each other that it becomes necessary once again to inquire into their respective authorization.

3. The recension which is found in Jīvānanda's and all other prints, and which, in the sequel, will be referred to as the Traditional Recension, has in its favour not only all available manuscripts, but also all ancient commentaries on the Compendium of Suśruta, as well as all such older medical works as adopt Suśruta's system of the skeleton. Or shortly, the Traditional Recension is supported by the whole body of existing witnesses.

4. As regards manuscripts, I have been able to examine the

following eleven copies, in all of which the existence of the Traditional Recension has been verified:

1. The Alwar Palace Library MS., No. 1703.[1]
2. The Benares College MS., No. 23 (old No. 64), fols. 18, 19.[1]
3. The Deccan College MS., No. 406, of 1895–8, fols. 37 *b*, 38; dated Saṁvat 1704 = A. D. 1647.
4. The Deccan College MS., No. 948, of 1884–7, fol. 14; undated.
5. The Deccan College MS., No. 949, of 1884–7, fols. 53 *b*, 54, 55 *a*, with Ḍallana's Commentary; undated.
6. The Deccan College MS., No. 956, of 1891–5, fol. 15; undated.
7. The Deccan College MS., No. 224, of 1882–3, fols. 23, 24 *a*; dated Saṁvat 1640 = A. D. 1583.[1]
8. The Bodleian MS. (Hultzsch), No. 349, fol. 31, in Śāradā characters, on paper, undated; a Kashmir MS.
9. The Bodleian MS., No. 739 (Wilson 290), fol. 19.
10. The India Office MS., No. 72 *b* (Cat. No. 2645), fol. 17; dated Saṁvat 1696 = A. D. 1639; contains only the *Śārīra Sthāna.*
11. The India Office MS., No. 1842 (Cat. No. 2646), fols. 21 *b*, 22 *a*; undated, contains Chandraṭa's revision of the text, based on the Commentary of Jaijjaṭa.

It should be observed that these MSS. come from widely separated Indian localities, and that three of them, Nos. 3, 7, 10, are of a considerable age—facts which enhance the value of their testimony as that of independent witnesses.

5. As to old commentaries, we have the two works, compiled by Gayadāsa and Ḍallana (§ 2). Of the former, I have been able to consult the unique MS. preserved in the Cambridge University Library, Add. 2491, fols. 48 *b*, 49 *a*; of the latter, the Deccan College MS., No. 949, of 1884–7, fols. 53 *b*, 54, 55 *a* (see above, No. 4). Of the latter, there is also the edition published by Jīvānanda, Calcutta, 1891. Both commentaries are based on the Traditional Recension, and contain not the remotest indication of being acquainted with the recension printed by Gangādhar. A number of other old commentaries are known by name, for

[1] A copy of the statement on the skeleton from MS. No. 1 was most kindly supplied to me by Major P. T. A. Spence, British Political Agent; from No. 2, by the Principal of the Benares College; and from Nos. 3–7, by Professor K. B. Pathak, of the Deccan College.

which Dr. Cordier's *Récentes Découvertes*, pp. 13, 14, may be consulted. But no copies of any of them—so far, at least, as the Anatomical Section (*Śārīra Sthāna*) is concerned—have as yet come to light.

6. As to older medical works which explicitly adopt Suśruta's system of the skeleton, we have the following two (§ 2):

(1) The *Śārīra Padminī*, by Bhāskara Bhaṭṭa (c. A.D. 1000), a manuscript of which is in the possession of Dr. P. Cordier (*Récentes Découvertes*, p. 30), dated Saṁvat 1735 = A.D. 1678; and from which a copy of the statement on the skeleton was very kindly supplied to me by the owner.

(2) The *Bhāva Prakāśa*, by Bhāva Miśra, in the sixteenth century, edited by Jīvānanda, and others.

Both works contain independently versified versions of the prose statement of Suśruta, made by the authors themselves, but based on the Traditional Recension of that statement.

7. As regards Gangādhar's recension, I have not been able to discover for it any authority whatsoever. It will be shown in the sequel (§§ 29–33) that the Traditional Recension is obnoxious to several very serious difficulties; and it is probable that the recension of Gangādhar (§ 35) is a reconstruction of his own to meet those of the difficulties which he had noticed. Though in some respects, his reconstruction is an improvement on the Traditional Recension, it cannot be accepted as satisfactory, because it fails to meet the most serious of the difficulties of that recension.

§ 27. *The Traditional Recension of Suśruta*

1. The Traditional Recension of Suśruta's statement (Original Text in § 88) on the human skeleton runs as follows:

'The professors of General Medicine (*āyurveda*) speak of three hundred and sixty bones.[1] But books on surgical science (*śalya-tantra*) know only of three hundred. Of these there are one hundred and twenty in the extremities; one hundred and seventeen in the pelvic cavity, sides, back, abdomen (*udara*), and breast; and from the neck upwards there are sixty-three. In this wise the total of three hundred bones is made up. Now in each toe of the foot, there are three bones; this makes altogether

[1] The reference here is to the doctrine of Ātreya and his school, preserved for us in the Compendia of Charaka and Bheḍa (§§ 4, 12).

fifteen. Those bones which constitute the sole, cluster, and ankle are ten. In the heel there is one; in the leg there are two; in the knee there is one; so also in the thigh. Thus there are thirty bones in one lower limb. The same count applies to the other lower limb, as well as to the two upper limbs. In the pelvic cavity there are five bones. Of these there are four in the anus, pubes, and hips; and the fifth constitutes the triangular (*trika*) sacrum. There are thirty-six bones in one side, and as many in the other. In the back there are thirty; eight in the breast; two in what are called the collar-bones (*akṣaka-saṁjña*); nine in the neck; four in the windpipe; and two in the jaws. The teeth number thirty-two. In the nose there are three bones. There is one in the palate; also one each in either cheek, ear, and temple; and there are six in the cranium.'

2. This detailed enumeration works out a total of 300 bones, as shown in the subjoined table:

I. FOUR EXTREMITIES.

1.	Phalanges (*aṅguli*)	15 × 4 =	60	
2.	Soles (*tala*)[1]			
3.	Clusters (*kūrca*)[1]	10 × 4 =	40	
4.	Ankle-bones (*gulpha*)			
5.	Heels (*pārṣṇi*)	1 × 4 =	4	
6.	Legs (*jaṅgha*)	2 × 4 =	8	
7.	Knees (*jānu*)	1 × 4 =	4	
8.	Thighs (*ūru*)	1 × 4 =	4	— 120

II. TRUNK.

9.	Pelvic cavity (*śroṇi*)		5	
10.	Sides (*pārśva*)	36 × 2 =	72	
11.	Back (*pṛṣṭha*)		30	
12.	Breast (*uras*)		8	
13.	Collar-bones (*akṣaka*)		2	— 117

III. NECK AND HEAD.

14.	Neck (*grīvā*)	9	
15.	Windpipe (*kaṇṭha-nāḍī*)[1]	4	
16.	Jaws (*hanu*)	2	
17.	Teeth (*danta*)	32	
18.	Nose (*nāsā*)	3	
19.	Palate (*tālu*)	1	
20.	Cheeks (*gaṇḍa*)	2	
21.	Ears (*karṇa*)	2	
22.	Temples (*śaṅkha*)	2	
23.	Cranium (*śiras*)	6	— 63
	Grand total		300

[1] *Tala*, *kūrca*, and *kaṇṭha-nāḍī* are identical with Charaka's *śalākā*, *sthāna*, and *jatru* (§ 4) respectively.

§ 28. *Suśruta's List compared with Charaka's*

Comparing Suśruta's list of bones with that of Charaka the following five points present themselves:

1. The Principle of Position. Suśruta divides the body into three parts, and explicitly enumerates the bones in accordance with their position in those divisions. Charaka (as representing Ātreya) also refers to this principle, but does not explicitly apply it to his enumeration. In fact, if the Traditional Recension (§ 4) is correct, he does not strictly adhere to it (§ 5).

2. The Principle of Homology. The osteological system of Suśruta is strictly based on the principle of homology, according to which the several organs of the right and left, and of the upper and lower halves of the body, correspond to each other. This comes out clearly in the Table in § 27, where the bones of the four extremities are succinctly enumerated on that principle. On the other hand, Ātreya-Charaka does not appear to have fully realized the homologies of the skeleton. The order in which he enumerates the bones of the four extremities (Nos. 8–15 in § 14), no doubt, indicates some degree of recognition of the principle of homology; and the manner in which he arrives at his total number of the vertebral column is intelligible only on the implication of the same principle (§§ 59, 61). But in the latter case, it is not applied by him with the thoroughness of Suśruta, and it fails him entirely with respect to the cranial and facial bones, which are treated by Suśruta alone on the homological principle (§§ 63, 66). The clearness with which that principle was recognized by Suśruta is shown by the subjoined statement (Original Text in § 96, cl. 1) in the sixth chapter of his Anatomical Section, which is devoted to an enumeration of the so-called 'vital spots' (*marman*) in the body.

'In particular, just as there are in the leg (or lower limb) the three mortal spots: ankle, knee, and ischio-pubic arch,[1] so there are in the arm (or upper limb) the three mortal spots: wrist, elbow (*kūrpara*), and collar-bone. Just as between the hip-bone and the scrotum there is the ischio-pubic arch, so between the breast-bone and the armpit there is the clavicular arch.'

[1] The *viṭapa*, or ischio-pubic arch, is formed by the combined rami of the os pubis and the ischium. See Figs. 4 and 20.

On the other hand (see §§ 41, 47) Suśruta carries his principle of homology to undue lengths in postulating three joints in each of the phalanges, and (at least, according to the Traditional Recension [1]) the existence of heels in the hand.

3. Alteration of Terms. The list of Suśruta introduces three new terms. These are No. 2, *tala*, No. 3, *kūrca*, and No. 15, *kaṇṭha-nāḍī*, which take the place, respectively, of Charaka's terms *śalākā*, *sthāna*, and *jatru*. The identity of the organs indicated by these alternative terms will be discussed in the Third Section (§§ 48, 49, 62). A fourth new term, which does not occur in the list, but is mentioned in the passage just quoted, is *kūrpara*, which is an alternative for Charaka's *kapālikā*, elbow-pan (No. 13 in § 4), and for the false term *kapola* of the Non-medical Version (No. 11 in § 16; see § 19, p. 52).

4. Alteration of Items. Suśruta omits from his list the thirty-two sockets of the teeth which occur in the list of Charaka (No. 2 in § 4). On the other hand, he introduces the two ears (*karṇa*), and (as may be mentioned here in anticipation of § 30) also the two eyes (*akṣi*). The omission of the sockets is due to Suśruta's counting two jaws in the place of Charaka's one (lower) jaw (No. 26 in § 4). The insertion of the ears and eyes is due to Suśruta's counting cartilaginous structures among the bones of the body (§ 30). The whole subject, however, of these alterations, as well as of others affecting the numbers of the bones in each item, will be discussed in full detail in the Third Section.

5. Alteration respecting Structure. With regard to two points Suśruta's views of the skeleton differ very considerably from those of Ātreya-Charaka. These are the structure of the vertebral column and of the skeletal face. On both points, as

[1] On this point, however, the Traditional Recension is wrong; see § 32.—A neat statement of the homologies of the four extremities occurs in Aruṇadatta's Commentary to the *Aṣṭāṅga Hṛdaya*, *Śārīra Sthāna*, ch. 3, verses 14, 15 *b* (vol. ii, p. 549 in the first edition): 'the bones of the two upper limbs are homologous to those of the two lower limbs. They may be detailed as follows: The hand corresponds to the foot, the base of the hand to the heel, and the wrist to the ankle. The cluster exists alike in both. The forearm corresponds to the leg, the elbow to the knee, and the arm to the thigh.'

will be fully explained in §§ 59, and 65, 66, the system of Suśruta marks a distinct advance in anatomical knowledge.

§ 29. *Difficulties and Inconsistencies of the Traditional Recension*

1. The Traditional Recension of the statement of Suśruta is beset with many difficulties and inconsistencies, both in respect of form and matter, which render it impossible to accept it as the genuine production of Suśruta.

2. As regards the form, there are two points which deserve consideration. In the first place, with reference to the bones of the trunk, the Traditional Recension states that they are distributed over 'the pelvic cavity, sides, back, abdomen, and breast' (§ 27). That this is the true reading of the Traditional Recension is proved by the fact that the two medical works, *Śārīra Padminī* and *Bhāva Prakāśa*, which adopt the statement of Suśruta, giving it, however, in a versified form of their own (§§ 26, 36), also name the abdomen (*udara*) in this connexion. The mention of the abdomen as a seat of bones may well cause surprise, and a suspicion that there must be some error in the text. The suspicion is confirmed when we find that in the subsequent enumeration of the bones in their several seats, the collar-bones (*akṣaka*) take the place of the abdomen (*udara*). As the collar-bones form a part of the shoulder-girdle, it suggests itself that the Sanskrit text of the statement of Suśruta, in its original and genuine form, must have read *aṁsa*, shoulder, instead of *udara*, abdomen. A very probable explanation of the origin of the error in the Traditional Recension may be given. In the classification of the bones according to their shape (§ 30), the text of the Traditional Recension has the compound word *pṛṣṭh-odara* (i. e. *pṛṣṭha*, back, and *udara*, abdomen). In this connexion the introduction of the term *udara*, abdomen, has a good reason. It is to indicate the position of the pubic arch (§ 60, cl. 2) as located in the anterior (or ventral) part of the pelvis. The latter organ comprises five bones (§ 27), viz. the two hip-blades (*nitamba*), the sacrum (*trika*), the coccyx (*guda*), and the pubic arch (*bhaga*). These five bones belong to two different classes: the hip-blades and the sacrum (incl. coccyx) belong to

the pan-shaped (*kapāla*), while the pubic arch belongs to the ornament-like (*valaya*). Hence, in classifying them according to their shape, the term *śroṇi*, pelvis, indicative of their common locality, could not be used; but each bone had to be indicated by its peculiar locality. Hence the sacrum and coccyx are indicated by the back (*pṛṣṭha*), and the pubic arch by the ventral part (*udara*) of the pelvis. The compiler of the Traditional Recension, failing to understand this, introduced the term *pṛṣṭh-odara* also into the enumeration of the bones according to their position in the body. But here the term is quite out of place. For the common locality of the five bones is already defined by the term *śroṇi*, pelvic cavity, while the locality of the bones of the shoulder-girdle (*aṁsa*) is entirely ignored. It can, therefore, hardly be doubted that the reading *pṛṣṭh-odara*, back and abdomen, of the Traditional Recension is an erroneous substitute for the true reading *pṛṣṭh-āṁsa*, back and shoulder.

3. In the second place, it will be shown in the next paragraph that the Traditional Recension omits all mention of the two shoulder-blades. These have their seat in the shoulder-girdle along with the collar-bones. One expects, therefore, in the enumeration of the 117 bones of the trunk, to find them mentioned in the clause respecting the collar-bones. As a fact, however, the Traditional Recension, while mentioning the two collar-bones, omits the shoulder-blades altogether. But it is noteworthy that the clause in question is worded in a very peculiar way. The Recension says: 'two in what is called the collar-bone' (*dve akṣaka-saṁjñe*).[1] The expression 'what is called' (*saṁjña*) is not employed in connexion with any other part, or bone, of the body. Yet there is nothing in the name *akṣaka*, for collar-bone, that calls for the use of the phrase *saṁjña*, 'what is called.' It suggests itself that that word *saṁjña* is a false reading, and that in all probability a word expressive of the missing shoulder-blades originally stood in its place. The ordinary term for shoulder-blade is *aṁsa-phalaka*; but the shorter word *aṁsa-ja*, literally 'shoulder-born', or

[1] *Saṁjñe* is here taken as the locative singular. It might also be taken as the nominative dual, 'two so-called collar-bones.' The argument is not affected thereby.

'issuing from the shoulder', would not be inappropriate, and might also be used. It is significant that the Non-medical Version of the system of Ātreya employs a synonym of the latter word, *aṁsa-samudbhava*, 'issuing from the shoulder,' to denote the shoulder-blade (see No. 13 in § 16). It will be shown in § 33, with respect to another point, that the Non-medical Version betrays marks of having been influenced by the system of Suśruta; and it suggests itself that the author of that Version was led to the choice of the term *aṁsa-samudbhava* by the occurrence of the synonymous term *aṁsa-ja* in the statement of Suśruta. It may be suggested, therefore, that, in the latter statement, in its original form in which we may suppose it to have left the hand of Suśruta, the clause respecting the collar-bones probably ran (not *dve akṣaka-saṁjñe*, but) *dve akṣak-āṁsaje*, 'two in the collar-bones and shoulder-blades'[1]; and that the word *aṁsaje* became corrupted into *saṁjñe*.

§ 30. *Continuation*

1. In respect of the matter of the statement, the Traditional Recension labours under three great difficulties.

In the first place, the list is incomplete. It omits two of the most conspicuous bones of the skeleton, namely, the shoulder-blades (*aṁsa-phalaka*, No. 16 of Charaka's list in § 4). It also omits the two eyeballs (*akṣi-koṣa*). In omitting these two items Suśruta's list, as it stands in the Traditional Recension, is inconsistent with another statement of his. Immediately following the list of bones in which Suśruta enumerates them according to their position in the body, he continues with another list dividing the bones into five classes according to their shape. This class-list (Original Text in §§ 88, 89) runs as follows:

'These bones are of five kinds, namely, pans (*kapāla*), sharp-ones (*rucaka*), tender-ones (*taruṇa*), ornaments (*valaya*), and reeds (*nalaka*). From among them the pan-shaped bones occur in the knees, elbows, hips, shoulders (*aṁsa*), cheeks, palate, temples, interiliac space (i.e. sacrum), and cranium. The sharp

[1] Or alternatively, 'two collar-bones and two shoulder-blades.'

bones are the teeth. The tender bones occur in the nose, ears, neck [1], and eyeballs (*akṣi-koṣa*). The ornament-shaped bones occur in the hands, feet, sides, back, abdomen, and breast. The remainder of the bones are termed reed-shaped.'

2. A comparison of the two lists, as given in the subjoined table, shows that all the items of the number-list reappear in the class-list with the exception of two which the latter contains in excess.

Number-list (as in § 27).	*Class-list.*	*Class-name.*
1. Phalanges	ditto	reed
2. Soles	ditto	reed
3. Clusters	ditto	ornament
4. Ankle-bones, wrist-bones	ditto	ornament
5. Heels	ditto	ornament
6. Legs, forearms	ditto	reed
7. Knees, elbows	ditto	pan
8. Thighs, arms	ditto	reed
9 *a*. Hip-blades, anal, sacral	ditto	pan
9 *b*. Pubic arch	ditto	ornament
10. Sides (i. e. ribs)	ditto	ornament
11. Back-bones	ditto	ornament
12. Breast-bones	ditto	ornament
13. Collar-bones	ditto	reed
14, 15. Neck, windpipe [2]	ditto	tender
16. Jaws	ditto	reed
17. Teeth	ditto	sharp
18. Nose	ditto	tender
19. Palate	ditto	pan
20. Cheeks	ditto	pan
21. Ears	ditto	tender
22. Temples	ditto	pan
23. Skull-bones	ditto	pan
24. —	Shoulder-blades	pan
25. —	Eyeballs	tender

3. Seeing that the class-list is intended to distribute all the items of the number-list into five kinds, it is evident that

[1] The reference, of course, is to the *jatru* or *kaṇṭhanāḍī*, the windpipe in the neck; see § 62, cl. 3.

[2] See the preceding note. The neck contains two organs, the neck-bones or cervical column, and the windpipe. In the class-list, of course, the latter is intended. The former, being a portion of the vertebral column, counts with No. 11, and belongs to the ornament-shaped class. The use of the term *grīvā* here is rather inaccurate, as it is usually employed to denote the cervical column.

the number-list, in the form in which it is found in the Traditional Recension, cannot be correct, but that, in its original and genuine form, it must have contained those two additional items: No. 24, shoulder-blades, and No. 25, eyeballs. It is true that, with reference to No. 24 in the class-list, the Traditional Recension employs the term *aṁsa,* which, in the Compendium of Suśruta, ordinarily denotes the collar-bone; but from the context it is quite obvious that, in the present case, it can refer only to the shoulder-blades. For the bones, here called *aṁsa,* are classed as pan-shaped (*kapāla*)—a description which is applicable only to the shoulder-blades. The collar-bones could only be described as reed-shaped (*nalaka*); and these bones, therefore, must be taken as referred to in the last class or the 'remainder' of the list. In literary Sanskrit the word *aṁsa* denotes, in a general way, the shoulder; in medical Sanskrit, at least of the Compendium of Suśruta, the several parts of the shoulder have specialized names: *aṁsa* is the collar-bone, *aṁsa-phalaka* (or *aṁsa-ja*), the shoulder-blade; *aṁsa-kūṭa,* the acromion process, and *aṁsa-pīṭha,* the glenoid cavity. The author of the Traditional Recension would seem to have been a person, who was imperfectly familiar with the anatomical terminology of Suśruta, and used the term *aṁsa* in the undefined literary sense; or more probably it is a scribal error for *aṁsa-ja* or *aṁsa-phalaka.* For a fuller discussion, see §§ 55, 56.

4. As regards the eyeballs, the class-list explicitly enumerates them among the 'tender' bones. In agreement herewith, speaking of the structure of the eye in the Supplementary Section (*Uttara Tantra*) of his Compendium, Suśruta describes the sclerotic coat of the eyeball as made of bone (*asthi*). The statement in question, describing the eye as seen in the sagittal section (Fig. 1), runs as follows:

'The outer one of the protecting covers[1] of the pupil consists of a luminous fluid, and the next one of flesh. The third is

[1] *Paṭala* denotes the protecting covers of the *dṛṣṭi,* or pupil, the supposed seat of vision. The composite nature (the 'tunics', incl. retina, choroid) of the 4th cover does not seem to have been known to the early Indian anatomists; nor the lens, which they thought to be a morbid accumulation of phlegm.

made of fat, and beyond it there is one consisting of bone.' (Original Text in § 96, cl. 2.)

It may be noticed also as a significant fact that the Non-medical Version of the system of Ātreya (§ 16) includes the eyeballs in the list of bones of the human body. The genuine list of Ātreya, as handed down by Charaka (§ 4) and Bheḍa (§ 12), does not count the eyes among the bones. The author of the Non-medical Version of that list, therefore, must have obtained the eyes from some other source; and this source cannot well have been any other than Suśruta's statement on the skeleton. If so, it follows that the latter statement, at the time of the

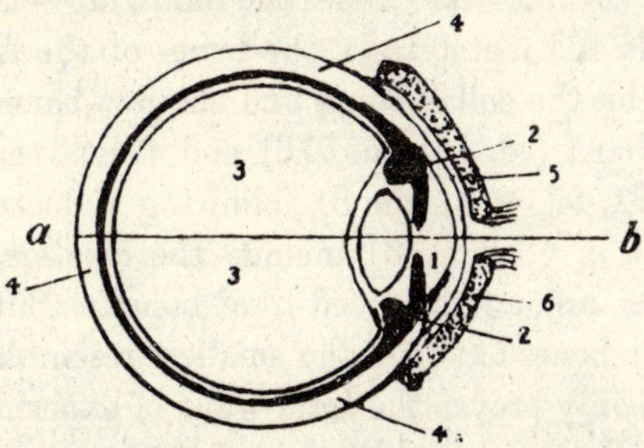

FIG. 1. DIAGRAM OF THE EYE, in Sagittal Section.
a–b. Optic Axis.

1. Outer cover, *Bāhya paṭala*, of luminous fluid, *Tejo-jala* (Aqueous humour).
2. Cover of muscle, *Piśita paṭala* (Ciliary body).
3. Cover of fat, *Medas paṭala* (Vitreous humour).
4. Cover of bone, *Asthi paṭala* (Sclerotica).

5, 6. Covers of eyelids and eyelashes, *Pakṣma-vartma paṭala*.

composition of the existing Law-book of Yājnavalkya, must have differed from the now existing Traditional Recension, and must have included the eyes in its list of bones.

5. It is clear, then, that Suśruta's list of bones of the human body, in its genuine form, must have contained four additional bones; viz. two shoulder-blades and two eyeballs. As regards the shoulder-blades, it has been shown in the preceding paragraph that their omission, in all probability, is due to a misreading of the term *saṁjña* for *aṁsaja*. As to the eyes, they

would appear simply to have dropped out of the penultimate clause (§ 27) which should run : 'one each in either cheek, eye, ear, and temple.'

Note.—With regard to the terms which occur in the class-list, *nalaka* means a reed, but not necessarily a hollow reed; it may be solid like the male bamboo. As used by the Indian anatomists it denotes any long bone, whether tubular or solid. Suśruta does not specify the bones which he likens to a *nalaka* or reed, but only says that they are 'the remainder', that is, that they are all those bones which do not fall into any of the other four classes. The process of exhaustion thus indicated shows that he classed as 'reed-like' bones the following—the phalanges, the metacarpals and metatarsals, the bones of the forearms, legs, arms, and thighs, the collar-bones and the jaw-bones. The commentators Ḍallana (ed. Jīv., p. 576) and Gayadāsa (Cambridge MS., Add. 2491, fol. 49 *a*, line 3), following a doctrine of Bhoja (Original Text in § 96, cl. 3), include the clusters, ankle-bones and wrist-bones among the 'reed-like' bones. But seeing that these particular bones have not the smallest resemblance to reeds, their inclusion only proves the total want of experimental knowledge of them on the part of Bhoja and the commentators.

Valaya is the name of a certain kind of personal ornament, such as bracelets, anklets, necklets, waist-bands, &c. They are well seen on the figures of the Bharhut Stūpa (of about the 2nd century A. D.), called Chulakokā and Suchiloma, shown in Figs. 2 and 3.[1] Suśruta states that these *valaya* bones are found in the hands and feet, and in the sides, back, abdomen, and breast. Those in the hands and feet are the clusters (carpus and tarsus), wrist-bones (styloid processes), ankle-bones (malleoli) and heels : they resemble bracelets and anklets. The latter are shown in Fig. 2. The other bones indicated by him are the ribs, the bones of the vertebral column, also the costal cartilages and sternum, all of which resemble a necklace (Fig. 2), and the pubic arch which resembles the bow of a waist-band (Fig. 3).

By the term *taruṇa*, tender bones, cartilages are denoted.

[1] Reproduced from Sir A. Cunningham's Report. See also Professor Hultzsch, in the *Journal of the German Oriental Society*, vol. xl, p. 63, No. 26.

The statement of Dr. Wise (*Hindu System of Medicine*, p. 52) that 'the difference [between Suśruta's total 300 and Charaka's total 360] is owing to their counting the cartilages with the bones' is hardly correct. Both writers include cartilages in their counts, though in different ways. The difference in their totals is mainly due to Charaka's counting the thirty-two sockets of the teeth as separate bones, and his including the twenty nails, neither of which are admitted in the count of Suśruta. See § 38, col. IV in the Table (p. 93).

§ 31. *Continuation*

1. In the second place the number ten, given in the Traditional Recension as the aggregate of the bones of the sole, cluster, and ankle (Nos. 2, 3, 4 in § 27), is inconsistent with other explicit statements of Suśruta. His commentator Ḍallana[1] explains that number ten in the following way:

'The term sole (*tala*) refers to the five long bones (*śalākā*) and to the single bone that connects them. The cluster (*kūrca*) and the ankle (*gulpha*) contain two bones each. Hence we have ten.' (Original Text in § 96, cl. 4.)

Ḍallana, therefore, identifies Suśruta's sole (*tala*) with Charaka's long bones (*śalākā*) and base (*sthāna*), that is, with Nos. 5 and 6 in § 4. He thus obtains six bones for the sole. Adding to them two cluster-bones and two ankle-bones, he makes up the aggregate ten. It has been pointed out in § 9, cl. 1 *b*, that the terms cluster (*kūrca*) and base (*sthāna*) are merely two different names, employed by Suśruta and Charaka respectively, for the same portion of the hand and foot, viz. the carpus and tarsus. Differentiating them, after the manner of Ḍallana, argues a want of anatomical knowledge such as cannot be attributed to Suśruta. In fact, as will be shown in § 40, the person responsible for this incongruity is, in all probability, Vāgbhaṭa I. But in any case, it is quite sufficient by itself to discredit the genuineness of the Traditional Recension.

[1] The earlier commentator Gayadāsa also mentions ten as the aggregate, though he does not enter into further details.

2. But further, the aggregate ten conflicts with the explicit statements of Suśruta himself regarding the number of clusters (*kūrca*) and ankle-bones (*gulpha*). On Ḍallana's theory there would be two clusters and two ankle-bones in either foot, and homologously two clusters and two wrist-bones (*maṇibandha*) in either hand. This results in an aggregate of eight clusters (*kūrca*), four ankle-bones (*gulpha*) and four wrist-bones (*maṇibandha*). On the other hand, Suśruta teaches explicitly that there are only four clusters in the hands and feet, two ankle-bones and two wrist-bones. Thus in the fifth chapter of the Anatomical Section (*Śārīra Sthāna*) he says:

'There are six clusters (*kūrca*) in the hands, feet, neck, and penis: namely, two in the hands, two in the feet, and one each in the neck and penis.' (Original Text in § 96, cl. 5.)

That is to say, there is one cluster in each hand and foot, making four; also one each in the neck and penis, making two; or an aggregate of six.[1] Again in the sixth chapter of the same Section, Suśruta says:

'There are two ankle-bones (*gulpha*) and two wrist-bones (*maṇibandha*).' (Original Text in § 96, cl. 6.)

3. It is evident, therefore, that Ḍallana's explanation of the aggregate ten involves a doctrine which was not held by Suśruta. It is, as will be shown in § 39, in reality the doctrine of Vāgbhaṭa I. An aggregate of ten, in fact, directly conflicts with the explicit doctrine of Suśruta. According to the latter, the sole (*tala*) consists of five long bones (*śalākā*, § 28, cl. 3); and

[1] *Kūrca* simply means a cluster of something, but not necessarily a cluster of true bones. In the case of the hands and feet, it is a cluster of small bones; but in the case of the neck, it refers to the cluster, or series, of imperfect cartilaginous rings which compose the windpipe (trachea), and apparently a similar view was held of the structure of the penis.—There are several other passages in the Compendium of Suśruta which confirm his doctrine of there being only four clusters in the hands and feet. They occur in the sixth chapter, on the 'vital spots'. There Suśruta speaks of 27 such spots in the sinews (*snāyu-marmāṇi*, Jīv. ed., p. 337, cl. 10) and 44 such spots causing weakness (*vaikalya-karāṇi marmāṇi*, Jīv. ed., p. 338, cl. 13). These numbers will not work out correctly, unless the clusters included in them are counted as being only four. The peculiar force of these passages lies in the indirectness of their evidence.

there are one cluster (*kūrca*) and one ankle-bone (*gulpha*). The true aggregate, therefore, can be no more than seven; and it follows that Suśruta's list of the bones, in its genuine form, must have contained that aggregate, but not ten.

§ 32. *Continuation*

1. In the third place, the number one hundred and twenty, given in the Traditional Recension, as the aggregate of the bones of the four extremities, involves (as may be seen from the Table in § 27) the incongruity of counting four heels. That count is based on a misconstruction of the explanatory direction of Suśruta. He enumerates the bones of one lower extremity (*sakthi*) as amounting to thirty, and proceeds to explain that in the same way the count of the bones in the other lower extremity, as well as in the two upper extremities, must be made. Now his aggregate, thirty, of the lower extremity includes the heel bone, but it does not follow, therefore, that the same way of counting, when applied to the upper extremities, must also include a heel bone. In short, Suśruta intended his explanation to be understood *cum grano salis*. In the case of the lower extremities which contain a heel, the aggregate is thirty; but in the case of the upper extremities which do not contain a heel, the aggregate, of course, must be twenty-nine. This means that no more than two heels may be counted, in making up the aggregate of the bones of the four extremities.

2. I know of no direct evidence as to the exact number of heels held by Suśruta, such as was available in the case of the two difficulties discussed in §§ 30 and 31. But neither is there any direct evidence for Suśruta's holding four heels, including two for the hands. It is also worth noting that the list of Charaka includes only two heels; and there is no reason for imputing to Suśruta a more incongruous view than Charaka held. On the whole, therefore, it is only reasonable to believe that the statement of Suśruta, in its genuine form, cannot have been intended to teach the existence of more than two heels.

§ 33. *Continuation*

1. The result of the discussion in the preceding paragraphs (§§ 30–2) is the reduction of the total of the bones, as enumerated in the Traditional Recension, from 300 to 290.

Thus:

Total of Traditional Recension (§ 27) . . .		300
Add 2 shoulder-blades and 2 eyes (§ 30) . .		4
Total .		304
Deduct 4 bases, 4 clusters, 2 ankle-bones, 2 wrist-bones (§ 31)	12	
Also deduct 2 heels (§ 32)	2	
	—	14
Balance		290

2. This resultant shortage of ten bones, of course, must be compensated in some way. A comparison of the lists of Charaka and Suśruta, as shown in the subjoined Table, suggests a solution of the difficulty.

	Charaka (§ 7).	*Suśruta* (§ 27).
1. Teeth	32	32
2. Sockets of teeth . . .	32	—
3. Nails	20	—
4. Phalanges	60	60
5. Long bones	20	20
6. Clusters, or bases . . .	4	4
7. Ankle-bones and wrist-bones	8	8
8. Heels	2	2
9. Legs and forearms. . .	8	8
10. Knees and elbows . . .	4	4
11. Thighs and arms . . .	4	4
12. Shoulder-blades . . .	2	2
13. Collar-bones	2	2
14. Back and pelvis . . .	45	35
15. Breast	14	8
16. Ribs, &c.	72	72
17. Neck and windpipe . .	16	13
18. Palate	2	1
19. Facial bones	4	9
20. Temples	2	2
21. Cranial bones . . .	4	6

3. The diverging items in the two lists are Nos. 2, 3, 14, 15, 17, 18, 19, 21. From among these, No. 3, nails, has no place

in the system of Suśruta, and the divergences in Nos. 2, 14, 17, 19, 21 depend on differences of anatomical theory which will be satisfactorily explained in the Third Section. There remain Nos. 15 and 18. It is noteworthy that these are precisely the two items in which the Traditional Recension agrees with the list of Vāgbhaṭa I (Nos. 13, 24 in § 37). Seeing that in two other points, already mentioned in § 31, the Traditional Recension has been unfavourably influenced by the list of Vāgbhaṭa I, it suggests itself as probable that in these two items also the same influence has been at work in causing the numbers eight and one to be adopted for the bones of the breast and palate respectively. As regards No. 18, palate, the list of Charaka gives two as the number of the bones of the palate; and there is no apparent reason why Suśruta should be credited with changing it in his list (see § 67). As to No. 15, we have a significant hint in the Non-medical Version of Ātreya's list of the bones (§ 16). The genuine list of Ātreya, as handed down by Charaka and Bheḍa, has only fourteen bones for the breast (No. 24 in §§ 4, 12, and No. 21 in § 7). The Non-medical Version of that list must have obtained its false number seventeen from some extraneous medical source; and it suggests itself that this source can have been no other than the list of Suśruta, as it stood at the time when the Non-medical Version was composed.

4. From these considerations it appears very probable that the original and genuine recension of the list of Suśruta allotted seventeen bones to the breast and two to the palate, instead of eight and one—the numbers which we now find in the Traditional Recension. The difference between these two sets of numbers ($17+2 = 19$, and $8+1 = 9$) is ten, that is to say, precisely the number we require to make good the shortage that results from the adjustments discussed in §§ 30–2. This coincidence tends to confirm the conclusion that the list of Suśruta, in its genuine form, must have given seventeen bones to the breast, and two bones to the palate.

§ 34. *Restored Recension of Suśruta's Statement*

1. We are now in a position to sum up the defects of the Traditional Recension, and restore what must have been the genuine form of the list of Suśruta.

2. The Traditional Recension is wrong in the following five points:

(*a*) It contains two misreadings (§ 29); viz. abdomen (*udara*) for shoulder (*aṁsa*), and the phrase 'what is called collar-bone' (*akṣaka-saṁjña*) for 'collar-bone and shoulder-blade' (*akṣak-āṁsaja*).

(*b*) It omits four bones; viz. the two shoulder-blades and the two eyeballs (§ 30).

(*c*) It gives the aggregate of its Nos. 2, 3, 4 wrongly as ten, instead of seven (§ 31), resulting in the wrong aggregate, thirty, for the bones of a lower extremity, instead of twenty-seven.

(*d*) It counts wrongly four heels, instead of two (§ 32), resulting in the false aggregate 120 of the bones of the four extremities, instead of 106.

(*e*) It counts wrongly eight bones of the breast, and one bone of the palate, instead of seventeen and two respectively (§ 33). And these false counts, together with those named in lit. *b*, result in the wrong aggregates 117 of the bones of the trunk, and 63 of the neck and head (§ 27), instead of 128 and 66 respectively.

3. Accordingly, the genuine statement of Suśruta must have run as follows, the restorations being in *italics*:

'The professors of General Medicine speak of three hundred and sixty bones; but books on Surgical Science know only of three hundred. Of these there are *one hundred and six* in the extremities; *one hundred and twenty-eight* in the pelvic cavity, sides, back, *shoulder*, and breast; and from the neck upwards, *sixty-six*. In this wise the total of the three hundred bones is made up. Now in each toe of the foot there are three bones; this makes altogether fifteen. Those bones which constitute the sole, cluster, and ankle are *seven*. In the heel there is one; there is also one in the thigh. Thus there are *twenty-seven* bones in one lower limb. The same count applies to the other lower limb, and *similarly* to the two upper limbs. In the pelvic cavity there are five bones. Of these there are four in the anus, pubes, and hips; and the fifth constitutes the triangular sacrum. There are thirty-six bones in one side, and as many in the other. In the back there are thirty; *seventeen* in the breast; two each in the *collar-bone and shoulder-blades*; nine in the neck; four in the windpipe, and two in the jaws. The teeth number thirty-two. In the nose there are three bones; *two* in the palate; one each in either cheek, *eye*, ear, and temple; and six in the cranium.' (Original Text in § 89.)

4. The genuine list of bones as thus restored is shown in the subjoined Table:

	I. Four Extremities.			
1.	Phalanges (*aṅguli*)		15 × 4 = 60	
2.	Soles (*tala*)	5 }		
3.	Cluster (*kūrca*)	1 }	7 × 4 = 28	
4.	Ankle-bone (*gulpha*)	1 }		
5.	Heel (*pārṣṇi*)		1 × 2 = 2	
6.	Legs (*jaṅgha*)		2 × 4 = 8	
7.	Knee (*jānu*)		1 × 4 = 4	
8.	Thighs (*ūru*)		1 × 4 = 4	
			—	106
	II. Trunk.			
9.	Pelvic cavity (*śroṇi*)		5	
10.	Sides (ribs, *pārśva*)		36 × 2 = 72	
11.	Back (*pṛṣṭha*)		30	
12.	Breast (*uras*)		17	
13.	Collar-bones (*akṣaka*)		2	
14.	Shoulder-blades (*aṁsaja*)		2	
			—	128
	III. Neck and Head.			
15.	Neck (*grīvā*)		9	
16.	Windpipe (*kaṇṭhanāḍī*)		4	
17.	Jaws (*hanu*)		2	
18.	Teeth (*danta*)		32	
19.	Nose (*nāsā*)		3	
20.	Palate (*tālu*)		2	
21.	Cheeks (*gaṇḍa*)		2	
22.	Eyeballs (*akṣikoṣa*)		2	
23.	Ears (*karṇa*)		2	
24.	Temples (*śaṅkha*)		2	
25.	Cranium (*śiras*)		6	
			—	66
			Grand total	300

§ 35. *Gangādhar's Recension of Suśruta's Statement*

1. Gangādhar's Recension of Suśruta's statement on the skeleton runs as follows:

'In the surgical text-book of Suśruta the number of the bones of the human body is given as only three hundred. Of these there are one hundred and eight in the extremities; one hundred and twenty-six in the pelvic cavity, sides, back, collar-bones (*akṣa*), and breast; and from the neck upwards, sixty-six. In this wise, the total of three hundred is made up. Now in each toe of the foot there are three bones; this makes altogether fifteen. Those bones which constitute the sole, cluster, and ankle are seven. In the heel there is one; in the leg there are two; in the knee there is one; also in the thigh there is one. Thus there are twenty-seven bones in one lower limb. The same count applies to the other lower limb, as well as to the two upper limbs. This makes up a total of one hundred and eight bones. In the pelvic cavity there are five bones; of these there are two in the hips; and the arms, pubes, and sacrum are constituted each of one bone. In one side there are thirty-six bones, and as many in the other. In the back there are thirty; two are in what is called the collar-bone; seventeen in the breast; eleven in the neck; four in the windpipe; and two in the jaws. The teeth number thirty-two. In the nose there are three bones, two in the palate; one each in either cheek, ear, and temple, making together six; and there are six in the cranium. These make altogether sixty-six. Thus the grand total of three hundred is made up. This is the list of the bones of the skeleton.' (Original Text in § 90.)

2. The list may be shown in tabular form, thus:

I. Four Extremities.

1. Phalanges (*aṅguli*)		15 × 4 = 60
2. Soles (*tala*)	5	
3. Clusters (*kūrca*)	1	7 × 4 × 28
4. Ankles (*gulpha*)	1	
5. Heels (*pārṣṇi*)		1 × 4 = 4
6. Legs (*jaṅgha*)		2 × 4 = 8
7. Knees (*jānu*)		1 × 4 = 4
8. Thighs (*ūru*)		1 × 4 = 4
		— 108

II. Trunk.

9.	Pelvic cavity (*śroṇi*)	5	
10.	Sides (ribs, *pārśva*)	36 × 2 = 72	
11.	Back (*pṛṣṭha*)	30	
12.	Breast (*uras*)	17	
13.	Collar-bone (*akṣaka*)	2	
		—	126

III. Neck and Head.

14.	Neck (*grīvā*)	11	
15.	Windpipe (*kaṇṭhanāḍī*)	4	
16.	Jaws (*hanu*)	2	
17.	Teeth (*danta*)	32	
18.	Nose (*nāsā*)	3	
19.	Palate (*tālu*)	2	
20.	Cheeks (*gaṇḍa*)	2	
21.	Ears (*karṇa*)	2	
22.	Temples (*śaṅkha*)	2	
23.	Cranium (*śiras*)	6	
		—	66
		Grand total	300

3. Comparing the above list with that given in the preceding paragraph, it will be seen at once that it is really an attempt made by Gangādhar to restore the genuine text of the statement of Suśruta. Moreover, it is made on much the same lines, though some of the more important defects of the Traditional Recension have escaped his attention. Thus he still counts four heels, instead of two, and omits the two shoulder-blades; and consequently his aggregates for the four extremities and the trunk are 108 and 126, instead of the true aggregates 106 and 128. He also fails to notice the omission of the two eyeballs; and hence, to make up the required total 300, he wrongly counts eleven neck-bones instead of nine. On the other hand, he rightly recognizes the error of the Traditional Recension in respect of the true number of the clusters and ankle-bones, and thus arrives at the true aggregates seven and twenty-seven, instead of ten and thirty. Similarly he recognizes the error with respect to the number of the bones of the breast and palate, restoring their true numbers seventeen and two, instead of eight and one. Further, he recognizes the misreading *udara*, abdomen, for which, however, he substitutes the insufficient reading

akṣa (short for *akṣaka*), collar-bone.[1] On the other hand, his failure to realize the omission of the shoulder-blades prevented him from recognizing the misreading involved in the phrase *akṣaka-saṁjña* (§ 29).

§ 36. *Suśruta's Statement in other Medical Works*

1. It has been mentioned in § 26 that the Traditional Recension of the statement of Suśruta is found in the two medical works, *Śārīra Padminī* and *Bhāva Prakāśa.*

2. In the *Śārīra Padminī* (verses 70 and 71) it runs as follows:

'In the sequel, the skeleton (*kīkasa*) is explained as numbering three hundred bones in accordance with the count of the ancient Surgical Text-book. There are altogether one hundred and twenty bones in the extremities; one hundred and seventeen in the pelvic cavity, sides, abdomen, breast, and back; and sixty-three in the neck and upwards. Counting them, item by item, there are three hundred; but in respect of their shape, they are divisible into five classes.' (Original Text in § 91.)

3. In the *Bhāva Prakāśa* the statement runs as follows:

'In the Surgical Text-book the number of bones is stated to be three hundred. These, as well as their position in the body, are as follows: One hundred and twenty bones are said to be in the extremities. In the two sides, hips, breast, back, and abdomen,—in all these, one should know, there are altogether one hundred and seventeen. In the neck and upwards there exist sixty-three bones.' (Original Text in § 92.)

C. The System of Vāgbhaṭa I

§ 37. *The Statement of Vāgbhaṭa I*

1. The system of Vāgbhaṭa I regarding the bones of the human body is contained in the fifth chapter of the Anatomical Section (*Śārīra Sthāna*) of his Summary, and runs as follows:

[1] Possibly suggested to him by Chandraṭa's revised text; see below, § 40.

'In the body there are three hundred and sixty bones. Of these there are one hundred and forty in the extremities; one hundred and twenty in the trunk, and one hundred in the head. That is to say, in each lower limb there are five nails; three bones in each toe, aggregating fifteen; five long bones with one bone to support them; two bones each in the cluster, ankle, and leg; and one bone each in the heel, knee, and thigh. All these, nails and bones, exist also in the upper limbs exactly as in the lower. There are twenty-four ribs, and just as many sockets and tubercles. There are thirty bones in the back, eight in the breast, one each in the pubes and sacrum; two in the two hips, and as many severally in the collar-bones, shoulder-peaks (*aṁsa*), and shoulder-blades, as well as in the windpipe (*jatru*) and palate jointly; thirteen in the neck; four in the windpipe (*kaṇṭhanāḍī*); and two in the jaws. There are thirty-two teeth, and as many sockets. There are three bones in the nose, and six in the cranium.'

2. The total 360, detailed in the above statement, works out as shown in the subjoined Table:

I. Four Extremities.

1.	Nails (*nakha*)	5 × 4 = 20	
2.	Phalanges (*aṅguli*)	3 × 5 × 4 = 60	
3.	Long bones (*śalākā*)	5 × 4 = 20	
4.	Bases (*pratibandhaka*)	1 × 4 = 4	
5.	Clusters (*kūrca*)	2 × 4 = 8	
6.	Ankle-bones (*gulpha*)	2 × 4 = 8	
7.	Legs (*jaṅgha*)	2 × 4 = 8	
8.	Heels (*pārṣṇi*)	1 × 4 = 4	
9.	Knee (*jānu*)	1 × 4 = 4	
10.	Thigh (*ūru*)	1 × 4 = 4	
			— 140

II. Trunk.

11.	Ribs (*pārśvaka*) 24 Sockets (*sthālaka*) 24 Tubercles (*arbuda*) 24	72	
12.	Back (*pṛṣṭha*)	30	
13.	Breast (*uras*)	8	
14.	Pubes (*bhaga*)	1	
15.	Sacrum (*trika*)	1	
16.	Hips (*nitamba*)	2	
17.	Collar-bones (*akṣaka*)	2	
18.	Shoulder-peaks (*aṁsa*)	2	
19.	Shoulder-blades (*aṁsa-phalaka*)	2	
			— 120

III. Head [and Neck].

20. Cheeks (*gaṇḍa*)	2
21. Ears (*karṇa*)	2
22. Temples (*śaṅkha*) . . .	2
23. Windpipe (*jatru*) . . .	1
24. Palate (*tālu*)	1
25. Neck (*grīvā*)	13
26. Windpipe (*kaṇṭhanāḍī*) . .	4
27. Jaw-attachments (*hanu-bandhana*)	2
28. Teeth (*danta*)	32
29. Sockets (*ulūkhala*) . . .	32
30. Nose (*nāsā*)	3
31. Cranium (*śiras*)	6
	100
Grand total	360

§ 38. *Criticism of the Statement of Vāgbhaṭa I*

1. A comparison of the statement of Vāgbhaṭa I with the Traditional Recensions of the statements of Charaka and Suśruta shows plainly that the former is a combination of the two latter. The list of Suśruta contains 300 bones; that of Charaka 360. Vāgbhaṭa I adopts the list of Suśruta, and enlarges it by adopting from the list of Charaka such items as appear to be omitted by Suśruta. He does not explain his reason for proceeding in this manner; but it may be surmised to have been something of this kind. It has been pointed out in § 30 that the traditional list of Suśruta is incomplete in respect of the shoulder-blades. The omission is too conspicuous to be easily overlooked; and it would seem that Vāgbhaṭa I had recognized it, and that he was thus caused to mistrust the exhaustiveness of Suśruta's list of 300 bones, especially as he knew that the list of Charaka included no less than 360 bones. Noticing that the list of Charaka contained several items which were absent from that of Suśruta, he concluded that the number 360 was the true total of the bones of the skeleton, and that this number might be secured by inserting, from the list of Charaka into that of Suśruta, all the apparently missing items. Of course, such a proceeding is altogether superficial and theoretical, and proves a total want of experimental knowledge of the composition of the skeleton; for, in reality (as will be shown in the Third Section, see the Table in § 46), both systems, of Suśruta as

well as Charaka, are, from their respective points of view, exhaustive. The procedure, here imputed to Vāgbhaṭa I, may seem strange; but the evidence for it, set out in the sequel, is very strong.

2. The case may be illustrated by the subjoined Table:

	I. Vāgbhaṭa	II. Suśruta § 27	III. Charaka § 4	IV. Adopted from Charaka
1. Nails . . .	20	—	20	20
2. Phalanges . .	60	60	60	
3. Long bones . .	20	20	20	
4. Bases (*sthāna*) .	4	4	4	
5. Clusters (*kūrca*) .	8	8	—	
6. Ankle-bones and wrist-bones .	8	8	6	
7. Legs and forearms	8	8	8	
8. Heels . . .	4	4	2	
9. Knees and elbows .	4	4	4	
10. Thighs and arms .	4	4	4	
11. Ribs, sockets, &c. .	72	72	72	
12. Back . . .	30	30	45	
13. Breast . . .	8	8	14	
14. Pubes . . .	1	1	1	
15*a*. Sacrum . .	1	1	—	
15*b*. Anus . . .	—	1	—	
16. Hips . . .	2	2	2	
17. Collar-bones . .	2	2	2	
18 Shoulder-peaks .	2	—	2	2
19. Shoulder-blades .	2		2	2
20. Cheeks . . .	2	2	0[1]	
21*a*. Ears . . .	2	2	—	
21*b*. Eyes . . .	—	—	—	
22. Temples . . .	2	2	2	
23. Windpipe (*jatru*) .	1	—	1	1
24. Palate . . .	1	1	2	
25. Neck (*grīvā*). .	13	9	15	
26. Windpipe (*kaṇṭha*).	4	4	—	
27. Jaws . . .	2	2	3[1]	
28. Teeth . . .	32	32	32	
29. Sockets of Teeth .	32	—	32	32
30. Nose . . .	3	3	1[1]	
31. Cranium . .	6	6	4	
Totals .	360	300	360	57

[1] To Vāgbhaṭa's Nos. 20, 27, 30, aggregating 7, correspond Charaka's Nos. 26, 27, 28 (§ 4), aggregating 4.

3. The following points may be observed. In the first place, the list of Vāgbhaṭa contains every item of the Suśrutiyan Traditional Recension (§ 27). To these it adds Nos. 1, 18, 19, 23, 29 from the list of Charaka (§ 4), aggregating 57. This aggregate is short of the required sixty by three. From Nos. 15 *b* and 25, in column II, it appears that Vāgbhaṭa I obtained the required three by adding four to No. 25 and deducting No. 15 *b*; that is to say, he counted thirteen neck-bones, instead of nine, and omitted the anal bone as a separate item. The reason for his adopting this, apparently, very arbitrary proceeding can only be conjectured. The following however suggests itself. It is significant that Vāgbhaṭa's No. 25 numbers thirteen, the exact sum of Suśruta's Nos. 25 and 26. Both these two items constitute the same part of the body: in Sanskrit, both *grīvā* and *kaṇṭha* denote the neck, the former referring more especially to the posterior, the latter to the anterior portion. This being so, Vāgbhaṭa placed to the credit of No. 25 the aggregate amount thirteen, which Suśruta had divided between Nos. 25 and 26. But as he thus obtained one bone in excess (i. e. four instead of three) he saved one bone by counting the two bones in Nos. 15 *a* and 15 *b* as constituting a single bone. He could do this all the more readily as he could not help observing that in the system of Charaka (as will be shown in § 60) the sacrum and coccyx (or anal bone) constitute but a single bone, which that system includes among its forty-five bones of the vertebral column.

4. The explanation of Vāgbhaṭa's procedure, here suggested, of course, involves the assumption of his failing to note that he counted the four bones of No. 26 (i. e. the windpipe) twice over; that is, once separately, in No. 26, and again as included in the thirteen bones of No. 25. But this is, by no means, the only instance of such inattention on the part of Vāgbhaṭa I. We have another conspicuous example in his Nos. 4 and 5, where he also counts the same bones twice over, once in No. 4 as bases (*sthāna*) and again in No. 5 as clusters (*kūrca*), these being the Charakiyan and Suśrutiyan terms respectively for the same organ (see § 49). There is a third instance in Vāgbhaṭa's Nos. 23 and 26, where he counts the windpipe twice over;

once in No. 23 under the Charakiyan term *jatru*, and again in No. 26, under the Suśrutiyan term *kaṇṭhanāḍī*. In fact, if the explanation, suggested above, is correct, Vāgbhaṭa I actually counts the windpipe thrice over, in Nos. 23, 25, and 26.

5. The inconsistencies, or incongruities, mentioned above are not the only ones of the list of Vāgbhaṭa I. There are others, affecting his Nos. 5, 6, and 8. In No. 5, he counts eight clusters (*kūrca*), that is, two in either hand and foot. But in the same fifth chapter of his Anatomical Section (*Śārīra Sthāna*) he says that there are altogether only six clusters, of which, moreover, two are in the neck (*grīvā*) and penis (*meḍhra*), leaving only four for the hands and feet (Original Text in § 96, cl. 5). According to his own statement, therefore, there is only one cluster in either hand and foot. Again in No. 6, Vāgbhaṭa I counts eight bones in the ankles, that is to say, according to the homological principle of his list, four ankle-bones (*gulpha*) in the feet, and four wrist-bones (*maṇibhanda*) in the hands. But in the seventh chapter of his Anatomical Section, treating of the 'vital spots' (*marman*), he counts only two ankle-bones and two wrist-bones (Original Text in § 96, cl. 6). Again in No. 8, Vāgbhaṭa I counts four heels; that is to say, one in each of the four limbs; and thus commits the incongruity of ascribing a heel to either hand.

6. There is another incongruity in Vāgbhaṭa's No. 27, he counts two *hanu-bandhana*, or jaw-attachments. Suśruta counts two *hanu*, or jaws, and Charaka counts two *hanumūla-bandhana*, or attachments at the base of the (lower) jaw. Both are consistent views; for, as will be explained in § 65, in the system of Suśruta the two *hanu* signify the two maxillary bones (superior and inferior), while in the system of Charaka the two *bandhana* signify the two rami of the inferior maxillary. Vāgbhaṭa I, noticing the terminological difference, but not understanding its reason, sought to compromise it by adopting the contracted term *hanu-bandhana*, or jaw-attachment, and treating it as a synonym of the simple term *hanu*, jaw; the two jaws being, in his view, as it were two attachments to the face.

7. There is a further inconsistency in Vāgbhaṭa's omitting to count the two eyeballs (*akṣikoṣa*) in his number-list, while he

mentions them in his class-list of the very same bones (Original Text in § 93) which he adopts from Suśruta. He also adopts from Suśruta the description of the outer cover, or shell, of the eyeball as made of bone (§ 30, Original Text in § 96, cl. 2). The fact is interesting, because it shows that the text of the Compendium of Suśruta, on which Vāgbhaṭa I based his anatomical theories, was already in his time in a corrupt state. It is not probable that if Vāgbhaṭa I had found the eyeballs included among the bones in the number-list of Suśruta, he would have omitted them from his own number-list, while it is quite credible, considering his other inconsistencies, that he should not have recognized their wrongful omission from the list of Suśruta.

8. The inconsistencies and incongruities as exposed above clearly prove that Vāgbhaṭa I possessed no experimental knowledge of the skeleton, but that he constructed his list of its bones theoretically from the information provided in the Compendia of Charaka and Suśruta—which compendia, as we shall see in the following paragraph, he cannot have possessed in their original and genuine form, and which, from want of anatomical knowledge, he was unfitted to use critically.

§ 39. *Relation of Vāgbhaṭa's List to the Traditional List of Charaka and Suśruta*

A comparison of the list of Vāgbhaṭa I with the traditional lists of Charaka and Suśruta, as exhibited in the Table in the preceding paragraph, brings out the following points:

1. The principle on which the list of Vāgbhaṭa I is constructed is to take the list of Suśruta as its basis, and add to it such items of the list of Charaka as do not occur in it.

2. The list of Suśruta which forms the basis of the list of Vāgbhaṭa is, in every point, identical with the traditional list of Suśruta as it at present exists (§ 27). This is proved by the fact that the list of Vāgbhaṭa shows every one of the inconsistencies which have been exposed in §§ 30–3 as existing in the Traditional Recension of Suśruta's list. That is to say: (*a*) both reckon the aggregate of Nos. 3–5 (§ 37, or Nos. 2–4 in § 27) as

ten, resulting in the aggregate forty for the four extremities; (*b*) in order to make up that aggregate ten, both count eight clusters, and four ankle-bones and four wrist-bones; also they count four bases in addition to the four clusters; (*c*) both count four heels; (*d*) both omit the two shoulder-blades[1] and the two eyeballs; (*e*) both count wrongly eight bones and one bone in Nos. 13 and 24 respectively.

3. The list of Vāgbhaṭa I is indebted to the list of Charaka in two ways: (*a*) in order to raise the grand total from 300 to 360, the former adopts Nos. 1, 18, 19, 23, 29 from the latter; and (*b*) in order to obtain the aggregate ten for Nos. 3–6, it similarly adopts No. 4, bases (§ 31).

4. The list of Charaka on which Vāgbhaṭa I has drawn for his additions, is identical with the Traditional Recension of it as we have it in the manuscripts of the present day (§ 4). This is proved by the fact that both lists possess No. 18, shoulders, and No. 19, shoulder-blades. It has been shown in § 6 that the repetition of *aṁsa*, shoulder, by the side of *aṁsa-phalaka*, shoulder-blade, is an ancient corruption of the traditional text of the list of Charaka. Seeing that Vāgbhaṭa I adopts the error into his own list, it is evident that he read the list of Charaka, as we still have it, in the traditional text of our own day. The procedure of Vāgbhaṭa I, however, explains a peculiarity of his system. The shoulder-girdle contains only two separate bones, the collar-bone (*akṣaka*, No. 17) and the shoulder-blade (*aṁsa-phalaka*, No. 19), see § 56, cl. 2. Finding, in his text of Charaka, the apparent mention of *aṁsa* as a third bone, and not suspecting an error, he appears to have explained it by taking *aṁsa* to refer to the so-called 'shoulder-peak' (*aṁsa-kūṭa*), or the acromion process (§ 55, cl. 5). In this explanation he would probably have felt himself justified by the practice, observed by Charaka and Suśruta, of occasionally counting 'processes' of bones as separate bones (§ 44, cl. 1); but in doing so, he failed to notice that with those two writers *aṁsa*, in its technical sense, is a synonym of *akṣaka* and denotes the collar-bone, while, when used in a loose way, it indicates the shoulder generally (§ 55, cl. 4).

[1] The two shoulder-blades, it is true, appear in the list of Vāgbhaṭa I, but they have been adopted into it from the list of Charaka.

Vāgbhaṭa I's ill-conceived interpretation of the term *aṁsa* led to another unfortunate result, inasmuch as it appears to have served as the basis of the definition of *aṁsa*, which is given in the *Amarakośa*, the famous Vocabulary of Amarasiṁha, and which, in its turn, led to the misinterpretation of the term *jatru*; see § 62, cl. 8.

§ 40. *The Relative Date of the Three Lists*

1. We are now in a position to draw certain conclusions regarding the approximate dates of the traditional lists of Charaka and Suśruta in relation to the list of Vāgbhaṭa I.

2. It has been shown in the preceding paragraph that the list of the bones of the human body as constructed by Vāgbhaṭa I is substantially identical with the lists of Charaka and Suśruta as we possess them in the manuscripts of the present day. Moreover, at least three corruptions of the latter two lists, viz. the repetition of *aṁsa*, shoulder, in the list of Charaka (§ 6), and the omission of the shoulder-blades and the eyeballs in the list of Suśruta (§ 30), must have existed in their texts already in the time of Vāgbhaṭa I; for, as explained in the two preceding paragraphs the construction of his list presupposes them. Accordingly both lists, in their traditionally corrupted form, must be anterior to the date of Vāgbhaṭa I whatever the latter may be. On the other hand, it has been shown (pp. 76, 79, 85), regarding the omission of the shoulder-blades and eyeballs, and the count of seventeen bones in the neck, that the Non-medical Version of Atreya's system presupposes the knowledge of a recension of Suśruta's text which was more correct, and therefore presumably older than the corrupt traditional text. Similarly the Non-medical Version which ignores the erroneous repetition of *aṁsa*, shoulder (§§ 6, 16, 17), presupposes the knowledge of an older and more correct recension of the text of Charaka. Accordingly at the time when the Non-medical Version was composed, both the lists of Charaka and Suśruta must have existed in the earlier uncorrupted form, and the corrupt recension, traditionally handed down, must have come into existence at a later date: that is to say, between the date

of the Law-book of Yājnavalkya, which contains the Non-medical Version, and the date of the construction of the list of Vāgbhaṭa I. As the date of the Law-book is about 350 A.D. (§ 14), the origin of the two traditional recensions cannot be placed earlier than the fourth century A.D.

3. The question suggests itself whether Vāgbhaṭa I himself might not be the author of the Traditional Recension of the statement of Suśruta on the bones of the human body. The evidence is not sufficient to return a decided answer; but whatever evidence there is seems certainly to point in that direction. The statement of Suśruta (§ 27) gives the aggregate of the bones contained in Nos. 2, 3, 4 of his list, but does not detail the number of bones of each item: sole (*tala*), cluster (*kūrca*), and ankle (*gulpha*). Whoever fixed the details so as to make the sole (*tala*) to include not only the five long bones (*śalākā*) but also the base (*sthāna*), must have been led to do so by noticing that the list of Charaka mentions the base (*sthāna*), while the list of Suśruta does not name it. He concluded, therefore, that Suśruta's term sole (*tala*) must cover both the long bones (*śalākā*) as well as the base (*sthāna*). In other words, whoever fixed the details proceeded on the principle of adding to the list of Suśruta such items from the list of Charaka as did not appear to be contained in it explicitly. This, as has been shown in § 39, is precisely the principle on which Vāgbhaṭa I worked in constructing his own list. It seems probable, therefore, that it was Vāgbhaṭa I who for the purpose of preparing his own list, constructed the Traditional Recension of the list of Suśruta.

4. It is a well-known fact that the text of Suśruta's Compendium, after a time, fell into some disorder, which necessitated revision or reconstruction. Several such revisions, or reconstructions, must have been undertaken at different times. The first reconstruction may have been that to which we owe the addition of the Supplementary Section (*Uttara Tantra*). This is traditionally ascribed to Nāgārjuna, in the second century A.D. (§ 2). Seeing that the traditional text of neither Charaka nor Suśruta existed about 350 A.D., the approximate date of the Law-book of Yājnavalkya, it follows that Nāgārjuna, if he made any recon-

struction of the text of Suśruta's Compendium, can at all events not be credited with the particular reconstruction of Suśruta's statement on the skeleton. Another revision was made by Chandraṭa, the son of Tīsaṭa. He states this fact himself at the end of his revised text, which he calls a *pāṭha-śuddhi* or 'Emendation of the Text'. We have a copy of this revised text in the unique manuscript of the India Office Library, No. 1842 (Cat. No. 2646), described on pp. 927, 928 of the catalogue. So far as a cursory examination permits one to judge, it does occasionally, though not very materially, differ from the Traditional Recension of the Compendium. But in the statement on the skeleton there occurs a noteworthy *varia lectio.* Instead of the erroneous reading *udara*, abdomen, of the traditional text (§ 29), Chandraṭa's text has *akṣa*, collar-bone.[1] This circumstance—so far as it goes—makes against the hypothesis that Chandraṭa was the author of the Traditional Recension. But there are two stronger objections to it in Chandraṭa's late date and comparative obscurity. The date of Chandraṭa is not known; but it cannot well be earlier than the ninth or tenth century, because in his Commentary on the *Cikitsā-kalikā*[2] of his father Tīsaṭa he quotes from the complement of Charaka's Compendium, which was made by Dṛiḍhabala; and the date of the latter must be in the eighth or ninth century (§ 2, cl. 9). He does not quote Bhoja[3], while both Chakrapāṇidatta and Gayadāsa quote him, but do not quote each other. Hence it appears probable that the last-mentioned two authors were near contemporaries who were preceded by Bhoja who himself was preceded by Chandraṭa. As the date of Chakrapāṇidatta is about 1060 A.D., the date of Chandraṭa may be referred to about 1000 A.D. As to the point of obscurity, so much may be taken as certain, that whoever was the author of the Traditional

[1] Also adopted by Gangādhar (§ 35); possibly from Chandraṭa.

[2] See Professor Jolly's article in the *Journal, German Oriental Society*, vol. lx, pp. 413 ff.

[3] Once however, Bodleian MS. (Fraser No. 21, Cat. No. 852), fol. 96 *b*, he quotes Bhoja the elder (*vṛddha Bhoja*). The earliest mention of Chandraṭa, known to me, occurs in Śrīkaṇṭhadatta's commentary on the *Siddhayoga* (Poona ed., p. 552). The date of Śrīkaṇṭha, a pupil of Vijaya Rakshita, is about 1260 A.D.

Recension must have been a person of great reputation; for otherwise it is inconceivable how his recension should have obtained such paramount authority as to supersede every other recension, and to be the only one found in all existing manuscripts, and exclusively commented on in all known commentaries.[1] Chandraṭa certainly cannot be said to have held such a position. The only ancient medical author who by the uniform tradition of India holds a place equal to that of Charaka and Suśruta is Vāgbhaṭa I. He is the third in the traditional triad of great representatives of Indian medicine: Charaka, Suśruta, Vāgbhaṭa.[2] It has been shown (§§ 38, 39) that the principle on which the Traditional Recension of the statement of Suśruta is made is certainly one on which Vāgbhaṭa I worked in constructing his own statement. The conclusion therefore seems unavoidable that it was Vāgbhaṭa I who is the author of that Traditional Recension. The fact that the older recensions still existed in the fourth century A.D., at the date of the Law-book of Yājnavalkya, and the consideration that a sufficient interval must be conceded for the text to have fallen into such a state of corruption as to necessitate a thorough revision, or reconstruction, will accord with the early seventh century A.D. as the date of Vāgbhaṭa I, already suggested by other considerations (see § 2). It should, however, be distinctly understood that these conclusions regarding the date and authorship of Vāgbhaṭa I are not put forward as established facts. They are, for the present, no more than historical speculations, or rather a working hypothesis, based on more or less conclusive evidence.

NOTE.—Whatever may be thought of the suggested authorship of the traditional text of Suśruta, there is distinct evidence of the text of Suśruta's Compendium having been liable to be affected by the theories of Vāgbhaṭa I. For example, according to Suśruta's doctrine, in the Anatomical Section (*Śārīra Sthāna*),

[1] This remark refers particularly to the Traditional Recension of the statement on the skeleton, which is the only one known to, and commented on by Gayadāsa and Ḍallana. They give no indication of being aware of the existence of any other recension of that particular passage.

[2] See Professor Jolly's *Indian Medicine*, § 9. See also p. 10 for the testimony of the Chinese pilgrim Itsing.

chapter v, clause 33 (Original Text in § 94, cl. 1), there are altogether 500 muscles in the human body. Of these 500 muscles, 400 go to the four extremities, while there are 66 in the trunk and 34 in the neck and head. This is the traditional reading of that doctrine, as printed by Jīvānanda, p. 334, and supported by existing manuscripts. Ḍallana, in his Commentary (Jīv. ed., p. 578), accepts that reading, but expressly states that Gayadāsa's Commentary followed a different reading, which allotted 60 muscles to the trunk and 40 to the neck and head; and he adds that this distribution of the muscles is also taught by Vāgbhaṭa I. Ḍallana's statement is verified by the Cambridge MS. of Gayadāsa's Commentary,[1] and the printed text of Vāgbhaṭa's Summary (*Aṣṭāṅga Saṁgraha*), vol. i, p. 225, line 21.

§ 41. *The Origin of the Traditional Recension*

1. The homological character of the skeletal structure is too conspicuous in the four extremities to have escaped the notice of Ātreya-Charaka. But that he did not fully realize it, is shown, *inter alia*, by his treatment of the cranial bones, as compared with that of Suśruta (see §§ 28, 63). It was the latter who first recognized that the homological principle dominated the whole structure, and who explicitly used it as the basis of his classificatory list of the bones. This is shown, e.g., by his distribution of the ribs into two sets of 36 bones each (§ 27), and by his hemisection of the vertebral column and of the frontal and other bones of the head (§§ 44, 59, 63). In one point, however, viz. the ascription of three bones to each digit (p. 73), Suśruta pressed the homological principle too far; see § 47. Vāgbhaṭa I adopted that principle from Suśruta, but pressed it one point farther, extending it, still more erroneously (at least, in the sense in which he applied it) to the heels, of which he counted four, ascribing heels to the two hands as well as to the two feet.

[1] Unfortunately the clause referring to the muscles is very badly mutilated in the MS., but sufficient of it still remains to confirm Ḍallana's statement. See my Article on the *Commentaries on Suśruta*, in the *Journal of the Royal Asiatic Society* for 1906.

2. It is Vāgbhaṭa's extended application of the homological principle which explains the origin of the Traditional Recension of Suśruta's list of the bones. That list (§ 27) states only the aggregate of the three items (Nos. 2, 3, 4), sole (*tala*), cluster (*kūrca*), ankle (*gulpha*). In order to determine the details of this aggregate, Vāgbhaṭa I consulted the list of Charaka. Here (§ 4) he found the three items, No. 5, long bones (*śalākā*), No. 6, base (*sthāna*), No. 8, ankle (*gulpha*). Failing to notice that the bases of Charaka were equivalent to the clusters of Suśruta, he concluded that Suśruta's sole (*tala*) must include the long bones (*śalākā*) as well as the bases (*sthāna*) of Charaka's list; and he thus set up four items: long bones, base, cluster, ankle, as identical with Suśruta's three items: sole, cluster, ankle. Further, noticing that the list of Charaka counted four ankle-bones in the two feet (No. 8 in § 4), he allotted two bones to Suśruta's ankle, and similarly two bones, to his cluster, forgetting that Suśruta himself had elsewhere allotted only one bone to either, the cluster and the ankle.[1] Such would seem to have been the consideration on which Vāgbhaṭa I arrived at the details of his own four (or Suśruta's three) items; as thus:

sole {	long bones,	5 bones	aggregate 10 bones.
	base,	1 bone	
	cluster,	2 bones	
	ankle,	2 bones	

Next, on the principle of homology, he multiplied this aggregate by four, obtaining forty as the grand aggregate of the bones of his four items in the four extremities. By a further, but erroneous, application of the same principle to Suśruta's No. 5, heel (*pārṣṇi*), he obtained his four heels; and the correct application of it to Suśruta's Nos. 6, 7, 8 (§ 27) gave him another set of sixteen bones. Totalling the sums so far obtained (i.e. $40 + 4 + 16 = 60$), and adding the sixty phalanges (No. 1 in § 27), Vāgbhaṭa arrived at the grand total of one hundred and twenty for the bones of the four extremities.

3. Let us remember that the list of Suśruta in its original

[1] The fact that Suśruta looked upon the ankles of the foot as constituting but one bone, is illustrated by the term *valaya*, anklet, which he applies to them. The *valaya* is a heavy bangle worn on the foot; see Fig. 2 illustrating § 30.

form counted seventeen bones in the breast and two in the palate (§ 33). The numbers in that list must have been as below:

Trunk.			*Neck and Head.*		
9.	Pelvis	5 bones	14.	Neck	9 bones
10.	Sides	72 „	15, 16.	Windpipe, jaw	6 „
11.	Back	30 „	17.	Teeth	32 „
12.	Breast	17 „	18, 19.	Nose, palate	5 „
13.	Collar-bones	2 „	20–3.	Cheeks, &c.	12 „
	Total	126 „		Total	64 „

Accordingly Suśruta's list would have contained the following totals:

Four Extremities (as calculated by Vāgbhaṭa I)	120
Trunk	126
Neck and Head	64
Grand total	310

This grand total having ten bones in excess of the required 300, it became necessary for Vāgbhaṭa I to make a corresponding reduction somewhere. He determined to make it in the bones of the breast and palate, reducing their numbers from seventeen and two (= 19) to eight and one (= 9) respectively—an operation which gave him just the required ten (19 – 9). It may be asked what made him select for reduction just those two items, the breast and palate. The answer to this question can only be conjectured; but what may be said on the subject will be found explained in the Third Section (§§ 57 and 67). Of course the process here suggested by which the Traditional Recension of Suśruta's statement on the skeleton was constructed is purely speculative: it may or may not have so happened; but to myself it appears to possess much probability.

D. The System of the Vedas

§ 42. *The Statements in the Śatapatha Brāhmaṇa*

1. It may be useful to present in their entirety those passages from the *Śatapatha Brāhmaṇa* to which I have briefly referred in some of the preceding paragraphs. They occur in the tenth and

twelfth sections (*kāṇḍa*) of that work, in the course of describing the erection of the fire-altar. In the building of it, 360 bricks were used together with the chanting of hymns consisting of a varying number of verses. With these bricks and hymns the body and certain of its parts are compared in a mystical way.

2. *Total Number of Bones.* In the tenth section (*kāṇḍa*), fifth chapter (*adhyāya*), fourth paragraph (*brāhmaṇa*), and twelfth clause the total number of the bones of the human body is compared to the 360 bricks of the fire-altars, as follows[1]:

'But indeed that fire-altar also is the body—the bones are the enclosing stones, and there are 360 of these, because there are three hundred and sixty bones in man; the marrow-parts are the *yajuṣmati* bricks, for there are three hundred and sixty of these, and three hundred and sixty parts of marrow in man.' (Vol. iv, p. 387; Original Text in § 99, cl. 1.)

Again in Section XII, 3, 2, clauses 3 and 4:

'There are three hundred and sixty nights in the year and three hundred and sixty bones in man; and these (two) now are one and the same;—there are three hundred and sixty days in the year, and three hundred and sixty parts of marrow in man, and these (two) now are one and the same. And there are seven hundred and twenty days and nights in the year, and seven hundred and twenty bones and parts of marrow in man, and these (two) now are one and the same.' (Vol. v, p. 169; Original Text in § 99, cl. 1.)

3. *Bones compared to Hymns.* The number of bones in certain parts of the body are compared to certain hymns in Section XII, 2, 4, clauses 9–14, as follows (Original Text in § 99, cl. 3):

'(9) The three-versed hymn-form (*trivṛt*) is the head (*śiras*), whence that (head) is threefold—skin, bone, and brain. (10) The fifteen-versed hymn-form (*pañcadaśa*) is the neck-bones (*grīvāḥ*); for fourteen of these are the transverse processes (*karūkara*); and their strength (*vīrya*) is the fifteenth; hence by means of them, though small, man can bear a heavy load. Therefore the fifteen-versed hymn is the neck-bones. (11) The seventeen-versed hymn-form (*saptadaśa*) is the breast (*uras*); for there are eight costal cartilages (*jatru*) on the one side, and eight on the other, and the breast-bone (*uras*, sternum) is the seventeenth.

[1] The translations are taken from, or based on, Professor Eggeling's Translation in the *Sacred Books of the East*, vols. iv and v.

Therefore the seventeen-versed hymn is the breast. (12) The twenty-one-versed hymn-form (*ekaviṁśa*) is the abdominal portion (*udara*) of the spine. For within the abdomen there are twenty transverse processes (*kuntāpa*), and the abdominal portion of the spine is the twenty-first. Therefore the twenty-one-versed hymn is the abdominal portion of the spine. (13) The thrice-nine-versed (or 27-versed) hymn-form (*triṇava*) is the two sides (*pārśva*). There are thirteen ribs (*parśu*) on the one side, and thirteen on the other; and the two sides make up the thrice-ninth (or 27th). Therefore the thrice-ninth hymn is the two sides. (14) The thirty-three-versed hymn-form (*trayastriṁśa*) is the thoracic portion (*anūka*) of the spine; for there are thirty-two transverse processes (*karūkara*) in it, and the thoracic portion of the spine is the thirty-third. Therefore, the thirty-three-versed hymn is the thoracic portion of the spine.' (Vol. v, pp. 163–5.)

4. *Position of Costal Cartilages.* The position of the costal cartilages is described in Section VIII, 6, 2, clauses 7 and 10, as follows:

'(1) The *triṣṭubh* (metres) are the breast-bone (*uras*): he (i.e. the sacrificer) places them on the range of the two *retaḥsic* (bricks), for the *retaḥsic* (bricks) are the back-bones (*pṛṣṭi*), and the back-bones lie over against the breast-bone. (10) The *bṛihatī* (metres) are the ribs (*parśu*); the *kakubh* (metres) are the thoracic vertebrae (*kīkasa*). The *bṛihatī* he places between the *triṣṭubh* (metres) and *kakubh* (metres), whence these ribs (*parśu*) are fastened, at either end, to the thoracic vertebrae (*kīkasa*) at the back and (interiorly) to the costal cartilages (*jatru*) in front.' (Vol. iv, p. 114; Original Text in § 99, cl. 4.)

5. *Date of Śatapatha Brāhmaṇa, and its Relation to Charaka and Suśruta.* The traditional author of the *Śatapatha Brāhmaṇa* is Yājnavalkya, who is said to have flourished at the court of Janaka, the famous king of Videha, and contemporary of Ajātaśatru, king of Kāśī (Benares). The latter, the celebrated ruler of Magadha and Kāśī, was a contemporary of Buddha. His accession took place approximately in 491 B.C. Accordingly Yājnavalkya may be dated about 500 B.C.[1] The anatomical

[1] On the dates see Weber's *History of Indian Literature* (3rd English ed.), pp. 116 ff.; Prof. Eggeling's Translation of the *Śatapatha Brāhmaṇa* in vol. xii of the *Sacred Books of the East*, Introd., pp. xxxv ff.; Prof. Rhys Davids' *Buddhist India*, pp. 12–16;

comparisons, quoted above, show that in his time both the medical schools of Ātreya and Suśruta were in existence, and that he possessed some knowledge of their respective theories on the skeleton. For he derived from Suśruta the allotment of seventeen bones to the breast (§§ 33, 34), Ātreya-Charaka counting only fourteen (§ 4); while he got the total of 360 bones of the skeleton from Ātreya, Suśruta having only 300. In his choice of particulars from the two systems, of course, he was guided by the requirements of his mystic treatment of the fire-altar. As to Suśruta's surgical text-book, it may be noted that Yājnavalkya was a native of Eastern India, and that Indian surgical science, in all probability, took its origin in that part of India (§ 2, cl. 3).

6. *Acquaintance with Suśruta.* Yājnavalkya's acquaintance with the system of Suśruta is further shown by the curious circumstance that he counts 360 marrow-parts, that is, as many as there are bones. Clearly, he believed that every bone contained a 'marrow-part'. This belief is closely related to Suśruta's doctrine, which also ascribes what may be called a 'marrow-part' to every bone. Charaka has left no statement on the subject, but Suśruta, in the Introductory Section (*Sūtra Sthāna*) of his text-book (ch. xiv, verse 6, Jīv. ed., p. 48; Original Text in § 99, cl. 2), teaches that 'from fat (*medas*) originates bone, and from the latter marrow (*majjā*)'. In the Anatomical Section (*Śārīra Sthāna*, ch. iv, cl. 9, Jīv., p. 319; Original Text in § 99, cl. 2), he further states that 'fat (*medas*) occurs in the abdomen, and in both the small and large bones of all beings'; and, *ibid.*, cl. 10, he explains that 'the fat which is found in the interior cavity of the large bones is called marrow (*majjan*), while that which is found in all other bones is called bloody (*sa-rakta*, or red) fat; further the grease (*sneha*) which attaches to clean flesh (of the abdomen) is known as suet (*vasā*), while in all other conditions fat (*medas*) is simply denoted grease (*sneha*)'. In the view of Suśruta, therefore, all bones contain the same fatty tissue (*medas*): only it is red in the small bones, and yellow in the large ones, the

Mr. V. Smith's *Early History of India*, pp. 26 ff.; Messrs. Hoernle and Stark's *History of India*, p. 21.

latter kind being distinguished as marrow (*majjan*). The author of the *Śatapatha Brāhmaṇa* only differs in employing the term *majjan* in the sense in which Suśruta uses the term *medas*.[1]

7. *Confused Counting in the Śatapatha Brāhmaṇa.* In the enumeration of the bones of the trunk, the author of the *Śatapatha Brāhmaṇa*, not being a medical man, but a theologian, is rather confused. The items of his count are:

In the Neck	. . .	15 bones
„ Breast	. . .	17 „
„ Lower Spine 21 } „ Upper Spine 33 }	.	54 „
„ Ribs	. . .	27 „

Here the first two items are correct, being taken from Ātreya-Charaka (§ 4) and Suśruta (§ 35) respectively. But the numbers of the bones of the spine and the ribs, 54 and 27 respectively, are very strange. It almost looks as if they were due to a misreading, or false recollection, reversing the true numbers 45 and 72.[2] The former (i.e. 45) is the total of the bones of the spine in the system of Ātreya-Charaka (§ 4), while the latter (i.e. 72) is the total number of the ribs with their sockets and tubercles in both systems, of Ātreya as well as of Suśruta.

8. *Continuation.* But further, the principle of counting is no less confused. Suśruta counted the bones of the breast on a principle different from that on which he counted the bones of the neck and back (that is, of the whole spine). The breast he counted by taking it to consist of a median bone (*sternum*), giving off an equal number of branch bones (costal cartilages)

[1] It deserves notice that also modern Anatomy distinguishes between red and yellow marrow, the latter being found in the medullary cavity of the long bones, the red in the cancellous parts of those bones as well as in all other bones. The red marrow has its name from the blood-vessels in it, while the yellow has its name from the oil gradually developed in it. The yellow kind is what is popularly known as marrow, and which Suśruta distinguishes as *majjan*. See Gerrish, *Textbook of Anatomy* (2nd ed., 1903), pp. 53, 113.

[2] Misreading would be an obvious solution, if we could assume that at the time of the composition of the *Śatapatha Brāhmaṇa* the system of numeral notation based on 'the value of position' was already known. With the older system of notation by means of distinct signs for the tens and for the units, the theory of misreading is far less intelligible. It must, then, be a case of false recollection.

on either side. But in the spine, he counted each vertebra separately without any median column. Ātreya-Charaka, less correctly, had applied the former method of counting also to the neck (§ 61). In the *Śatapatha Brāhmaṇa*, even more confusedly, it is extended to the whole of the spine. The latter is supposed to consist of a median column, divided into an upper (*anūka*) and a lower (*udara*) portion, either of them giving off an equal number of branch bones (transverse processes) on either side.

9. *Continuation.* As to the ribs, the very non-anatomical view is taken of counting the collar-bones as a species of ribs, and thus obtaining a total of thirteen ribs on either side of the sternum. This explanation of the otherwise unintelligible count of thirteen ribs has been suggested by Professor Eggeling in his Translation of the *Śatapatha Brāhmaṇa* (*Sacred Books of the East*, vol. xliv, p. 164, footnote 2), and is undoubtedly correct. The fanciful count itself, of course, is due to the mystical exigencies of the author of the *Śatapatha Brāhmaṇa*.

10. *Continuation.* Finally, another quite non-anatomical procedure of the same author is the description of the head (or rather, cranium, *śiras*) as consisting of skin, bone, and brain.

§ 43. *Statement in the Atharva Veda*

1. The hymn on the creation of man, which is referred to in § 2, cl. 2, is the second in the tenth book of the Atharva Veda. Its composition is traditionally ascribed to a certain sage (*ṛṣi*) Nārāyaṇa. This sage is the traditional author also of the famous hymn on the sacrifice of man (*puruṣa-sūkta*), which is found both in the Rigveda and the Atharva Veda, and is regarded as 'one of the very latest poems of the Rigvedic age'—an age 'which can hardly be less remote than 1000 B.C.'[1] It seems probable that he is identical with the Nārāyaṇa, to whom Indian medical tradition ascribes the composition of certain very ancient medical formulae,[2] and who, from all these considerations, comes

[1] See *Rigveda*, x. 90, and *Atharva Veda*, xix. 6; Professor Macdonell's *Sanskrit Literature*, pp. 44, 47, 133.

[2] One formula for the preparation of a medicated oil has the very early authority of the Bower MS., Part III, verses 37–53. Another formula for preparing a compound powder is recorded in

within the semi-mythical period of the history of Indian medicine (§ 2, cl. 2).

2. The initial eight verses of the hymn in question run as follows[1] (Original Text in § 100):

Verse 1. By whom were fixed the two heels of man? By whom was the flesh constructed? By whom the two ankle-bones; by whom the slender digits; by whom the apertures; by whom the two sets of long bones, in the middle? Who made their bases?

Verse 2. How did they (the devas) make the two ankle-bones of man below, and the two knee-caps above? The two legs, furthermore—how, pray, did they insert (them)? and the two knee-joints—who conceived them?

Verse 3. A four-sided (frame) is formed by their ends being firmly knit together. Above the two knees (there is) the pliant abdomen. The two hips and the two thighs that there are, who has created them, (those props) through which the trunk becomes so firmly set up?

Verse 4. How many devas, and who among them, contributed to build up the (bones of the) breast and the (cartilages of the) windpipe of man? How many disposed (the ribs of) the two breasts; who, the two shoulder-blades? How many piled up the neck-bones; how many, the back-bones?

Verse 5. Who constructed the two arms of his for the exertion of strength? Which deva hoisted the two collar-bones on his trunk?

Verse 6. Who pierced the seven apertures in the head: the two ears, two nostrils, two eyes, the mouth—these (organs of sense) in whose surpassing might quadrupeds and bipeds walk their way in all directions?

Verse 7. For within the two jaws he fixed the tongue, and installed the far-reaching mighty voice. The devas pervade the

Mādhava's *Siddhayoga*, ch. xxxvii, verses 18–25 (p. 307), and Dṛiḍhabala's complement to the *Charaka Saṁhita, Cikitsita Sthāna*, ch. xviii, verses 122–9 (p. 649, ed. 1895).

[1] Several of the Sanskrit terms, occurring in this hymn, are very rare. On these and other philological matters my *Studies in Ancient Indian Medicine*, No. II, in the *Journals of the Royal Asiatic Society* for 1906, pp. 915 ff., and 1907, pp. 1 ff., may be consulted.

(three) worlds, they dwell in the waters, but which of them conceived it?

Verse 8. Whoever first constructed that brain of his, the brow, the facial bone, the cranium, and the structure of the jaws, and having done so, ascended to heaven, who of the many devas was he?

3. The significance of these verses comes out very clearly, when the system of the bones of the human body disclosed in them is compared with the osteological systems of Ātreya-Charaka and Suśruta. The three systems are shown in the subjoined Table, the arrangement of which follows the order of the verses in the hymn of the Atharva Veda. The systems of Charaka and Suśruta, in columns V and VI, are quoted from § 7 and § 34 respectively; and the bracketed numbers in the columns refer to the order of the bones in those paragraphs.

I. Ver.	II. No.	III. Name of Bone	IV. Atharva Veda	V. Ātreya-Charaka (§ 7)	VI. Suśruta (§ 34)
1	1	Heel	*pārṣṇi*	*pārṣṇi* (7)	*pārṣṇi* (5)
	2	Ankle-bone	*gulpha*	*gulpha* (8) and *maṇika* (9)	*gulpha* (4)
	3	Digit	*aṅguli*	*aṅguli* (4) with *nakha* (3)	*aṅguli* (1)
	4	Long bones	*uchlakha*	*śalākā* (5)	*tala* (2)
	5	Base	*pratiṣṭhā*	*adhiṣṭhāna* (6) (or *sthāna*)	*kūrca* (3)
2	6	Knee-cap	*aṣṭīvat* (or *jānu*)	*jānu* (12) and *kapālika* (13)	*jānu* (7)
	7	Leg-bones	*jaṅgha*	*jaṅgha* (11) and *aratni* (10)	*jaṅgha* (6)
					Here brief notice of Upper Limbs (*bāhu*)
3	8	Pelvic cavity	*śroṇi*	*śroṇi-phalaka* (18) with *bhaga* (19)	*śroṇi* (9)
	9	Thigh-bone	*ūru*	*ūru-nalaka* (14) and *bāhu-nalaka* (15)	*ūru* (8)
4	10	Breast-bone	*uras*	*uras* (21)	*uras* (12)
	11	Windpipe	*grīvā*	*jatru* (24) (or *grīvā*, § 62)	*kaṇṭhanāḍī* (16) (or *jatru*, or *grīvā*)
	12	Rib-piece (ribs)	*stana*	*pārśvaka* with *sthālaka*, *arbuda* (22^{a-c})	*pārśva* (10)
	13	Shoulder-blade	*kaphoḍa*	*aṁsa-phalaka* (16)	*aṁsaja* (14) (or *aṁsa-phalaka*)
	14	Neck-bones	*skandha* (plur.)	*grīvā* (23)	*grīvā* (15)
	15	Back-bones	*pṛṣṭi* (plur.)	*pṛṣṭhāsthi* (20)	*pṛṣṭha* (11)
5		The Upper Extremities (*bāhu*) here briefly mentioned			
	16	Collar-bone	*aṁsa*	*akṣaka* (17) (or *aṁsa*, § 55)	*akṣaka* (13) (or *aṁsa*)
8	17	Brow	*lalāṭa*	*nāsikā-gaṇḍakūṭa-lalāṭa* (28)	*nāsā* (19), *gaṇḍa* (21), *akṣi-koṣa* (22), *karṇa* (23)
	18	Central Facial Bone	*kakāṭikā*		
	19	Cranium with Temples	*kapāla*	*kapāla* (30) with *śaṅkha* (29)	*kapāla* (25) with *śaṅkha* (24)
	20	Structure of Jaws	*hanvoḥ citya*	*danta* (1) with *dantolūkhala* (2)	*danta* (18)
				tālūṣaka (25)	*tālu* (20)
				hanvasthi (26) with *hanu-mūla-bandhana* (27)	*hanu* (17)

4. It will be noticed in the preceding table that while the several items, taken singly, do not follow one another in the Atharvic column IV in exactly the same order as in the Charakiyan and Suśrutiyan columns V and VI, they do so nevertheless, if regard is had mainly to their grouping in the Atharvic verses (col. I). The only exception to this rule is the collar-bone (No. 16 in col. II), which occupies a rather different place in columns V and VI. It is not difficult, however, to see the reason of this exception. The Atharvic hymn mentions the collar-bone, in verse 5, in connexion with the mention of the upper limb (*bāhu*) which serves to join it to the trunk.

5. A much more important point to observe is that, as the table shows, the system of the Atharva Veda more nearly approaches the system of Ātreya-Charaka than that of Suśruta. The only point of agreement in the Atharvic and Suśrutiyan systems is that both content themselves with a brief reference to the bones of the upper extremities (as being alike to those of the lower extremities), but do not enumerate them separately as the Charakiyan system does. This, however, is a merely formal and unimportant point. A really important circumstance is that the Atharvic system shares with the Charakiyan one of the most striking points, in which the latter differs from the system of Suśruta, namely, the assumption of a central facial bone in the structure of the skull (Nos. 17 and 18 in the Table; see also § 11, cl. 5; § 13, cl. 4; § 17, cl. 4; § 23, cl. 3 *b*). This is a point which will be found fully explained in § 66. It may be added that the Atharvic term *pratiṣṭhā* for the base of the long bones (No. 5 in the Table) obviously agrees with the Charakiyan term *adhiṣṭhāna*, and widely differs from the Suśrutiyan *kūrca*. The closer agreement of the system of the Atharva Veda with that of Ātreya-Charaka is nothing more than might have been expected from their closer chronological position, as explained in § 2, cl. 4. The two circumstances suggest mutual confirmation.

6. It also deserves notice that the Atharvic system knows only of two bones as constituting the shoulder-girdle—viz. the collar-bone (*aṁsa*, No. 16 in the Table) and the shoulder-blade (*kaphoḍa*, No. 13). It thus serves to confirm the correctness

of omitting the item *aṁsa* from the osteological summary of Charaka (§ 6, and § 25, Note). The two systems, of the Atharva Veda and Ātreya-Charaka, being in other respects in such close agreement, it becomes increasingly probable that the latter system likewise knew only of two bones in the shoulder, viz. the collar-bone (*akṣaka*, No. 17 in § 7) and the shoulder-blade (*aṁsa-phalaka*, No. 16, *ibid.*).

SECTION III

ANATOMICAL IDENTIFICATIONS

§ 44. *Preliminary Remarks*

1. Before proceeding to the detailed identification of the bones which, according to the early Indian anatomists, compose the human skeleton, it may be useful to note the following preliminary points.

2. According to modern Anatomy, there are about 200 bones in the adult human skeleton.[1] The early Indian anatomists, on the other hand, count either 360 (Ātreya) or 300 (Suśruta) bones. This large excess is principally due to the fact that (besides including the teeth, nails, and cartilages) they counted prominent parts of bones, such as are now known as 'processes' or 'protuberances', as if they were separate bones. Their reasons for counting in this manner were mainly three.

3. Sometimes processes, or protuberances, of bones were popularly known by special names, and regarded as special bones. Examples are the malleoli, or ankle-bones, and the styloid processes, or wrist-bones. In such cases it was probably a mere concession, made by the early Indian anatomists, to popular usage that they enumerated them in their lists as separate bones. In other cases the separate enumeration of processes or protuberances was due to an exaggerated regard for the homological principle. For example the right and left halves of the skeleton were regarded as homologous. Hence, seeing that the vertebral column lay in the median line, the transverse processes on the right and left of the several vertebrae were counted as separate homologous bones (§ 59). Sometimes, again, it was a fancy for artificial symmetry which led to the multiplication of bones. To this cause, probably, is due the

[1] See Dr. Gerrish's *Textbook of Anatomy*, p. 113.

assumption of the existence of a third joint in the thumb and great toe (§ 47), and of twelve costal tubercles instead of ten (§ 58).

4. All these cases are examples of the multiplication of bones; but the opposite process of unification also occurs. Here a number of bones is counted as a single bone, either from deference to an older or popular theory, or because they were thought to constitute a peculiar unity. Conspicuous examples are the bones of the carpus and tarsus (§ 49), and, in Suśruta's system, the ankle-bones (§ 52).

§ 45. *The Practice of Dissection*

1. Allowing for the modifying causes explained in the preceding paragraph, the views of the early Indian anatomists are surprisingly accurate. This is due to the fact that they were accustomed to the practice of preparing the dead human body for actual examination, and that, therefore, their views were the direct result of an experimental knowledge of the skeleton. It is true that the Compendium of Charaka contains no reference whatever to the practice of human dissection; and it must, therefore, remain doubtful whether, and to what extent, that practice was observed in the school of Atreya. But there can be no doubt as to the practice being known and observed in the school of Suśruta; for his Compendium contains a passage which gives detailed instructions regarding the procedure to be adopted in preparing a dead body for anatomical examination.

2. The passage in question occurs at the end of the fifth chapter of the Anatomical Section (*Śārīra Sthāna*) of the Compendium, and runs as follows:

'No accurate account of any part of the body, including even its skin, can be rendered without a knowledge of anatomy. Hence any one who wishes to acquire a thorough knowledge of anatomy must prepare a dead body, and carefully examine all its parts. For it is only by combining both direct ocular observation and the information of text-books that thorough knowledge is obtained. For this purpose one should select a body which is complete in all its parts. It should also be the body of a person who was not excessively old, nor who died of poison or of a protracted disease. Having removed all excrementitious matter from the entrails, the body should be wrapped in rush, or bast, or grass, or hemp, and placed in a cage. Having firmly secured the latter, in a hidden spot, in a river with no strong current, the body should be allowed to decompose. After an interval of seven days the thoroughly decomposed body should be taken out, and very slowly scrubbed with a whisk made of grass-roots, or hair, or bamboo, or bast. At the same time, every part of the body, great or small, external and internal, beginning with the skin, should be examined with the eye, one after the other, as it becomes disclosed in the course of the process of scrubbing.' (Original Text in § 95.[1])

3. The procedure, thus described, will doubtlessly enable the observer to recognize such structures as the clusters (*kūrca*) of small bones which make up the carpus and tarsus. But it would hardly suffice to enable him to discover bones lying interiorly; such, for example, as the ethmoid, sphenoid, vomer, and others in the interior of the head. As a matter of fact, we do not find these latter bones mentioned even in the more accurate list of Suśruta.

§ 46. *Conspectus of the Ancient Indian and Modern Systems*

1. The subjoined comparative table, setting side by side the system of Modern Anatomy and the systems of Ātreya-Charaka and Suśruta, as well as the skeleton shown in Figs. 4 and 5, may serve as a guide to the detailed identification of bones discussed in the succeeding paragraphs. Column I on Modern Anatomy is based on Dr. Samuel O. L. Potter's *Compend of Human Anatomy* (5th ed., 1893), pp. 9, 10; column II on §§ 4, 7; and column III on § 34.

[1] A German translation is given in Professor Jolly's *Indian Medicine*, pp. 44, 45, in the Cyclopedia of Indo-Aryan Research. See also Dr. Wise's *Hindu System of Medicine* (new issue), pp. 68, 69.

	I. Potter.		II. Charaka.		III. Suśruta.		
	A. Four Extremities.						
1	Phalanges, or joints of fingers and toes	56	pāṇi-pād-aṅguli	60	pāṇi-pād-aṅguli	60	§ 47
2	Metacarpus and Metatarsus, Long bones	20	śalākā	20	tala	20	§ 48
3	Carpus and tarsus, Clusters, or Bases	30	adhiṣṭhāna	4	kūrca	4	§ 49
4	Os calcis, heel		pārṣṇi	2	pārṣṇi	2	§ 50
5	Forearm (Radius, Ulna)	4	aratni	4	aratni	4	§ 51
6	Styloid processes, wrist-bones		maṇika	4	maṇibandha	2	§ 52
7	Olecranon, elbow-pan		kapālikā	2	kūrpara	2	§ 53
8	Leg (tibia and fibula)	4	jaṅgha	4	jaṅgha	4	§ 51
9	Malleoli, ankle-bones		gulpha	4	gulpha	2	§ 52
10	Patella, knee-cap	2	jānu	2	jānu	2	§ 53
11	Arm (humerus)	2	bāhu-nalaka	2	bāhu	2	§ 54
12	Thigh (femur)	2	ūru-nalaka	2	ūru	2	§ 54
		120		110		106	
	B. Trunk.						
	Shoulder:						
13	Clavicle, collar-bone	2	akṣaka	2	akṣaka	2	§ 55
14	Scapula, shoulder-blade	2	aṁsa-phalaka	2	aṁsa-ja	2	§ 56
15	Thorax: Ribs	24	pārśvaka, &c.	72	pārśvaka, &c.	72	§ 58
16	Sternum, breast-bone	1	uras	14	uras	17	§ 57
17	Vertebrae, thoracic and lumbar	17	} pṛṣṭha	} 45	pṛṣṭha	30	§ 59
18	Pelvis: Sacrum	1	}	}	trika	1	§ 60
19	Coccyx	1	}	}	guda	1	§ 60
20	Ilium, ischium }	} 2	śroṇi-phalaka	2	nitamba	2	§ 60
21	Pubes }	}	bhag-āsthi	1	bhaga	1	§ 60
		50		138		128	

	I. Potter.		II. Charaka.		III. Suśruta.		
	C. Head and Neck.						
22	Cervix : Vertebrae, Neck-bones	7	grīvā	15	grīvā	9	§ 61
23	Trachea, bronchi, windpipe		jatru	1	kaṇṭha-nāḍī	4	§ 62
24	Cranium,						
	Frontal } pan-	1	}				
	Parietal } shaped	2	} śiraḥ-kapāla	4	śiraḥ-kapāla	6	§ 63
	Occipital } bones	1	}				
	Sphenoid	1					
	Ethmoid	1					
25	Temporal	2	śaṅkhaka	2	śaṅkha	2	§ 64
26	Face :						
	Superior Maxillary } jaws	2			}		
	Inferior do. }	1	hanu, hanumūla	3	} hanu	2	§ 65
	Superciliary ridges, brows		lalāṭa }				§ 66
27	Malar	2	gaṇḍa-kūṭa }	1	gaṇḍa	2	§ 66
28	Nasal	2	nāsikā }		nāsā	3	§ 66
29	Palate bones	2	tālūṣaka	2	tālu	2	§ 67
	Lachrymal	2					
	Inferior turbinated	2					
	Vomer	1					
	Hyoid	1					
30	Additional :						
	Teeth		danta	32	danta	32	§ 68
	Sockets of teeth		ulūkhala	32			§ 68
	Nails		nakha	20			§ 69
	Eyeballs				akṣi-koṣa	2	§ 70
	Ears				karṇa	2	§ 71
	Total :	30		112		66	
	Grand total :	200		360		300	

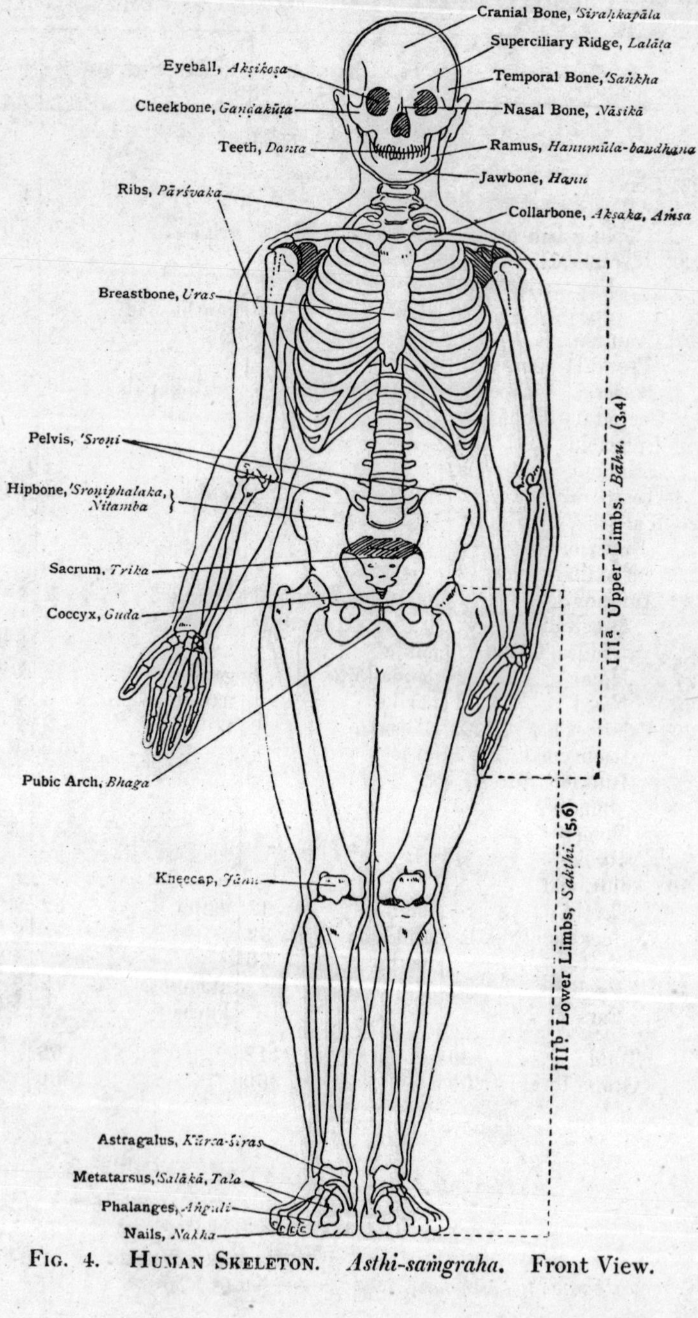

FIG. 4. HUMAN SKELETON. *Asthi-saṁgraha.* Front View.

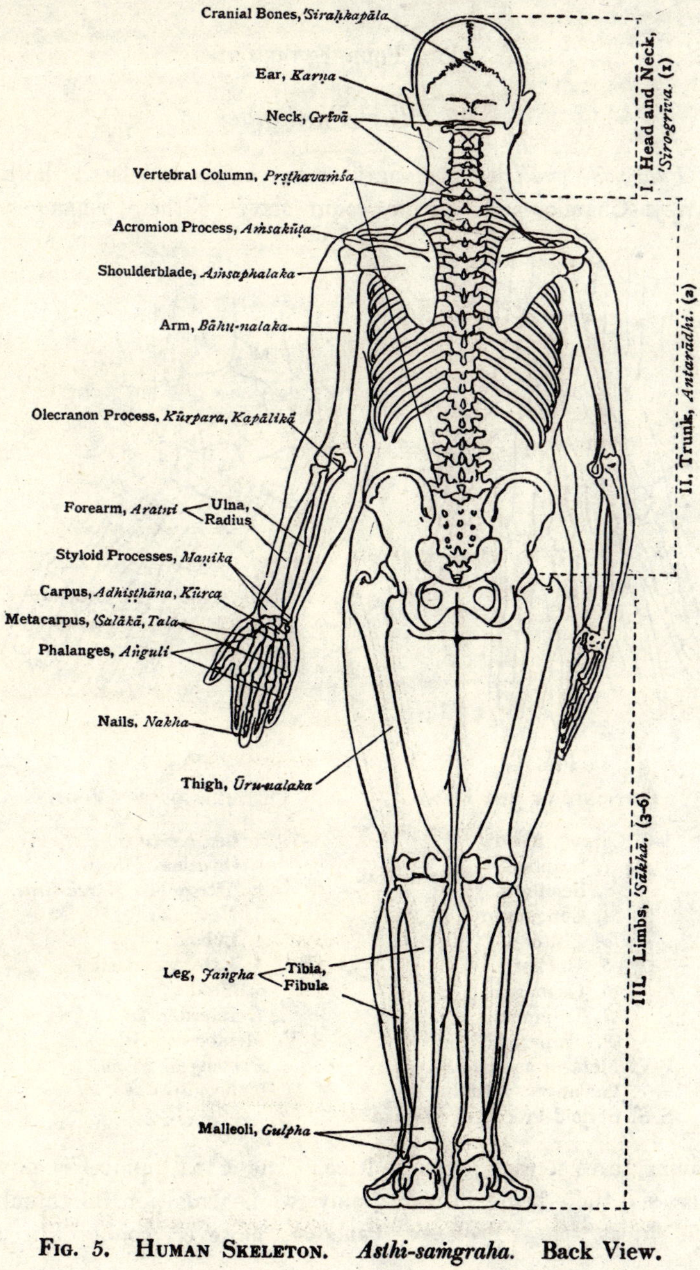

FIG. 5. HUMAN SKELETON. *Asthi-saṁgraha.* Back View.

A. The Four Extremities

§ 47. *The Phalanges*

Pāṇi-pād-aṅguli, or phalanges of the hands and feet. Both Atreya-Charaka and Suśruta count sixty of these phalanges,

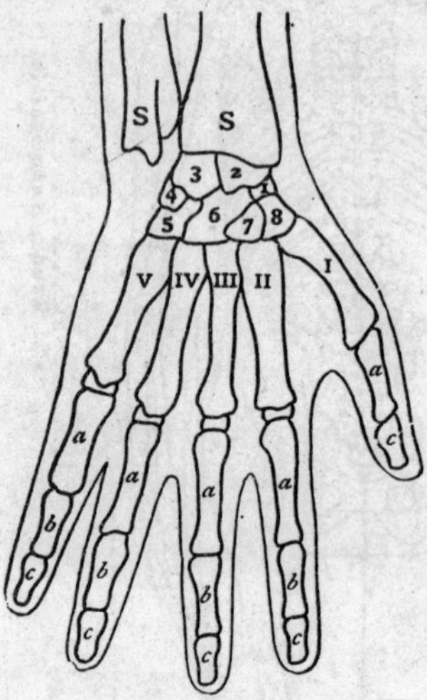

Fig. 6.

Outlines of the Hand.

1-8. Carpus, *Kūrca*.
- 1. Scaphoid } *Kūrca-śiras*.
- 2. Semilunar }
- 3. Cuneiform.
- 4. Pisiform.
- 5. Unciform.
- 6. Os magnum.
- 7. Trapezoid.
- 8. Trapezium.

I-V. Metacarpus, *Śalākā*.
a-c. Phalanges, *Aṅguli*.
S. S. Styloid Processes, *Maṇika*.

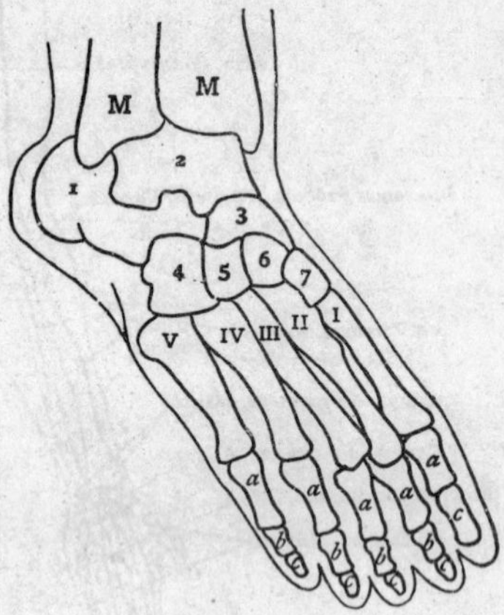

Fig. 7.

Outlines of the Foot.

1-7. Tarsus, *Kūrca*.
- 1. Os calcis, *Pārṣṇi*.
- 2. Astragalus, *Kūrca-śiras*.
- 3. Navicular.
- 4. Cuboid.
- 5. External cuneiform.
- 6. Middle ,,
- 7. Internal ,,

I-V. Metatarsus, *Śalākā*.
a-c. Phalanges, *Aṅguli*.
M. M. Malleoli, *Gulpha*.

giving three to each finger and toe. The actual number is only fifty-six, there being in reality only two phalanges in the thumb and great toe. Professor Pancoast, however, counts fifteen phalanges in either hand, classing the first metacarpal bone among the phalanges of the thumb,[1] and thus making the total of the phalanges to be fifty-eight. He would seem to consider the trapezium (Fig. 6), one of the carpal bones with which the first metacarpal articulates, to be the real metacarpal of the thumb, and the real homologue of the metacarpals of the other four fingers. According to the usual view the clusters of carpal and tarsal bones contain eight and seven bones respectively. Professor Pancoast's theory would equalize their numbers by the exclusion of the trapezium. It is interesting to observe that Chakrapāṇidatta's somewhat obscure remarks on the phalanges seem to indicate his having held a similar view. For he says (§ 11): 'As to the third joint of the thumb and great toe, it must be understood to be contained within the respective hand or foot,' that is, within the palm or sole or, in other words, among the metacarpal or metatarsal bones. And he adds: 'The long bones belonging to the thumb and great toe are also of small size'; that is, he appears to have identified the trapezium as the first metacarpal, and the internal cuneiform bone of the tarsus (Fig. 7) as the first metatarsal. How far the explanation of Chakrapāṇidatta may be the survival of an ancient tradition going back to the time of Atreya and Suśruta, it is, at present, impossible to say. But on the whole it seems more probable that the reckoning of sixty phalanges by the ancient Indian anatomists is based on fancied claims of symmetry (§ 44).

§ 48. *The Long Bones*

1. *Pāṇi-pāda-śalākā*, or the long bones of the hands and feet. These are the metacarpal and metatarsal bones. Charaka counts twenty of them, five in either hand and foot (§ 4), which agrees with the actual number. Suśruta, in his list (§ 27), aggregates them under the term *tala*, which signifies the palmar and plantar portion of the hand and foot respectively. The Atharva Veda (§ 43) denotes that portion by the term *uchlakha*.

2. It may here be useful to note that the combined term *taḷa-kūrca-gulpha*, sole-cluster-ankle, employed by Suśruta in his

[1] Dr. Potter's *Compend of Human Anatomy*, pp. 49, 50.

list (§ 88) denotes the whole (roughly rectangular) portion of the foot and hand, as shown in Figs. 6 and 7, exclusive of the phalanges. That is to say, it signifies the metatarsus (*tala*), tarsus (*kūrca*), and malleoli (*gulpha*) of the foot, and similarly the metacarpus (*tala*), carpus (*kūrca*), and styloid processes (*maṇibandha*) of the hand.

§ 49. *Bases or Clusters*

1. *Pāṇi-pāda-śalāk-ādhiṣṭhāna*, base (prop) of the long bones of the hand and foot; or simply *sthāna* or *pratiṣṭhā*, base; or *kūrca*, cluster (of bones). The first-mentioned term occurs in the lists of Charaka (§ 4) and Bheḍa (§ 12); the second and third in the lists (non-medical) of Yājnavalkya (§ 16) and the Atharva Veda (§ 43) respectively; the fourth in the list of Suśruta. See Figs. 6 and 7.

2. Ātreya, whose system is reported by Charaka and Bheḍa, appears to have held the opinion that the long bones (metacarpals and metatarsals) were fixed in one bone as their common base. He may have known that this base (the carpus, or tarsus) was really composed of a cluster of small bones, but the term *adhiṣṭhāna* (or *sthāna*) which he chose as its name, rather suggests that he thought it to be a single undivided bone. Actual examination of a prepared skeleton, such as Suśruta certainly practised (§ 45), would, of course, have set him right; but it may be doubted whether he ever went beyond a superficial examination of a dead body.

3. Suśruta's use of the term *kūrca*, cluster, which he substitutes for *adhiṣṭhāna*, base, is by itself sufficient to show that he was aware of the true nature of the 'base', as being made up of a cluster of small bones. It is not improbable that he knew even the exact number of the small bones which constitute each cluster (eight in the carpus and seven in the tarsus), but, so far as I know, there is no passage in his Compendium which definitely proves it. Rather inconsistently, but probably in deference to the older view, he continued, for the purpose of his list, to count his 'cluster' as one bone. But of course, properly

interpreted, this only means that he counted the 'cluster' as a composite bone, or rather as a set of bones.

4. The identity of the organ which Suśruta calls *kūrca*, cluster, may also be inferred from a passage in which he describes its position in the limb. In the sixth chapter of the Anatomical Section (*Śārīra Sthāna*), explaining his doctrine of the 'vital spots' (*marman*), he says:

'Between the great toe and the toe next to it, there lies the vital spot called *kṣipra*. Upwards of this *kṣipra*, both ways (i.e. exteriorly and interiorly), there lies the vital spot called *kūrca*.' (Original Text in § 97, cl. 1.)

Referring to Fig. 7, it will be seen that Suśruta's *kūrca*, or cluster (of bones), lies on the exterior and interior sides of the foot, beyond the great and second toes. As a matter of fact, the seven bones of the tarsal cluster are in modern Anatomy considered as 'placed in two rows, side by side, two bones in the external row, five in the internal, as follows: externally, os calcis (No. 1), and cuboid (No. 4); internally, astragalus (No. 2), scaphoid or navicular (No. 3), and the three cuneiform (Nos. 5, 6, 7).[1] *Mutatis mutandis* these remarks apply also to the carpal cluster. The eight bones of that cluster are now usually considered as 'placed in two rows, one in front of the other, with four bones in each row'.[1] But they may also be considered as placed (Fig. 6) in two rows, side by side, four bones externally (Nos. 3, 4, 5, 6, unciform, pisiform, cuneiform, os magnum); and four internally (Nos. 1, 2, 7, 8, scaphoid, semilunar, trapezoid, trapezium).

5. The only difficulty about Suśruta's *kūrca*, or cluster, arises from the fact that the Traditional Recension of his statement on the skeleton (§ 27) ascribes to him, by implication, the doctrine that there are eight *kūrca*, or clusters, in the four extremities, two in either hand and two in either foot. It has been shown, however, in § 31, that this is a complete error, foisted into the system of Suśruta, in all probability, from the system of Vāgbhaṭa I (§ 37, also pp. 99, 103). The true doctrine of Suśruta, stated by himself in explicit terms (§ 31),

[1] See Dr. Potter's *Compend of Human Anatomy*, pp. 48 and 53.

knows only four *kūrca*, or clusters, one in either hand, i.e. the carpus, and one in either foot, i.e. the tarsus.

6. It might be thought that Vāgbhaṭa I derived his doctrine that there are eight *kūrca*, two in either hand and two in either foot, from the circumstance, above referred to, that the small bones of the carpi and tarsi are placed in two rows. One would thus obtain eight rows of small bones, two in either hand and two in either foot; and it might be thought that Vāgbhaṭa I wanted to express that circumstance by his count of eight *kūrca*, or rows. In support of this view it might be said that Vāgbhaṭa I also counts four *gulpha*, or ankle-bones, as well as four *maṇibandha*, or wrist-bones (§ 37). Seeing that there are actually two malleoli (or ankle-bones) in either leg, and two styloid processes (or wrist-bones) in either forearm, it seems a very plausible conclusion that Vāgbhaṭa I was really thinking of the four malleoli and four styloid processes when in his list of bones he enumerates four *gulpha* and four *maṇibandha*; and similarly that he was thinking of the eight rows of small bones in the two carpi and tarsi, when he counted eight *kūrca*. But such a view would credit Vāgbhaṭa I with more consistency and more accurate knowledge of anatomy than he really possessed. How little of both qualities his statement on the skeleton exhibits has been already shown in § 38. A striking proof of his imperfect knowledge of the skeleton is the circumstance that in his list (§ 37) he enumerates both *adhiṣṭhāna* and *kūrca* as two distinct kinds of bone. By the former he understood the carpus and tarsus. This is clear from the term *pratibandhaka*, or interlocker, by which he calls them. He says: 'There are five long bones, and one bone interlocking them' (Original Text in § 93). This shows that (whatever Ātreya-Charaka's view of the real nature of *adhiṣṭhāna* may have been) Vāgbhaṭa I took it to be a single undivided bone, on which the five long bones articulated. But as he had thus provided for the carpus and tarsus, it is difficult to understand what he could have imagined the additional *kūrca* to be. Seeing that all actually existing bones (Figs. 6 and 7), phalanges, metacarpus (or metatarsus), carpus (or tarsus), and styloid processes (or malleoli) were already covered by the terms *aṅguli*, *śalākā*,

pratibandhaka (or *adhiṣṭhāna*), and *maṇibandha* (or *gulpha*), there was no bone left to be named *kūrca*. It may be doubted whether Vāgbhaṭa I had any idea as to what the Suśrutiyan term *kūrca* meant. He certainly failed to see that it signified the equivalent of the Charakiyan term *adhiṣṭhāna*; and his anatomical knowledge was too imperfect to prevent that failure. It thus came to pass that, dominated by his desire of combining the two systems of Suśruta and Charaka, he not only superfluously counted the *kūrca*, by the side of his *pratibandhaka* (Charaka's *adhiṣṭhāna*), but actually duplicated its numbers, counting eight *kūrca* instead of four.

7. In connexion with the cluster of bones (*kūrca*) it may be well to discuss the case of a bone which is not especially enumerated in the list of Suśruta, but which he mentions in the sixth chapter of his Anatomical Section (*Śārīra Sthāna*), in discussing the 'vital spots' (*marman*). It is there named by him *kūrca-śiras*, or head of the cluster, that is, head-bone within the cluster. He defines its position as follows:

'Below the ankle-joint, but not on both sides, there lies what is called the head of the cluster.' (Original Text in § 97, cl. 1.)

By referring to Fig. 7, it will be seen at once that the bone here described as the head of the cluster is the astragalus (No. 2). It forms the lower part of the ankle-joint, and lies below the distal ends of the tibia and fibula with both of which it articulates. In the list of Suśruta (§ 27) it is not specially enumerated, because, of course, it is included in the cluster (*kūrca*) of which it merely forms the head-bone. But in his chapter on the 'vital spots' it had to be mentioned separately by the side of the cluster, on account of its being the location of a particularly dangerous spot, in addition to another dangerous spot located in the remainder of the cluster (Nos. 3, 4, 5, 6). The astragalus (No. 2) and the os calcis (No. 1) are the two largest bones of the tarsal cluster, and Suśruta distinguishes them by the names 'head of the cluster' (*kūrca-śiras*) and 'heel' (*pārṣṇi*) respectively. That fact definitely proves that he was aware of the real nature of the tarsus as being composed of a cluster (*kūrca*) of bones. Ātreya-Charaka, on the other hand, knew nothing of a head of the cluster, and his heel (*pārṣṇi*), as we shall see in the next paragraph, is merely the projecting tuberosity of the os calcis. With him both the astragalus and the os calcis are included in his *adhiṣṭhāna*, or base, and there is nothing to prove definitely that he knew anything of the real composite nature of the organ which he called *adhiṣṭhāna*.

8. It should be mentioned that Suśruta teaches the existence of four *kūrca-śiras*, or heads of clusters. He says:

'There are two ankles, two wrists, and two pairs of cluster-heads. These eight an experienced surgeon should know to be vital spots that are apt to cause diseases.' (Original Text in § 96, cl. 6.)

What Suśruta means is, of course, that there is a head-bone in each of the four clusters (*kūrca*), that is, in either of the two carpi and tarsi. The head-bones of the two tarsi are their respective astragali. Those of the two carpi would appear to be their respective semilunar bones (No. 2 in Fig. 6). Charaka (i.e. Ātreya), as has been already indicated, does not mention the existence of any of these four head-bones.

§ 50. *The Heel*

Pārṣṇi, or the heel. See Fig. 7. This term, as used by Charaka, denotes the backward and downward projection of the os calcis, that is, that portion of it which can be superficially seen and felt, and is popularly known as the heel. Accordingly, in Ātreya's statement of the skeleton, as reported by Charaka and Bheḍa (§§ 4, 12), the number of heels is rightly said to be two. In the list of Vāgbhaṭa I (§ 37), rather grotesquely a heel is ascribed to each of the four extremities, two in the feet and two in the hands, giving a total of four heels. The reason of this incongruous conception has been explained in § 32. It arose from a false construction of Suśruta's direction regarding the method of counting the bones of the four extremities, and it actually succeeded, probably on the authority of Vāgbhaṭa I himself, in being received into the Traditional Recension of Suśruta's statement on the skeleton (§ 27). There can hardly be any doubt that the statement of Suśruta, in its original and genuine form, taught no more than two heels. From the general tenor of it, it is evident that Suśruta knew the true nature of the tarsus; namely, that it is a cluster (*kūrca*) of small bones. The two largest of these small bones he distinguished by special names; namely, the astralagus (No. 2) by *kūrca-siras*, or head of the cluster (§ 49), and the os calcis (No. 2), by *pārṣṇi*, or heel. In his detailed list of the bones (§ 27) he did not enumerate the 'head of the cluster' separately; for of course it was implicitly included in the term 'cluster' (*kūrca*). But the heel (*pārṣṇi*) he counted separately, either as a concession to the older system of Ātreya, and to popular usage, or, perhaps on the whole more probably, because he did not consider the os calcis as constituting one of the component bones of the cluster (*kūrca*). In all probability Suśruta's real view of the lower portion of the lower extremity (the portion shown in Fig. 7) was that it was formed by five constituents: 1, phalanges (*aṅguli*); 2, metatarsals (*tala* or *śalākā*); 3, tarsal cluster (*kūrca*) of six small bones (Nos. 2–7; 4, ankles (*gulpha*); and 5, os calcis or heel-bone (*pārṣṇi*, No. 1). The view of Ātreya-Charaka differed from the view of Suśruta only in considering the tarsus to consist, not of a cluster of bones, but of a single, undivided supporting bone (*adhiṣṭhāna*), which included the body of the os calcis, but excluded its posterior downward projection, the latter being counted separately and named *pārṣṇi*. In § 65 it will be shown that there exists a similar difference of opinion with respect to the term *hanu* between Suśruta and Ātreya-Charaka. The former uses it as denoting the whole lower jaw-bone (inferior maxillary), while with Ātreya it denotes its (roughly) triangular 'mental protuberance,' popularly known as the chin (Fig. 31).

§ 51. *Forearm and Leg*

Aratni or *prabāhu*, forearm, and *jaṅgha*, leg. The term *prabāhu* occurs only in certain manuscripts of the Vishnu Smriti (see § 84). In all the three statements, of Ātreya (that is, Charaka and Bheḍa, §§ 4, 12), Suśruta (§ 27), and Vāgbhaṭa I, (§ 37) these two organs are correctly described as consisting of two bones each—viz. the radius and ulna in the forearm, and the tibia and fibula in the leg. In the Atharva Veda (verse 3 in § 43) the figure made by the two bones of the leg is appropriately described as 'a four-sided frame having its ends firmly knit together'; and this description of course is intended also to apply to the bones of the forearm. See Figs. 8 and 9.

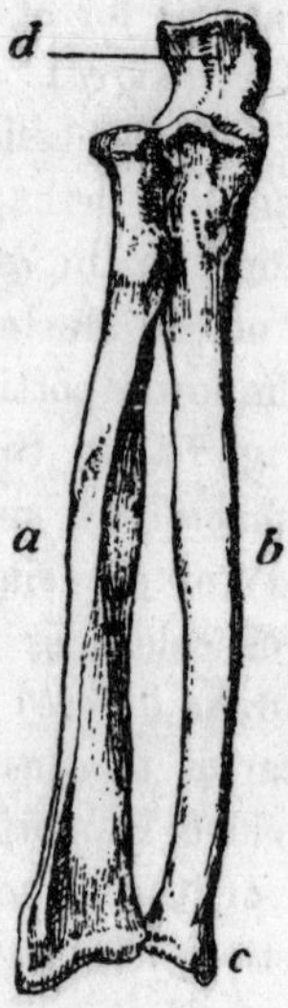

FIG. 8.

FOREARM, *Aratni*.

a. Radius.
b. Ulna.
c, c. Styloid processes, *Maṇika*.
d. Olecranon process, *Kapālikā*.

FIG. 9.

LEG, *Jaṅgha*.

a. Tibia.
b. Fibula.
c, c. Malleoli, *Gulpha*.

§ 52. *Ankles and Wrists*

Maṇika or *maṇibandha*, wrist-bone, and *gulpha*, ankle-bone. See Figs. 6 and 7. In literary Sanskrit these terms denote the wrist-joint and ankle-joint respectively; but as anatomical terms they signify more precisely the wrist-bones and ankle-bones, that is, the distal processes of the two bones of the forearm and leg which are known respectively as the styloid processes and the malleoli. By the ancient Indian anatomists, according to their peculiar method (§ 44, cl. 3), they are reckoned as separate bones; but while Ātreya counts them all singly, and thus in the list, reported by Charaka (§ 7), enumerates four wrist-bones and four ankle-bones, Suśruta counts them by pairs, and thus in his list (§ 34), has only two wrist-bones and two ankle-bones, one in each forearm, and one in each leg. The Traditional Recension, of the list of Charaka (§ 4), it is true, counts only two wrist-bones; but it has been shown in §§ 6 and 25 (p. 67) that the original and genuine list (§ 7) must have contained four wrist-bones. On the other hand, the Traditional Recension of Suśruta's list (§ 27) gives four wrist-bones and four ankle-bones. This, as shown in §§ 31, 41, is also an error, due to the influence of Vāgbhaṭa I (§ 37), who, in pursuance of his aim of combining and harmonizing the two systems of Charaka and Suśruta, adopted Charaka's way of counting the wrist-bones and ankle-bones.

2. The truth regarding the way in which Suśruta contemplated the styloid processes and malleoli is clearly brought out by the term *valaya*, wristlet or anklet, which he applies to them (§ 30). It is obvious from this comparison that he looked upon each pair of styloid processes and malleoli as forming but a single composite bone encircling the lower part of the forearm, or leg, like a wristlet, or anklet (see Fig. 2, p. 80). It must be admitted that this is a rather fanciful way of treating those organs. At the same time, it is quite consistent with Suśruta's methods; he treats the carpus and tarsus in exactly the same way. For him both are single, composite bones, or clusters (*kūrca*) as he calls them (§ 49). For the purpose of enumeration in the list of bones, the clusters, though consisting of a number of small bones, are reckoned each as a single bone, or—it would be better to say—as a single system of bones. Similarly, the pairs of styloid processes and malleoli are counted, in the list, each as a single bone, or rather as a single system of bones.

§ 53. *Elbow-pan and Knee-cap*

1. *Kapālikā* or *kūrpara*, elbow-pan, and *jānu* or *jānuka*, knee-cap. There can be no doubt regarding the bones to which these terms

refer. They are the olecranon process of the elbow, and the patella of the knee. The former, which 'in its function and structure resembles the patella',[1] is not a separate bone, but a process of the ulna (Fig. 8). But by the ancient Indian anatomists, according to their usual practice (§ 44), it is counted as a separate bone. They follow herein our own popular usage which speaks of it as the 'funny bone' or 'crazy bone'.

2. The term *kūrpara* is peculiar to Suśruta, who expressly defines it as denoting the homologue of *jānu*, the knee-cap (p. 72), and who may, therefore, have been the first to use it as a denotation of the olecranon process. The term *kapālikā* is peculiar to Ātreya (Charaka and Bheḍa). It means, literally, a small shallow dish, and is therefore identical in meaning with patella, the Latin name of the knee-cap. It well describes the appearance of the olecranon process, which presents, in the ventral view, a concave surface, the so-called great sigmoid cavity (Fig. 8). Accordingly, in this treatise, it has been rendered by 'elbow-pan'.

FIG. 10.

THE PATELLA, *Jānu*.
From the back, showing interior concave surface.

3. The term *kapola*, for the elbow-pan, which is found in the Non-medical Version (§ 16), is undoubtedly, as has been explained in § 19, cl. 4, an ancient misreading for *kapāla*, pan, of which *kapālikā* is a diminutive. By way of corroboration it may be mentioned that the Smaller Petersburg Dictionary quotes the form *kapolaka* as a misreading for *kapālaka*, pan. The antiquity of the misreading may be seen from the fact that ancient Sanskrit dictionaries mention *kapolī*, with the meaning knee-cap. The true form, of course, is *kapālī*, a feminine diminutive of *kapāla*, meaning a small pan, or any small pan-like bone, such as the knee-cap or elbow-pan. Similarly, *kapāla* itself is used to denote the larger pan-shaped bones of the cranium (§ 63).

4. The Atharva Vedic list (§ 43) has the two synonymous

[1] Dr. Potter's *Compend of Human Anatomy*, p. 47.

terms *jānu* and *aṣṭhīvat*. The latter literally means 'the organ (knee) which possesses a bone (patella)', and thus, like *jānu*, comes to denote specifically the knee-cap.

§ 54. *Arms and Thighs*

Bāhu, arm, and *ūru*, thigh. These two terms are employed by Suśruta (§ 27) and Vāgbhaṭa I (§ 37). Charaka uses the fuller terms *bāhu-nalaka*, reed-like or hollow bone of the arm, and *ūru-nalaka*, reed-like, or hollow bone of the thigh (§ 4). All three correctly ascribe to either organ a cylindrical bone, the humerus and the femur respectively, with a hollow shaft, the so-called medullary cavity. See Figs. 4 and 5.

B. The Trunk

§ 55. *The Clavicle or Collar-bone*

1. *Akṣaka* or *akṣa*, also *aṁsa* or *aṁsaka*, clavicle or collar-bone (Fig. 11). All three writers, Ātreya-Charaka, Suśruta, and Vāgbhaṭa I, in their lists (§§ 4, 27, 37), correctly state the number of these bones to be two.

Fig. 11.

The Right Clavicle, *Akṣaka*.

a. Shaft.
b. Sternal end.
c. Acromial end.

2. The first-named term, *akṣaka*, is the strictly technical denotation of the collar-bone. It is uniformly explained by the commentators to have that meaning. Thus Ḍallana, in his commentary on the thirty-fourth and forty-eighth verses of the third chapter of the Therapeutical Section (*Cikitsita Sthāna*) of the Compendium of Suśruta, explains it by saying: 'The *akṣaka* is located above the shoulder-joint,' and again, 'The *akṣaka*

is the part above the shoulder-joint' (Original Texts in § 97, cl. 2). Similarly Gangādhar, in his commentary on Charaka's skeletal statement, says: 'The two *akṣaka* are the two shoulder-bones (*aṁsaka*) which lie below the throat' (Original Text in § 97, cl. 2). But the matter is clinched by Chakrapāṇidatta, who (§ 11, p. 36) very aptly likens the two *akṣaka* to two *kīlaka* or 'pegs that run athwart the anterior part of the trunk'. Referring to Figures 4 and 12, it will be seen that the external end of the

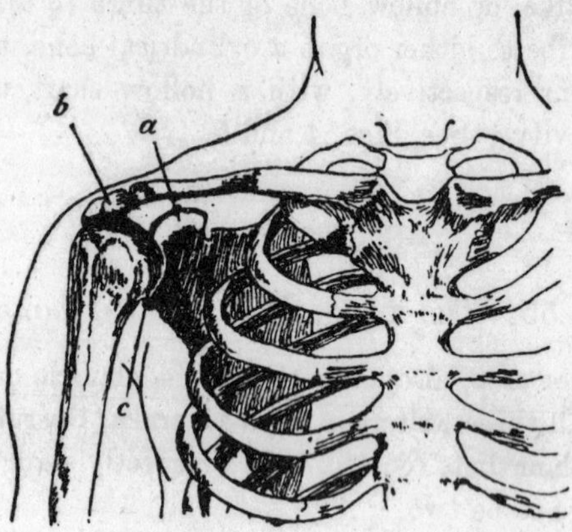

FIG. 12.

DIAGRAM OF RIGHT HALF OF SHOULDER-GIRDLE.

Ventral view showing—Clavicle, *Akṣaka*, above.
Scapula, *Aṁsa-phalaka*, below (shaded).
with *a*. Coracoid process.
b. Acromion process, *Aṁsa-kūṭa*.
c. Glenoid cavity, *Aṁsa-pīṭha*.

clavicle lies exactly above the shoulder-joint, and its internal end below the throat, while the whole clavicle runs, like a peg, across from the throat to the shoulder-joint.

3. In the shorter form *akṣa*, the term occurs only in the Non-medical Version of the system of Ātreya (§ 16),[1] where, however, as stated in § 20, cl. 4, it is wrongly explained by the

[1] It also occurs in the *Śatapatha Brāhmaṇa*: see Monier Williams's Dictionary, 2nd ed.

commentators of the Law-book of Yājnavalkya to signify 'a bone on the edge of the eye', or, 'a bone between the eye and the ear.' And this unintelligent guess at the meaning of *akṣa* was copied from them by Nanda Paṇḍita, in his Commentary on the Institutes of Vishnu, where he says that the term means 'the part below the temples, between the ear and the eye'.[1] In medical works the term never occurs with that meaning. The only other way in which I have noticed it used in a medical work is as a synonym of *indriya*, or organ of sense. With this meaning it occurs not unfrequently in the Compendium of Vāgbhaṭa II (e.g. *Sūtra Sthāna*, chap. I, verse 33; X. 2; XII. 17; *Śārīra Sthāna*, III. 5), where the commentator expressly says that 'the organs of sense are called *akṣa*' (*akṣāṇi indriyāṇi ucyante*). It may be noted, however, that Vāgbhaṭa I, in his Summary, in the corresponding passages never uses the term *akṣa*, but always *indriya* (*Sūtra Sthāna*, chap. XIX, vol. I, p. 96, l. 21; XIX, p. 106, l. 16; *Śārīra Sthāna*, chap. V, p. 220, l. 8).[2]

4. As to *aṁsa*, it is properly an indefinite term, denoting the shoulder-girdle generally. But in the Compendium of Suśruta it is frequently used as a synonym of *akṣaka* to denote the collar-bone, as distinguished from *aṁsa-phalaka*, which denotes the shoulder-blade or scapula. This usage is explicitly explained in a passage in the sixth chapter of the Anatomical Section (*Śārīra Sthāna*), where Suśruta defines the names and positions of those two parts of the shoulder-girdle. He says:

'In the upper part of the back, and on both sides of the vertebral column, there lie what are called the shoulder-blades (*aṁsa-phalaka*), being of triangular form (*trika-sambaddha*). Be-

[1] Curiously enough, in the exact position indicated by Nanda Paṇḍita, there is a small elongated bone, called the Zygomatic Process (see Figs. 211, 239, on pp. 184, 204, of Dr. Gerrish's *Textbook of Anatomy*, 2nd ed., 1903). But, even granting the improbable assumption that this process was known to the legal commentators, the explanation is out of place, because *akṣa* is enumerated, not among the bones of the head, but among those of the trunk.

[2] It is this meaning of *akṣa*, which appears to have suggested to Aparārka the interpretation of *akṣa-tātūṣaka*, as 'edge of the eye', see p. 55, footnote 1.

tween the head of the arms and the neck there lie what are called the collar-bones (*aṁsa*), connecting the shoulder-seat (*aṁsa-pīṭha*, i.e. the glenoid cavity)[1] with the nape of the neck. (Original Text in § 97, cl. 3.)

In another passage in the same sixth chapter, in which Susruta describes the forty-four 'vital spots which cause weakness' (*vaikalya-karāṇi marmāṇi*), he enumerates (Original Text in § 97, cl. 4) among their number the two *aṁsa* or collar-bones, and the two *aṁsa-phalaka* or shoulder-blades. Exceptionally, it would seem that Suśruta employed the term *aṁsa* also to denote the shoulder-blade. Thus in the passage, quoted in § 30, in which he divides the bones of the skeleton in five classes, according to their shapes, he places the bones which he there calls *aṁsa* among the pan-shaped ones. It is obvious from this very classification that by the term *aṁsa* Suśruta can there mean no other than the shoulder-blades, for these, as a fact, are pan-shaped, broad, and flat bones, while the collar-bones are short, cylindrical bones which belong to the class described by Suśruta as *nalaka*, or reed-like. In another passage of the fifth chapter, in which Suśruta enumerates the muscles (*peśī*) of the body, he says that 'there are seven muscles round about the collar-bone (*akṣaka*) and shoulder-blade (*aṁsa*, Original Text in § 97, cl. 4). Here again it is obvious that by the term *aṁsa* Suśruta cannot mean the collar-bones, which are already indicated by the term *akṣaka*. The term *aṁsa*, therefore, can only refer to the shoulder-blades. It is possible that Suśruta might have used the term *aṁsa*, which in the ordinary Sanskrit is only a general name for the shoulder, indifferently to denote sometimes the collar-bones, and at other times the shoulder-blades. But such a practice is obviously very inconvenient, and it is not at all probable that Suśruta was guilty of it. It is far more probable that the traditional text of the passages in which Suśruta is made to use the term *aṁsa* to denote the shoulder-blades is corrupt; and that in every such case, instead of *aṁsa* we should read *aṁsa-ja*,

[1] This is not quite correct. The clavicle does not connect with the glenoid cavity (*aṁsa-pīṭha*), but with the acromion process (*aṁsa-kūṭa*). Possibly the traditional reading of Suśruta's text is at fault.

'sprung from the shoulder.' The latter term quite properly describes the shoulder-blades as springing from the shoulder (Fig. 12). It has already been explained in § 29 that the term *saṁjña*, 'so-called,' which is so unaccountably found in the Traditional Recension of Suśruta's list of the skeletal bones, suggests itself to be a corruption of the term *aṁsaja*, caused by copyists unfamiliar with skeletal anatomy and its terms. It may be suggested that probably in the two passages above referred to we should also read *aṁsaja* instead of *aṁsa*.[1] It would thus appear that Suśruta employs the following pairs of terms: (1) *akṣaka* and *aṁsa*, to denote the collar-bones; (2) *aṁsa-phalaka* and *aṁsa-ja*, to denote the shoulder-blades; the last-mentioned term *aṁsa-ja* being misunderstood by copyists and changed either into *saṁjña* or simply into *aṁsa*.

5. In this connexion it may be useful to identify two other terms occasionally used by Suśruta, namely *aṁsa-kūṭa* and *aṁsa-pīṭha*. The former occurs in a passage of the sixth chapter of the Anatomical Section (*Śārīra Sthāna*), in which Suśruta describes two 'vital spots' (*marman*) of the body (see the Original Text in § 97, cl. 5), called by him *apalāpa* (apparently the upper attachment of the coraco-brachialis muscle: see Figs. 295, 303, 304, in Dr. Gerrish's *Textbook of Anatomy*, 2nd ed., pp. 274 and 277). These two vital spots (one, of course, on either side of the body) he says are situated 'below the two summits of the shoulder' (*aṁsa-kūṭa*). The 'two summits of the shoulder' (Fig. 22), are the two acromion processes of the right and left scapula, below which the caraco-brachialis attachment is situated. The *aṁsa-pīṭha*, lit. shoulder-seat, is mentioned in a passage in the fifth chapter of the Anatomical Section (Original Text on § 97, cl. 6), in which Suśruta describes eight kinds of differently shaped joints.[2] There two joints are described as being *sāmudga*, that is shaped like a round casket (*samudga*).

[1] It may be useful to collect the passages in question. They are (1) in the Number-list (§ 29), for *akṣaka-saṁjñe* read *akṣak-āṁsaje*; (2) in the Class-list (§ 30), for *aṁsa* read *aṁsaja*; (3) in the list of muscles, for *akṣak-āṁsau* read *akṣak-āṁsajau*.

[2] Another mention occurs in the passage on *aṁsa*, quoted earlier in this paragraph.

These are the shoulder-joint and the hip-joint. The former is called *aṁsa-pīṭha*, or shoulder-seat, and indicates the glenoid cavity, into which the head of the humerus is inserted (Fig. 13). The latter is described as being formed of the anal bone (*guda*, coccyx), pubic bone (*bhaga*, pubic arch), and hip-bone (*nitamba*, ilium and ischium), and indicates the acetabulum or cotyloid cavity, in which the head of the femur is lodged[1] (Fig. 20).

6. The longer form *aṁsaka* occurs, e. g. in the passage above quoted from the Commentary of Gangādhar. It is a derivative of *aṁsa*, shoulder, and means shoulder-bone, that is, collar-bone. A similar formation is that of *śaṅkhaka*, temporal bone, from *śaṅkha*, temple (§ 64), and *pārśvaka*, rib, from *pārśva*, side (§ 57).

§ 56. *The Shoulder-blade or Scapula*

1. *Aṁsa-phalaka*, flat bone of the shoulder, *aṁsa-ja* or *aṁsa-samudbhava*, (bone) springing from the shoulder. All three terms are employed to denote the shoulder-blade or scapula, but the first-named, *aṁsa-phalaka*, is the term which is commonly used by Ātreya-Charaka, Suśruta, and Vāgbhaṭa I. The term *aṁsa-ja* is conjectural and only occurs in the Compendium of Suśruta (§§ 29, 55). The term *aṁsa-samudbhava* is found only in the Non-medical Version of Ātreya's statement on the skeleton, and is probably a synonymous variation of the Suśrutiyan term *aṁsa-ja* (§§ 16, 17, 21). The Atharva Veda has the peculiar term *kaphoḍa* to denote the shoulder-blade (§ 43, cl. 6).

2. All three lists of Ātreya-Charaka (Bheḍa), Suśruta, and Vāgbhaṭa I, correctly state the number of shoulder-blades to be two; but there is a difficulty attending them which requires a word of explanation. The shoulder-girdle (Fig. 12) comprises two bones, and no more. These are the scapula or shoulder-blade, and the clavicle or collar-bone. Examining the traditional lists of Ātreya-Charaka, Suśruta, and Vāgbhaṭa I, we find a curious

[1] As a fact, the acetabulum is formed by the union of three bones, the ilium, ischium, and os pubis. The anal bone or coccyx does not enter into its formation, and should be omitted. The Suśrutiyan text is probably corrupt, as the confused manuscript readings indicate: see § 97, cl. 6.

state of things. Charaka apparently enumerates three bones (§ 4)—*aṁsa*, shoulder, *aṁsa-phalaka*, shoulder-blade, and *akṣaka*, collar-bone. Vāgbhaṭa I has the same threefold enumeration (§ 37). On the other hand, Suśruta appears to enumerate only a single bone, namely *akṣaka*, or the collar-bone (§ 27). As regards Charaka, it has been shown in § 6 that the separate mention of *aṁsa*, shoulder, is an early error of the manuscript text caused by an inadvertent repetition, by some scribe, of the word *aṁsa* inherent in *aṁsa-phalaka*. In reality, therefore, the genuine list of Charaka (§ 7) knows only two bones as comprised in the shoulder, viz. *akṣaka*, clavicle, and *aṁsa-phalaka*, scapula. It is different with the list of Vāgbhaṭa I. That list deliberately enumerates the shoulder-peak as a third bone by the side of the shoulder-blade and the collar-bone; for otherwise (see § 37) its total of 120 bones does not work out correctly. This, however, is only one of the numerous incongruities and blunders of the list of Vāgbhaṭa I; and how he came to be betrayed into committing it has been explained in § 39, cl. 4.

3. As regards Suśruta, it has been shown in §§ 29, 30, 56, that the omission of the shoulder-blades from his list is a textual error, due in all probability to an ancient misreading (or false emendation), by some ignorant scribe who wrote *saṁjña*, so-called, for *aṁsaja*, shoulder-blade; and that, as a matter of fact, Suśruta explicitly mentions the shoulder-blade as one of those bones which he classifies as pan-shaped (*kapāla*). In reality, therefore, the genuine list of Suśruta (§ 34) enumerates both bones which constitute the shoulder-girdle, the clavicle as well as the scapula. His explicit statement regarding the existence of the two bones, together with other evidence on the subject, has already been quoted in the preceding paragraph. An additional piece of evidence, however, may here be adduced. In the sixth chapter of his Anatomical Section (*Śārīra Sthāna*), in which Suśruta enumerates the so-called 'vital spots' (*marman*) in the body, he says that 'there are eight such places in the bones', and among these eight bones he enumerates the *aṁsa-phalaka*, or shoulder-blades (Original Text in § 97, cl. 4).

4. The scapula is a large, flat, triangular bone (Fig. 13). That the ancient Indian anatomists knew it to be a large, flat bone is shown by the fact of their calling it *phalaka*, which word means a board or slab. But it is Suśruta alone who also notes its triangular shape. In the passage quoted in the preceding paragraph he particularly describes it as *trika-sambaddha*, trebly bounded, that is, as being of a triangular form. For the same reason of its triangular shape the sacrum likewise is called

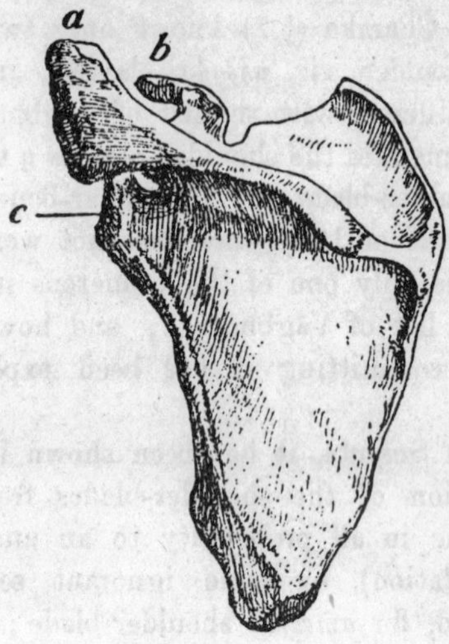

FIG. 13.

LEFT SCAPULA, *Aṁsa-phalaka*. Posterior View.
Showing—*a*. Acromion process, *Aṁsa-kūṭa*.
b. Coracoid process.
c. Glenoid cavity, *Aṁsa-pīṭha*.

trika: see § 60. In this connexion Dallana's explanation of the Suśrutiyan phrase *trika-sambaddha*, triangular in form, is significant as showing the decay of anatomical knowledge subsequent to the time of Suśruta. He says: 'The place where the two collar-bones connect with the neck, that place is meant by the term *trika*.'[1] This place, as may be seen by referring to Fig. 4,

[1] This explanation is also quoted in the *Bhāva Prakāśa* (Jīv. ed., p. 60). In the Bengali commentary, appended to the edition of that

has no apparent connexion with the scapula, and its mention in a description of the latter bone, accordingly, is quite out of place. The explanation of Ḍallana, however, would appear to be a tradition of considerable antiquity. For its incongruity would seem to have induced Vāgbhaṭa I to change the text of Suśruta's description of the scapula. In the seventh chapter of the Anatomical Section of his Summary, quoting Suśruta's description, Vāgbhaṭa I replaces the Suśrutiyan phrase *trika-sambaddha*, trebly bounded or triangular, by the phrase *bāhumūla-sambaddha*, joined to the root of the arm, i. e. to the head of the humerus. Here we see that Vāgbhaṭa I replaces the incongruous expression 'junction of the collar-bone with the neck' by the phrase 'junction with the head of the humerus'. Though this alteration doubtlessly now states a correct fact—the junction of the scapula with the head of the humerus in the glenoid cavity —it entirely abandons Suśruta's striking description of the triangular shape of the scapula, apparently because Vāgbhaṭa I also did not know what to make of the Suśrutiyan term *trika*.

§ 57. *The Thorax: Sternum and Ribs*

1. *Uras* or *vakṣas*, breast, chest; *pārśva*, region of the ribs; *pārśvaka* or *parśuka*, rib. The organs denoted by these terms, which are common to all three writers, Ātreya-Charaka, Suśruta, and Vāgbhaṭa I, form three sides of the thoracic cage (*pañjara*), the fourth side being formed by the *pṛṣṭha*, or back. The four sides of the thoracic cage are made up thus: the back by the thoracic vertebrae, which are included in the term *pṛṣṭha*, back (§ 58); the two sides by the ribs, denoted by the term *pārśvaka* or *parśuka* (§ 57), and the front, by the sternum and costal cartilages, which are jointly denoted by the term *uras* or *vakṣas*, breast.

2. Regarding the number of bones of the front of the thorax, that is, the breast (*uras*), the lists differ very considerably. Charaka's list (§ 4) counts fourteen, while the traditional

work by Debendranath and Upendranath Sengupta, p. 597, the place in question is explained as 'the most depressed spot of the vertebral column, well known under the name *trika*' (*merudatter sarva-nimna trika nāme prasiddha*)!

Recension of Suśruta's list (§ 27) counts only eight, and the list of Vāgbhaṭa I (§ 37) agrees with the latter. Again, the Non-medical Version of Ātreya's list counts not less then seventeen. It has already been shown to be very probable that the latter number represents the true count of Suśruta, and that the number eight is properly the count of the list of Vāgbhaṭa I, from which subsequently it was foisted into the list of Suśruta (§§ 33, 34, 40).

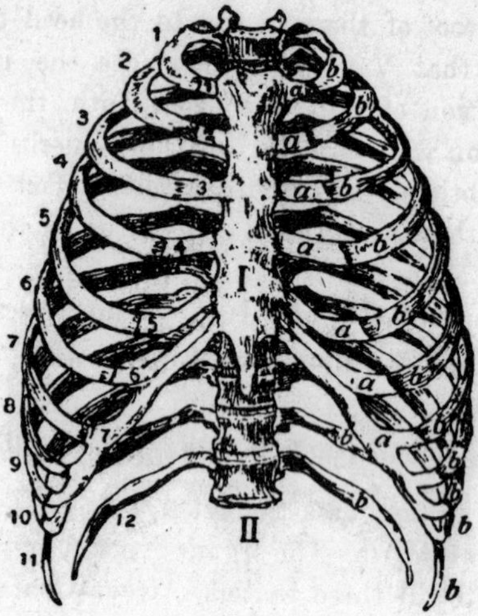

FIG. 14.

THE THORAX. Anterior View.

Showing—1-7, *a*. Costal cartilages, *Jatru*.
1-12, *b*. Ribs, *Pārśvaka*.
I. Sternum, *Uras*.
II. Vertebral column, *Pṛṣṭha-vaṁśa*.

3. The bones of the organs that constitute the sides and back of the thoracic cage are satisfactorily accounted for in the next two paragraphs. The only bones that remain to be accounted for are those of the organs that constitute the front, that is, the sternum and the costal cartilages (Figs. 14 and 16). It may, therefore, be justly concluded that these must account for the numbers mentioned by the Indian anatomists. The cartilages, we may remember (§ 30), are reckoned by them as 'tender'

(*taruṇa*) bones. The costal cartilages (1–7, *a*, in Fig. 14) form the links that connect the sternal end of the shafts of the ribs with the sternum. But only the seven upper ribs (distinguished as the 'true' ribs) are in this way connected. The cartilages of the upper three 'false' ribs (eighth, ninth, tenth) are attached to the cartilage of the seventh rib. The remaining two ribs (eleventh and twelfth) do not connect at all with the sternum, being 'floating' ribs. It will be seen that these facts admit of two ways of counting the number of costal cartilages. One may take them to be either seven or eight. We have only seven cartilages, if we take those of the seventh, eighth, ninth, and tenth ribs which are attached to one another as constituting but a single cartilage; or we obtain eight cartilages, if we count the cartilage of the seventh rib and the cartilaginous attachments thereto of the eighth, ninth, and tenth ribs as two distinct cartilages. Applying these alternative views to the whole of the cartilages, or 'tender' bones, of the breast, we have to count either seven or eight cartilages on either side of the sternum, that is, a total of either fourteen or sixteen cartilages, or 'tender' bones.

4. Both views are represented in the lists of the ancient Indian anatomists. Suśruta counts sixteen bones; and these sixteen, together with the median bone of the sternum, make up the seventeen bones of the *uras* or breast, which we find in the genuine form of his list (§ 34). Charaka, on the other hand, counts only fourteen bones (§ 4). The difficulty in his case is that apparently he ignores the existence of the sternum: one expects that he would count fifteen bones. Considering that the sternum is a very prominent bone which even a less experienced anatomist would have no difficulty in feeling under the skin, it is inconceivable that Charaka (or rather Ātreya, whose system Charaka reports) should have failed to recognize it. The probability is that Ātreya merely omitted to distinguish between bone and cartilage, that is, between the hard bone of the sternum and the 'tender' bone of the costal cartilages. To him probably the sternum appeared to be merely a continuation of the latter which he considered as meeting in the median line of the breast. He looked upon the front of the thoracic cage as formed by

a series of seven long bones, placed horizontally one above the other, and attached to one another in the median line. On the homological principle, he divided this series of bars into two halves, and thus obtained his total of fourteen bones.

5. Suśruta's treatment of the bones of the breast marks an anatomical advance, inasmuch as he distinguishes the sternum from the adjacent costal cartilages, and the cartilaginous attachments of the eighth, ninth, and tenth ribs from the cartilage of the seventh rib. Incidentally, moreover, Suśruta's count of seventeen bones of the breast has an important chronological bearing, inasmuch as the same count is found in the ritual *Śatapatha Brāhmaṇa* (see §§ 42, 62), the reputed author of which, Yājnavalkya, not being a medical expert himself, must have obtained his knowledge of the skeleton from the current surgical school of his time. Suśruta, therefore, must be placed earlier in date than the *Śatapatha Brāhmaṇa*.

6. It is not quite so easy to recognize a rational ground for the number eight of the list of Vāgbhaṭa I. The only explanation that can be suggested is that it arose from an unintelligent attempt at combining the doctrines of Ātreya-Charaka and Suśruta. While accepting the former's theory of a series of bars, Vāgbhaṭa I added to it an additional eighth bar, in conformity with the count of Suśruta. At the same time he abandoned the homological division into halves, which would have given him sixteen bones for the breast. The reason of this abandonment, probably, was that the duplication of the number eight (or, for that matter, of the number seven) would have interfered with his obtaining the requisite total of 360 bones for the whole skeleton (§§ 38, 41).

§ 58. *Continuation: the Ribs, and their Appendages*

1. *Pārśva*, region of the ribs; *stana*, breast; *pārśvaka* or *parśuka*, rib; *sthālaka*, socket; *arbuda*, tubercle. The last three terms are peculiar to the list of Ātreya-Charaka (§ 4), from which they are adopted into the list of Vāgbhaṭa I (§ 37). Suśruta uses only the first term, but that he agrees with the

theory of Ātreya-Charaka, implied in the use of the other three terms, is evident from the fact that both hold the same number of bones to constitute the *pārśva*, or region of the ribs. According to Ātreya-Charaka these bones number seventy-two, while according to Suśruta they number thirty-six on either side, and therefore seventy-two altogether. The term *stana* occurs in the list of the Atharva Veda (§ 43).

2. Suśruta does not explain how this number is arrived at, but Charaka states that there are twenty-four *pārśvaka* or *parśuka*, ribs, twenty-four *sthālaka*, sockets, and twenty-four *arbuda*, tubercles. And, of course, as indicated by Suśruta's manner of counting, it is to be understood that there are twelve of each kind, that is, altogether thirty-six, on each side. Each rib (Figs. 15, 16, 17) consists[1] of a shaft, and of a head with neck; also at the point of junction of these two parts there is a tubercle which articulates with the transverse process of the corresponding vertebra; and this transverse process has a facet, or very shallow cavity, for the reception of the tubercle. It is from this facet that the transverse process takes its name *sthālaka*, which word means a shallow socket. The transverse processes, though really a part of the vertebral system, are considered by the ancient Indian anatomists a part of the system of ribs by reason of their containing the sockets, or facets, for holding the ribs. The word *sthālaka* is a diminutive of the word *sthāla*, vessel, cup, or pan, and means a small or shallow cup or pan. In anatomical terminology the two words, *sthāla* and *sthālaka*, mean, respectively, socket for a tooth (§ 68) and shallow socket (or facet) for a rib. The name of the tubercle is *arbuda*, and the

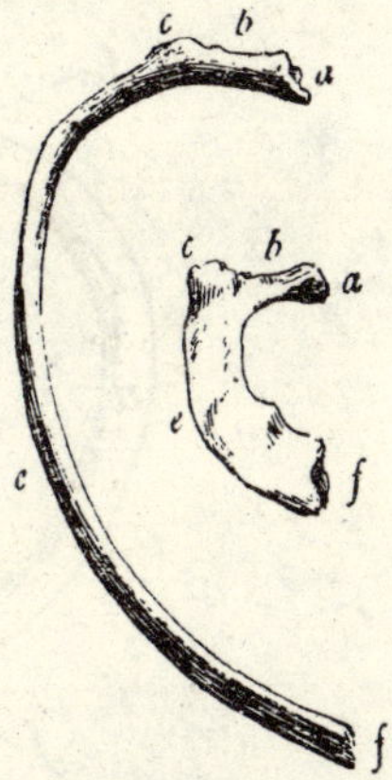

FIG. 15.
THE FIRST AND SIXTH RIBS.

a. Head } *Sthālaka.*
b. Neck }
c. Tubercle, *Arbuda.*
e. Shaft, *Pārśvaka.*
f. Extremity of Shaft, articulating with costal cartilage.

[1] See Dr. Potter's *Compend of Human Anatomy*, p. 38.

name of the shaft (including the neck), or rib proper, is *parśuka* or *pārśvaka*. Each of the three parts, the rib, its tubercle, and its corresponding transverse process, as usual with the ancient Indian anatomists (§ 44), is counted as a separate bone. It may be noted, however, that even admitting the Indian way of

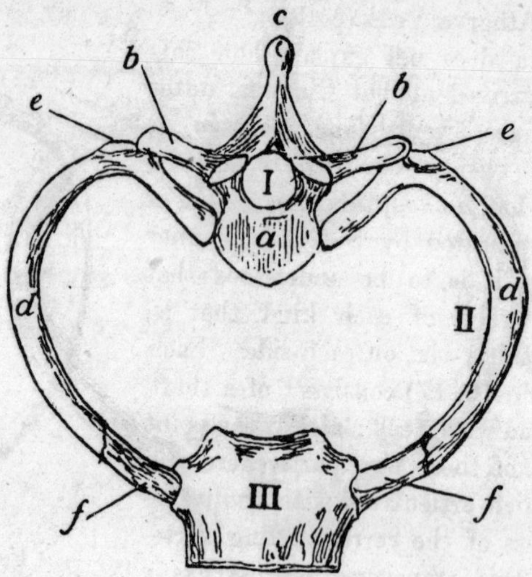

FIG. 16.

DIAGRAM OF TRANSVERSE SECTION OF THORAX.

Showing—I. Vertebra, *Pṛṣṭhāsthi*, with *a*. Body.
b, *b*. Transverse process, *Sthālaka*.
c, *c*. Spinous process.
II. Rib, with *d*, *d*. Shaft, *Pārśvaka*.
e, *e*. Tubercle, *Arbuda*.
f, *f*. Costal cartilage, *Uras*.
III. Sternum, *Uras*.

counting, there would strictly be only sixty-eight bones (or thirty-four on either side), because in reality there exist only ten tubercles on either side, the two lowest, or 'floating', ribs (the eleventh and twelfth) having no tubercles. But the Indian anatomists, owing to their usual fancy for symmetry (§ 44), count twelve tubercles, just as they count fifteen joints in the fingers and toes.

3. The only Indian writer, who, so far as I know, attempts to give a detailed explanation of the three terms *pārśvaka*, *sthālaka*, *arbuda*, and of their respective numbers, is Nanda Paṇḍita. As his explanation differs from that above given, it becomes necessary to consider its claims to acceptance. It occurs

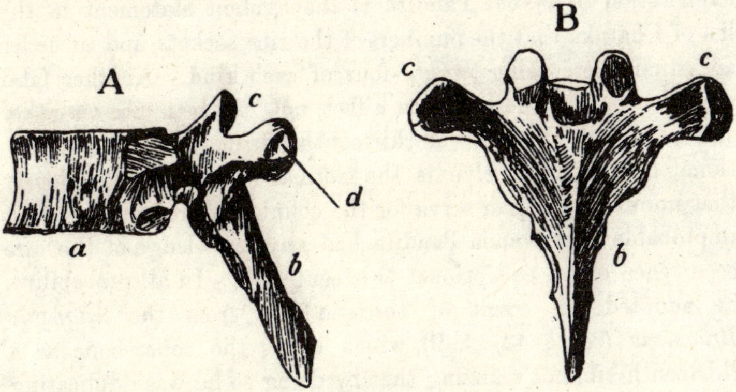

FIG. 17.

THORACIC VERTEBRA, *Kīkasā*.

A. Lateral View. B. Posterior View.

a. Body. *b*. Spinous process.

c, *c*. Transverse processes, *Sthālaka*, with *d*. Facet for tubercle of rib.

in his commentary on the Institutes of Vishnu, and runs as follows:

There are thirteen ribs (*pārśvaka*) on either side, which aggregate to twenty-six. The tubercles, (*arbuda*), being the bones which connect the ribs with the breast (*vakṣas*), are ten on either side, which make twenty. The sockets (*sthālaka*), being the bones which connect them with the back (*pṛṣṭha*), are thirteen on either side, which make twenty-six. In this way, the ribs together with their tubercles and sockets amount to seventy-two (i.e. 26 + 20 + 26 = 72). (Original Text in § 85.)

It is evident that in this explanation the tubercles (*arbuda*) are identified with the costal cartilages which connect the upper ten ribs with the sternum (Fig. 16). But the term tubercle, *arbuda*, would be most inappropriate as applied to the costal cartilages. Moreover, the latter do not belong to the 'region of the ribs' (*pārśva*), but to the front of the thoracic cage, or the breast (*uras*); see § 57. Further, there are, strictly speaking, not ten costal cartilages, but only seven; for the four lowest connected ribs have, between them, only one cartilage. On this last point, indeed, theories of counting might differ; but what is fatal to the explanation of Nanda Paṇḍita is the explicit statement in the list of Charaka that the numbers of the ribs, sockets, and tubercles are equal, there being twenty-four of each kind. Another fatal objection is that there are, as a fact, not 'thirteen ribs on either side', but only twelve. A thirteenth rib does occur in exceptional cases; but twelve is the normal number, and obviously that number alone can serve for the count. Moreover, it is most improbable that Nanda Paṇḍita had any knowledge of the rare occurrence of an exceptional thirteenth rib. In all probability, he adopted his count of thirteen ribs from the *Śatapatha Brāhmaṇa* (see § 42, cl. 9), which treats the collar-bone as a thirteenth rib, not realizing that by doing so he was duplicating the collar-bones which are separately enumerated in the list of the Institutes of Vishnu under the name *akṣa* (*akṣaka*).

§ 59. *The Vertebral Column*

1. *Pṛṣṭha*, back; *pṛṣṭha-vaṁśa*, lit. back-row, i. e. vertebral or spinal column; *pṛṣṭh-āsthi*, back-bone, or *pṛṣṭha-gat-āsthi*, bone belonging to the back, or *pṛṣṭi*, back-bone, all three denoting the vertebra. The first two terms are chiefly found in Suśruta; the next two chiefly in Charaka and in the Non-medical version of the Institutes of Vishnu. The last term, *pṛṣṭi* (or *pṛṣṭī*), which properly denotes the transverse process of a vertebra, and thence the vertebra itself, is peculiar to the Vedas (§§ 42, 43), where it occurs in the plural number to denote the series of vertebrae or the vertical column.[1]

[1] In the Vedas there occur the following further terms: *kīkasa* for the entire spinal column, or for its cervical, or thoracic, portion; *anūka* or *anūkya* and *karūkara*, for its truncal portion; *anūka*, for its thoracic, or lumbar portion, and *udara* for its lumbar portion; also *karūkara* and *kuntāpa* for the transverse processes of the vertebra. See § 42, cl. 3 and 4; also my article on *Ancient Indian Medicine*, in the *Journal of the Royal Asiatic Society* for 1907, pp. 2–10.

2. The actual number of the bones of the entire vertebral column is twenty-six, consisting of twenty-four simple and two composite bones. The former are the true vertebrae, and comprise the seven cervical, the twelve thoracic, and the five lumbar

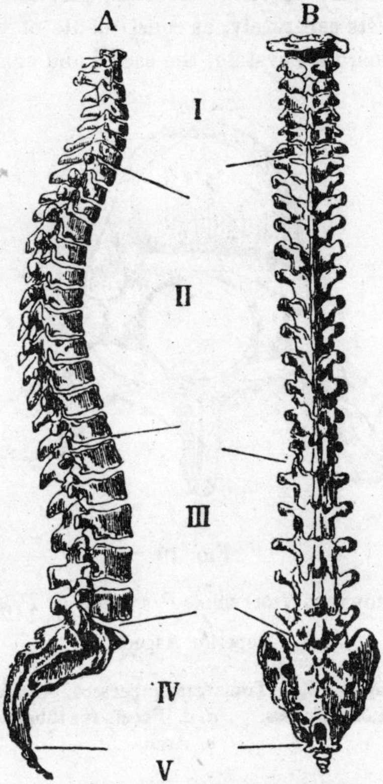

FIG. 18.

VERTEBRAL COLUMN, *Pṛṣṭha-vaṁśa.*

A. Lateral View. B. Dorsal View.

I. Cervical, *Grīvā.* II. Thoracic, *Anūka.* III. Lumbar, *Udara.* IV. Sacrum, *Trika.* V. Coccyx, *Guda.*

vertebrae. The two composite bones are the sacrum or sacral bone, and the coccyx or anal (caudal) bone (Fig. 18). Either of these consists of five vertebrae fused together, and hence known as the false vertebrae. It is to be noted, however, that the first sacral vertebra is of a transitional and partly lumbar character, and occasionally remains permanently separate.[1] It is this fact which appears to have caused Suśruta to count six lumbar vertebrae.

3. As regards the cervical vertebrae, they are counted by the Indian anatomists separately, as constituents of the neck (§ 61). Moreover, in Suśruta's system, the sacral and anal bones also are

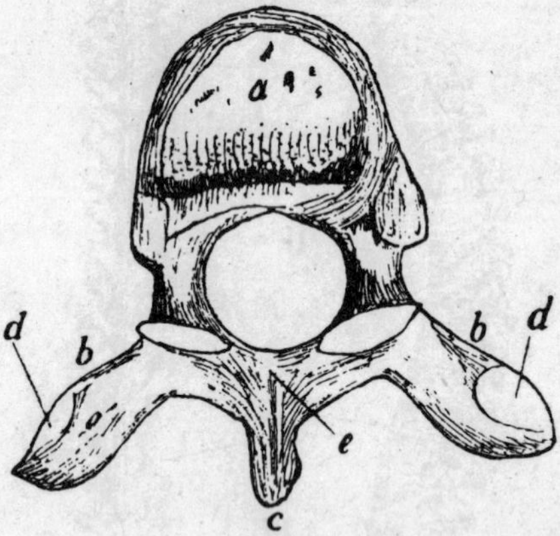

FIG. 19.

THORACIC VERTEBRA, *Pṛṣṭhāsthi* or *Pṛṣṭi*.

Superior Aspect.

a. Body. *b*, *b*. Transverse processes, *Sthālaka*.
c. Spinous process. *d*, *d*. Facets for tubercle of ribs.
e. Arch.

counted separately as constituents of the pelvis (§ 60). There remain, therefore, only the twelve thoracic and five lumbar vertebrae, altogether seventeen, or, if we include the sacral and anal bones, nineteen bones to be accounted for. Against these seventeen or nineteen bones Suśruta counts thirty, and Charaka forty-five. In order to appreciate these large numbers correctly, we must

[1] In some quadrupeds, e.g. the gibbon, the normal number of the lumbar is six, and of the sacral four. See Dr. Gerrish, *Textbook of Anatomy*, 2nd ed., p. 133, Dr. Wiedersheim, *Structure of Man*, p. 34.

remember the peculiar practice of the Indian anatomists to count 'processes' as separate bones (§ 44, cl. 1). Each vertebra (Fig. 19) consists of a 'body' and an 'arch', the latter being constituted of three particularly prominent 'processes', viz. the two transverse processes and the spinous process. Charaka counts these four parts, that is, the body and the three processes of the arch, as separate bones. On this point, Suśruta differs from Charaka; and it constitutes one of the two cardinal points of difference between the two systems (for the other, see §§ 65, 66). In the view of Suśruta, with his more thorough application of the principle of homology (§ 28, cl. 2), the body and spinous process, both of which lie in the median line of the body, constitute but a single bone, while the two transverse processes, being homologous on the right and left sides of the body, are separate bones. Accordingly, while Charaka counts four, Suśruta counts only three bones to each vertebra. Moreover, with regard to the thoracic vertebrae, another point must be remembered. Their transverse processes were reckoned by the Indian anatomists along with the ribs as their *sthālaka*, or sockets, and have been already disposed of in the preceding paragraph. It is only the body and spinous process of the thoracic vertebrae which are counted by them as 'bones belonging to the back' (*pṛṣṭha-gat-āsthi*).

4. The system of Suśruta counts thirty bones, exclusive of the vertebrae of the neck (§ 61) and the pelvis (§ 60). This number is made up thus:

12 thoracic vertebrae (excl. transverses) . . .	12 bones
6 lumbar vertebrae (incl. first sacral, and dividing each into body and two transverses) × 3 . .	18 bones
Total .	30 bones

In the case of the first sacral vertebra, its two alae (Fig. 20, *i i*) correspond to the two transverse processes of the ordinary lumbar vertebra.

5. The system of Charaka counts forty-five bones. Like Suśruta's system it excludes the vertebrae of the neck; but, unlike it, it includes those of the pelvis (the sacral and anal bones). Accordingly its numeration is made up thus:

12 thoracic vertebrae (excl. transverses, but separating body and spine) × 2	24 bones
5 lumbar vertebrae (separating body, spine, and two transverses) × 4	20 bones
1 pelvic bone (incl. sacrum and coccyx) . . .	1 bone
Total	45 bones

6. The treatment of the pelvic bones by Suśruta and Charaka respectively shows the former's advance in anatomical knowledge. That Charaka took the sacrum and coccyx to constitute a single bone is shown by the circumstance (*infra,* cl. 7) of Vāgbhaṭa I adopting that count from him. Suśruta's more intimate knowledge of the structure of the pelvis is shown not only by the fact that he recognized the separate existence of the sacrum and coccyx, but also by the fact that he realized the peculiar shape of the sacrum as being triangular (§ 60, cl. 3), and especially of its first vertebra as resembling that of the fifth lumbar, on which account, in fact, he counted the first sacral rather as a lumbar vertebra.

7. The system of Vāgbhaṭa I is peculiar. Its aim is to combine the systems of Charaka and Suśruta (§ 38). Following the doctrine of the latter, Vāgbhaṭa I counts thirty back-bones, excluding the sacral and anal bones from the vertebral column, and relegating them to the pelvis. But if he had reckoned these two as separate bones, he would not have been able to secure the required total of 360 bones for the whole skeleton. Accordingly, with regard to this count, he adopted the system of Charaka, and counted the sacrum and coccyx as constituting a single bone. In the system of Vāgbhaṭa I, therefore, the term *trika*, or triangular bone, which he took over from Suśruta, includes both the sacral and anal bones (§ 60, cl. 4).

§ 60. *The Pelvis: Hip-bones, Pubes, Sacrum, Coccyx*

1. *Śroṇi*, pelvis, or the pelvic cavity, consisting of *śroṇi-phalaka*, or *nitamba*, hip-blade; *bhaga* or *bhag-āsthi*, pubes or pubic bone; *trika*, sacrum or sacral bone; and *guda* or *gud-āsthi*, coccyx or anal (caudal) bone. The term *śroṇi-phalaka* is peculiar to the

list of Charaka (§ 4), while Suśruta (§ 27) and Vāgbhaṭa I (§ 37) use the term *nitamba.* The full form *bhag-āsthi,* bone of the pubes, or the pubic arch, is employed in the list of Charaka. The shorter form *bhaga* occurs in the lists of Suśruta and Vāgbhaṭa I. In literary Sanskrit, and in popular usage, the word *bhaga* has the narrower meaning of the external female sexual organ, the vulva[1] (*yoni*); but in medical usage it has a wider meaning, irrespective of sex. There it denotes the inferior part, or base, of the trunk, that is, in the male, the space between the anus and scrotum, or the perinaeum; in the female the space occupied by the vulva and the perinaeum. When not referring to the trunk as a whole, but to its bony constituents, *bhaga,* or more accurately *bhag-āsthi,* or bone of *bhaga,* denotes the bone contained in that inferior part, namely, the pubic arch, made up by the two ossa pubis and the symphysis (Figs. 4, 21). It is quite correctly described by Chakrapāṇidatta (§ 11, cl. 2, p. 36) as 'the cross (*tiryak*) bone which binds together the haunch-bones (ilium *plus* ischium) in front'. The full form *gud-āsthi,* or bone of the anus, anal (or caudal) bone, occurs in the Compendium of Vāgbhaṭa II.[2] But in the lists of Suśruta and Vāgbhaṭa I the shorter form *guda* is used. That word ordinarily means anus, but of course in the lists, being the denotation of a bone, it must signify the anal, or caudal bone, that is, the coccyx.

2. Suśruta, in his statement on the skeleton (§ 27), explicitly states that the pelvic cavity is constituted of five bones, namely, the anal bone (*guda*), the pubic bone (*bhaga*), the two hip-bones (*nitamba* or *śroṇi-phalaka*), and the triangular bone (*trika,* or sacrum). This agrees with the actual constitution of the pelvic cavity. For the pelvis includes the coccyx or caudal bone (*guda*),

[1] It is this circumstance which led to the absurdity, explained in § 9, of the inclusion of the male and female generative organs, *meḍhr-āsthi,* penis, and *bhaga,* vulva, by Gangādhar in his recension of Charaka's list of the bones of the skeleton. The usage of literary Sanskrit is taught in the great vocabulary, the *Amarakoṣa,* while the medical usage is defined in the medical vocabulary, *Rājanighaṇṭu*; see § 97, cl. 7.

[2] e.g. *Aṣṭāṅga Hṛdaya, Nidāna Sthāna,* chap. ix, verse 1, in 1st ed., vol. i, p. 758.

the triangular sacrum (*trika*), and the two ossa innominata. These last-mentioned bones consist, each of three parts, the ilium, ischium, and os pubis. The Indian anatomists prefer to divide the ossa innominata into two parts, namely a posterior and an anterior portion. The former, consisting of the ilium and ischium, exists in duplicate, one on the right, the other on the left side of the skeleton, and is named *śroṇi-phalaka* (or *nitamba*), blade of the pelvis, hip-blade. The latter is formed by the prominent pubic arch, and is called *bhag-āsthi*, bone of

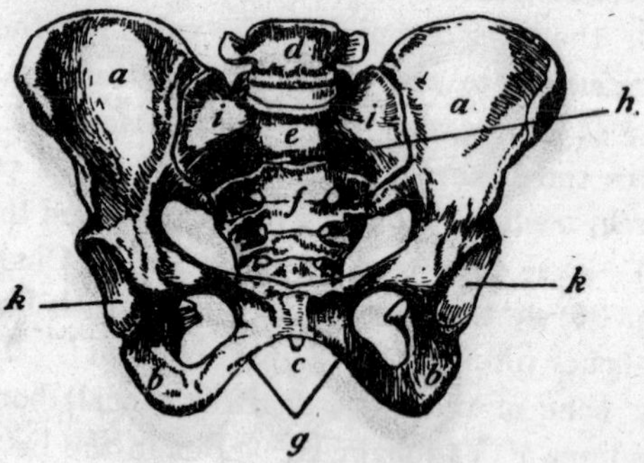

FIG. 20.

PELVIS, *Śroṇi*. Anterior View.

Showing—*a, a*. Ilium *plus* (below) Ischium, *Nitamba*.
b, b. Ischio-pubic arch, *Viṭapa*.
c. Coccyx, *Guda* (see Fig. 18).
d. Fifth lumbar vertebra.
e. First sacral or sixth lumbar vertebra.
f. Sacrum (2nd–5th vertebrae), *Trika*.
g. Pubic arch, *Bhag-āsthi*.
h. Ridge between first and second sacral vertebrae.
i, i. Alae of first sacral or sixth lumbar vertebra.
k, k. Acetabulum, *Guda-bhaga-nitamba*.

the pubes (Figs. 4, 20). As this bone lies in the median line of the skeleton it is not subject to duplication by the homological principle, but (like the penis and vulva to which it gives attachment) it is counted, in the Indian anatomical system, as a single bone. In fact, it corresponds, in the lower part of the body, to the breast-bone or sternum, in the upper part; and thus the ischio-pubic arch (*viṭapa*, § 28, footnote on p. 72), connecting the pubic arch with the ischium, is the homologue of the clavicular arch (*kakṣa-dhara*, clavicle), connecting the sternum with the shoulder. The pubic arch, of course, does not really consist of a single bone, but is made up of two bones, the ossa pubis, which form the two sides of the arch, and which are bound at the top of the arch by means of a cartilaginous disk forming the symphysis pubis. But it must be remembered that for the Indian anatomist cartilage is bone (§ 30), and from his point of view he was justified in regarding the whole arch as composed of a single bone. We must also remember that the mode of counting the bones of the skeleton is more or less arbitrary at all times. Modern anatomy counts the ilium and ischium as two separate bones, though, as a matter of fact, they are ankylosed in the adult: it does so as a matter of scientific convenience, and is justified in doing so by the circumstance that they are really separate in early life. Indian anatomists, on the other hand, having regard to the adult condition, count the ilium and ischium as constituting a single bone.

3. On the other hand, in the system of Ātreya-Charaka, the anal (*guda*) and sacral (*trika*) bones are not reckoned as parts of the pelvis, but as a portion of the vertebral column. In that system, indeed, those two bones are considered to constitute but a single bone, which is included among the forty-five vertebrae (§ 59, cl. 5) without being named separately. This, as has been stated (§ 59, cl. 6), is one of the marks of the divergent pelvic systems of Suśruta and Ātreya-Charaka. Suśruta seems to have been the first to count the sacrum and coccyx separately, and thus to recognize the distinction between true and false vertebrae. It is also not improbable that he was the first particularly to observe the triangular shape of the sacrum, and to give it the name *trika*, or triangle, which expresses that fact, and by which it is now generally known. It should be noted, however, that Suśruta's *trika* is not quite identical with the sacrum of modern anatomy. He treats the first sacral vertebra as belonging to the lumbar region, and as forming a sixth lumbar vertebra (§ 59, cl. 2, 4). His sacrum, therefore, comprises only four vertebrae, and it constitutes the triangular bone which is made up of these four, and which subtends the ridge

that connects the two uppermost foramina of the sacrum (Fig. 20, *h*).

4. Vāgbhaṭa I, as usual, attempts to combine the systems of Ātreya-Charaka and Suśruta. From the latter he adopts the transfer of the sacral and anal bones from the vertebral column (*pṛṣṭha*) to the pelvis (*śroṇi*). But he follows the former in counting them as forming together a single bone, which he names *trika*, or triangular (§ 38, cl. 3, § 39, cl. 7).

C. The Head and Neck

§ 61. *The Cervical Vertebrae, or Neck-bones*

1. *Grīvā*, neck. This term is used in all the three lists, of Ātreya-Charaka, Suśruta, and Vāgbhaṭa I, to denote the cervical column in the posterior part of the neck. The list in the Atharva Veda (§ 43) uses the term *skandha* in the plural number to denote the neck-bones.

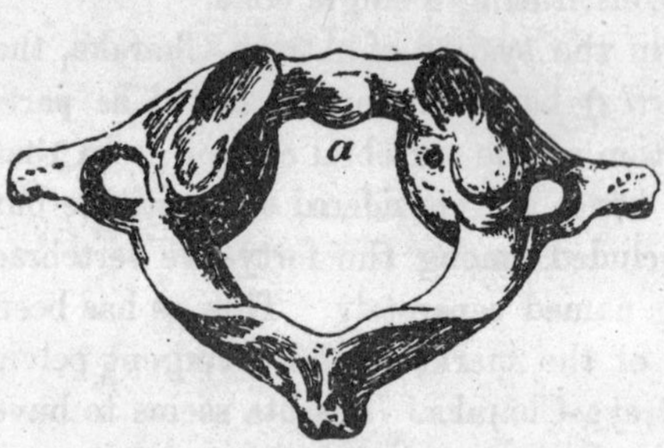

Fig. 21.

The Atlas, viewed from above.
a. Arch.

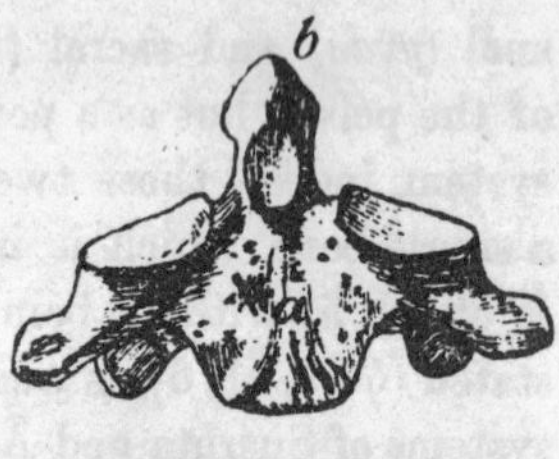

Fig. 22.

The Axis. Anterior View.
a. Body.
b. Odontoid process.

2. There is no part of the skeleton with regard to the number of bones of which the lists differ more widely. The list of Ātreya-Charaka (§ 4) makes the number of neck-bones to be fifteen. The Traditional Recension of the list of Suśruta (§ 27) makes it to be only nine, while the list of Vāgbhaṭa I (§ 37) makes it to be thirteen. As a matter of fact, the number of the cervical vertebrae is seven; but they greatly differ among

themselves in some respects. The first vertebra, called the atlas (Fig. 21), is practically a mere ring. It lacks the body and spinous process of the normal vertebra. The second vertebra, called the axis (Fig. 22) consists practically only of a large strong body, surmounted by the odontoid process, on which as a pivot the atlas rotates.[1] The remaining five vertebrae possess the normal type (§ 59, cl. 3), and consist of a body and three (one spinous and two transverse) processes; but these processes, in all except the seventh, are short and bifid at the extremity (Fig. 23), and hence not very prominent. The seventh vertebra is exceptional: it approaches in shape the upper thoracic

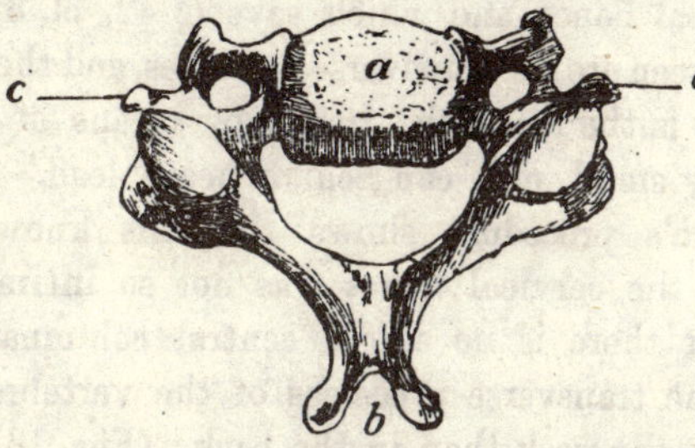

FIG. 23.

A CERVICAL VERTEBRA, viewed from above.

a. Body.
b. Bifid spinous process.
c, c. Transverse processes.

vertebrae, having a very long spinous process, whence it is called vertebra prominens, as well as large transverse processes.[2]

3. These considerations fully explain Suśruta's count of nine neck-bones. He counted each of the six upper vertebrae as a single bone; but the seventh he treated in the same way as he treated the thoracic vertebrae (§ 59, cl. 3), that is to say, he counted it as consisting of three bones; viz. a body *plus*

[1] See Dr. Gerrish's *Textbook of Anatomy*, 2nd ed., p. 117. The odontoid process, in fact, is the body of the atlas from which it has become separated, and become ankylosed to the axis.

[2] *Ibid.*, pp. 117, 124, 'The spinous processes of the upper vertebrae are not readily felt in the living body, until we reach the 7th or sometimes the 6th spine.'

spine, and two transverse processes. He thus obtained $6+3=9$ bones.

4. Ātreya-Charaka obtained his total of fifteen bones by treating the cervical column somewhat similarly to the vertebral column (§ 59). He gave two transverse processes to each vertebra, counting them as separate bones, and looked upon the bodies of the vertebrae as constituting together a single columnar bone. He thus had twice seven transverse processes, or fourteen bones, *plus* one columnar body, or a total of fifteen bones. That this was really Ātreya's procedure is shown by a statement of the *Śatapatha Brāhmaṇa*, which is evidently based on Ātreya's theory of the cervical bones, and which says (§ 42, cl. 3) of the neck-bones, 'Fourteen are the transverse processes, and their strength (or strong bone) is the fifteenth; hence by means of them, though they are very small, man can bear a heavy load.' At the same time, Ātreya's procedure shows that his knowledge of the structure of the cervical bones was not so intimate as that of Suśruta; for there is no single central columnar bone in the neck, and the transverse processes of the vertebrae are far less prominent in the neck than in the back[1] (Fig. 18).

4. As regards the count of Vāgbhaṭa I, his total of thirteen bones probably represents, as usual, a compromise between the systems of Ātreya-Charaka and Suśruta. He appears to have counted two bones (transverse processes) for each of the cervical vertebrae, except the first, which, being a mere bony ring, without body and spinous process, was reckoned as a single bone. He would thus obtain his total of thirteen bones (i.e. $6\times 2=12+1=13$).

§ 62. *The Windpipe*

1. *Kaṇṭhanāḍī*, lit. throat-pipe, or *jatru*, windpipe. The former term is peculiar to the list of Suśruta (§ 27), the latter is employed in the list of Ātreya-Charaka (§ 4). In the list of Vāgbhaṭa I both terms occur, though they denote the same organ, this being (as explained in § 38, cl. 4) one of its conspicuous incongruities.

[1] 'The transverse processes are rather short.'—*Ib.*, p. 116.

2. The windpipe consists of four parts, the larynx, trachea, and two bronchi (Fig. 24). These four parts are enumerated by Suśruta as four distinct bones. On the other hand, Ātreya-Charaka counts the whole organ as a single bone. Strictly speaking, of course, the organ consists not of bone at all but of cartilage; but by the ancient Indian anatomists cartilage is regarded as a kind of tender, or immature (*taruṇa*) bone (§ 30, p. 80).

3. The word *jatru*—so far as I am aware—is explained in all Sanskrit dictionaries (native Indian, as well as European) to

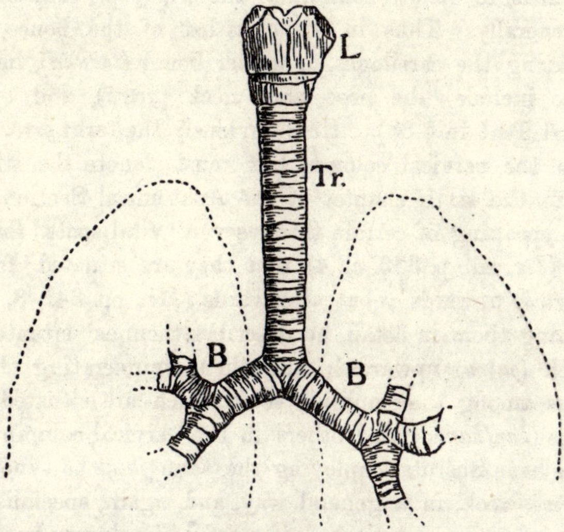

FIG. 24.

THE WINDPIPE, *Jatru* or *Kaṇṭhanāḍī*.

L. Larynx. *Tr.* Trachea. *B, B.* Bronchi.

mean, not the windpipe, but the clavicle or collar-bone. This—so far as the occurrence of the word in medical literature is concerned—is a total mistake. It becomes, therefore, necessary to discuss more fully the correct meaning of the word.[1]

4. In the earliest medical compendia the term *jatru* is either synonymous with *grīvā*, neck, or signifies more especially a

[1] See also a fuller discussion of this point in my article on 'Ancient Indian Medicine' in the *Journal of the Royal Asiatic Society* for 1906, pp. 922 ff.

particular aspect of it. The neck contains two structures, posteriorly the cervical column, denoted more particularly by the term *grīvā*, and anteriorly the windpipe, denoted more particularly by the term *jatru*. As the latter term, in a general way, also denotes the whole neck, Suśruta prefers, in his list of bones (§ 27), to employ the more specialized term *kaṇṭhanāḍī*, throat-pipe, to indicate the windpipe as distinguished from the cervical column. On the other hand, outside his list, he frequently uses the two terms *jatru* and *grīvā* as practically synonymous, to denote sometimes the windpipe, sometimes the neck generally. Thus in his class-list of the bones (§ 30), enumerating the cartilages, or tender bones (*taruṇa*), he makes them to include 'the nose, ears, neck (*grīvā*), and eyeballs' (Original Text in § 88). Here obviously the term *grīvā* cannot refer to the cervical column, but must denote the windpipe. Again in the sixth chapter of the Anatomical Section (*Śārīra Sthāna*), speaking of certain thirty-seven 'vital spots' (*marman*), he says (Jīv. ed., p. 336, cl. 4) that they are situated 'from the neck (*grīvā*) upwards'; but afterwards (Jīv., pp. 342–3, cl. 32), mentioning them in detail, he describes them as 'situated from the neck (*jatru*) upwards'; and then, enumerating them, he mentions among their number some which are situated in the windpipe (*kaṇṭhanāḍī*) and others in the cervical column (*grīvā*). Here we have Suśruta employing the term *jatru* as synonymous with *grīvā*, neck, in a general way, and, again, specializing, he uses *grīvā* for the posteriorly-lying cervical column, but *kaṇṭhanāḍī* for the anteriorly-lying windpipe. Similarly Vāgbhaṭa II (in his *Aṣṭāṅga-Hṛdaya*, II. 4, verse 2, in 1st ed., vol. I, p. 592), speaking of the same thirty-seven vital spots, says that they are situated *ūrdhvaṁ jatroḥ*, or upwards of the neck, using *jatru* synonymously with *grīvā*. Again in the fifth chapter of the Pathological Section (*Nidāna Sthāna*), speaking of the rheumatic disease *manyā-stambha*, or rigidity of the neck, Suśruta says (Jīv. ed., p. 249, verse 69) *grīvā apavartate*, 'the neck becomes awry.' Similarly Charaka, or rather Dṛiḍhabala[1] (VI. 26,

[1] The statement is really one of the Complementor Dṛiḍhabala, who wrote the chapter in question. He is expressly named as its author by Vijaya Rakshita, the commentator of the Nidāna (Jīv. ed., p. 152).

verse 41*a*, Jīv. ed., 1896, p. 775), referring to the same disease, says *grīvā antar-āyamyate*, 'the neck becomes bent inward.' On the other hand, Vāgbhaṭa I (*Aṣṭāṅga Saṁgraha*, III. 15, vol. I, p. 300, last line, quoted by Vāgbhaṭa II in *Aṣṭāṅga Hṛdaya*, III. 15, verse 22, in 1st ed., vol. I, p. 831), says *jatrur≠āyamyate.*[1] This shows that *grīvā* and *jatru* are synonymous terms. Again, in the thirteenth chapter of the same section, speaking of the Valmīka disease,[2] Suśruta tells us (Jīv. ed., p. 286) that, among other places, it occurs *grīvāyām≠ūrdhva-jatruṇi*, in the cervical column and upwards of the windpipe, that is, in the neck generally. Vāgbhaṭa I, speaking on the same subject (*Aṣṭāṅga Saṁgraha*, VI. 36, vol. II, p. 316, l. 3, quoted by Vāgbhaṭa II, in *Aṣṭāṅga Hṛdaya*, VI. 31, in 1st ed., vol. II, p. 682, verse 19*b*), says simply *jatrūrdhvaṁ*, from the neck upwards, omitting *grīvā*, and therefore using *jatru* as indicating the neck generally. On the other hand, Mādhava, in his *Nidāna* (Jīv. ed., p. 276), paraphrasing the statement of Suśruta, uses the two terms *grīvā*, cervical column, and *gala*, windpipe, instead of Suśruta's *grīvā* and *jatru*, thus showing that he took *jatru* to be synonymous with *gala*, windpipe. Again, in the fifteenth chapter of the Supplementary Section (*Uttara Tantra*), speaking of *hikkā*, or hiccough, Suśruta uses the term *jatru-mūlāt*, 'from the base of the neck' (Jīv. ed., p. 849, verse 9, quoted by Mādhava, in his *Nidāna*, p. 105). The same phrase is used by Charaka (or rather Dṛiḍhabala, VI. 19, in Jīv. ed., 1896, p. 689, verse 30*a*) and Vāgbhaṭa I (*Aṣṭāṅga Saṁgraha*, III. 5, vol. I, p. 270, l. 6, quoted by Vāgbhaṭa II in *Aṣṭāṅga Hṛdaya*, III. 4, verse 22, in 1st ed., vol. I, p. 716). Gayadāsa, in his commentary on the Compendium of Suśruta (according to Vijaya Rakshita, in the *Madhukoṣa*, Jīv. ed., p. 105), explains here *jatru* by *grīvā*, neck, or *kaṇṭha*, throat. The two terms *ūrdhva-jatru* and *jatrūrdhva* are synonymous, and denote one of the three parts into which the body is divided. These three parts are: (1) the four

[1] Both terms, *apavartate* and *āyamyate*, according to the commentators, are synonymous of *vakrī-bhavati* or *vakrī-kriyate*, 'it becomes crooked' (*Nidāna*, p. 152; *Aṣṭāṅga Hṛdaya*, p. 831).

[2] Suppurating scrofulous glands, according to Dr. U. C. Dutt's translation in his edition of the *Mādhava Nidāna*, p. 193.

extremities (*śākhā*), (2) the trunk or middle (*antarādhi* or *madhya*), and (3) the neck and head (*śiro-grīva*). It is the last-named portion which is also called *ūrdhva-jatru* or *jatrūrdha*, i.e. 'the portion from the neck upwards', and inclusive of the neck. Both forms of the term are frequently met with. Thus Suśruta, describing the respective scope of the various parts of Medical Science, in the first chapter of the Introductory Section (*Sūtra Sthāna*, Jīv. ed., p. 2), says of Minor Surgery, that it concerns itself with 'the cure of the diseases which have their seat in the portion of the body from the neck upwards (*ūrdhva-jatru*), that is, those maladies which affect the ears, eyes, mouth, nose, and other organs'. Chakrapāṇidatta, in his Commentary (*Bhānumati*, p. 20), here says that the term *jatru* means 'the base of the neck' (*grīvā-mūla*), and explains the phrase *ūrdhva-jatru* to mean 'from the neck (base of the neck) upwards' (*jatruṇa ūrdhvam*). Ḍallana, in his comment on the same phrase (Jīv. ed., p. 7), says that according to some '*jatru* means the base of the neck, and according to others, the point of junction of the sternum and clavicles'. In accordance with this definition, Suśruta, in the Anatomical Section, chap. III, cl. 7 (Jīv. ed., p. 337), enumerates certain vital spots (*marman*) as situated in the body from the neck upwards (*jatrūrdhvam*). In the Pathological Section, chap. I, verse 14, Suśruta again speaks of 'diseases seated in the organs from the neck upwards (*ūrdhva-jatru*); and Ḍallana (Jīv., p. 459) once more explains those diseases to be 'those affecting the eyes, mouth, nose, ears, and cranium'. Many other examples of this use of the phrase *ūrdhva-jatru* might be quoted from the Compendium of Suśruta, e.g. *Sūtra Sthāna*, XXI. 30 (Jīv. ed., p. 68, l. 20); *Cikitsita Sthāna*, XXXVI, 24 (Jīv., p. 569), &c. The same usage is very common in the Summary of Vāgbhaṭa I. The following examples may be quoted: the form *jatrūrdhva* occurs in *Sūtra Sthāna*, chap. XXIX (vol. I, p. 153, l. 14), and chap. XXXVI, (vol. I, p. 176, l. 19); *Nidāna Sthāna*, chap. XV (vol. I, p. 304, l. 5), and *Uttara Sthāna*, chap. XXXVI (vol. II, p. 315, l. 21), quoted by Vāgbhaṭa II in his Compendium (*Aṣṭāṅga Hṛdaya*), *Sūtra Sthāna*, chap. XX, verse 17; chap. XXVII, verse 11; *Nidāna Sthāna*, chap. XVI, verse 22; *Uttara Sthāna*, chap. XXXI, verse 16 (in 1st ed., vol. I, pp. 373, 433, 842; vol. II, p. 681). The other form *ūrdhva-jatru* occurs in the Compendium of Vāgbhaṭa II, *Sūtra Sthāna*, chap. XX, verse 1 (vol. I, p. 368), where he refers to *ūrdhva-jatru-vikāra*, that is, 'diseases affecting the body upwards from the neck.' The commentary of Aruṇadatta here explains the phrase to refer to 'headache and similar diseases'. (For the original texts of the passages quoted above, see § 98.)

5. We will now turn to the commentators. Suśruta, speaking about hiccough in the passage above quoted, mentions *jatru-mūla*, the base of the neck. His statement is quoted by Mādhava in the seventh verse of the twelfth chapter of his *Nidāna* (Jīv. ed., p. 105). Vijaya Rakshita, commenting on this statement, quotes the explanations of Jaijjaṭa and Gayadāsa, two of the oldest commentators on the Compendium of Suśruta. Jaijjaṭa explains *jatru-mūla* to be *kaṇṭh-orasoḥ sandhiḥ*, that is, the junction of the throat with the breast-bone.[1] This shows that he understood *jatru* to be synonymous with *kaṇṭha*, throat, and to denote the anterior part of the neck (*grīvā-purobhāga*). Gayadāsa explains *jatru-mūla* by *grīvā-mūla*, base of the cervical column, which shows that by him *jatru* was understood to be a synonym of *grīvā*, neck. Again Chakrapāṇidatta (c. 1070 A.D.), in his *Bhānumatī* commentary on Suśruta, explains the phrase *jatruṇa ūrdhvaṁ* in Suśruta I. 7, (Jīv. ed., p. 71, top line), by *hanu-sandhau*, 'at the point of junction of the jaw (apparently the temporo-mandibular articulation).' This shows that he also took *jatru* to denote the throat (*kaṇṭha*). Again Ḍallana, in his commentary on Suśruta, IV. 1, verse 139 (Jīv. ed., p. 644), explains *jatru* by *vakṣo-'ṁsayoḥ sandhī*, the point of junction of the breast-bone and clavicle, which points to the base of the neck. In fact, in his comments on Suśruta, I. 23, clause 2 (Jīv. ed., p. 91, top line), as well as on Suśruta, I. 21, clause 30 (Jīv. ed., p. 86, l. 20), he explicitly identifies *jatru* with *grīvā-mūla*, the base of the neck. Again Aruṇadatta in his comments on Vāgbhaṭa II's *Aṣṭāṅga*

[1] Ḍallana, in his commentary, also quotes that explanation. But Jīv. ed., p. 1249, reads it falsely *kakṣ-orasoḥ sandhiḥ*, junction of the armpit with the breast-bone, which makes no sense.

Hṛdaya, I. 20, verse 1 (in 1st ed., vol. I, p. 368), repeats the explanation of Ḍallana that *jatru* signifies *vakṣo-'ṁsayoḥ sandhi*, the articulation of breast-bone and clavicle. This definition is noteworthy as it modifies the meaning of *jatru*, which is no longer the throat or neck, but the base of the neck, and, for the first time, brings it into connexion with the clavicles. (For the original text of the passages, see § 98.)

6. The writers hitherto discussed are all medical. It will be observed that they never use the dual number with reference to *jatru*, as they would do if they were thinking of the pair of clavicles. They always use the singular number, indicating a single bone. Their evidence, on the whole, is uniformly and clearly in favour of *jatru* denoting in a general way the neck, or more particularly the throat, that is, the anterior part of the neck (*grīvā-purobhāga*), in short the windpipe. In the list of Suśruta (§ 27) *jatru* does not occur at all, but it enumerates the pair of bones, *grīvā* and *kaṇṭhanāḍī*, the cervical column and the windpipe. The list of Charaka (§ 4), on the other hand, does not name *kaṇṭhanāḍī*, but gives the pair *grīvā* and *jatru*. It is obvious that Suśruta's *kaṇṭhanāḍī* must be identical with Charaka's *jatru*, and that both those terms denote the same organ, that is, the windpipe.

7. Turning now to the non-medical evidence, we have the earliest in the Vedas. Here we find in the Rigveda, VIII. 1[12], *jatru* used in the plural number: *purā jatrubhya ātṛdaḥ*, i.e. 'before making an incision in the costal cartilages.' So also in Rigveda, XI. 3[10], *antrāṇi jatravaḥ*, i.e. 'the entrails are (represented by) the costal cartilages.' Whatever else *jatru* may mean, it can in these two passages not denote the clavicles, of which there are only two, and which would be expressed by the dual number. The plural excludes any reference to the clavicles. The meaning of *jatru* in the plural, however, is clearly indicated in a later Vedic work, the *Śatapatha Brāhmaṇa*. It says (§ 42, cl. 4), 'the ribs are fastened at either end, exteriorly to the thoracic vertebrae, and interiorly to the costal cartilages (*jatru*).' It even mentions their number to be sixteen (§ 42, cl. 3), 'there are eight costal cartilages (*jatru*) on the one side, and eight on the other; the sternum is the seventeenth (bone of the breast).'

At the same time, it may be noted that Sāyaṇa, in his great commentary on the Rigveda, commenting on the first of the two above-quoted passages, explains *jatrubhyaḥ* by *grīvābhyaḥ*. He, therefore, took *jatru* to mean the neck (*grīvā*). If his interpretation should be preferred, it might refer to the cartilaginous rings of the trachea of which there are from sixteen to twenty (Fig. 24). But the important point is that in the opinion of Sāyaṇa *jatru* does not denote the clavicles. In the Epics and Purānas, *jatru* seems to have always the meaning of the anterior part of the neck or the throat. Thus *Mahābhārata*, III. 713, *jatrudeśe vgavāsīdat*, i. e. he fell on his throat; and *Bhagavat Purāṇa*, VIII. 11^{14}, *jatrāvatāḍayat*, he struck him in the throat. The singular number shows that the clavicles are not intended. Again, in *Rāmāyaṇa*, I. 1^{12} and V. 32^{10}, we find the phrase *dṛḍha-jatru*, and in *Bhagavat Purāṇa*, I. 19^{27}, the phrase *nigūḍha-jatru*, both meaning 'strong-necked', in the description of a hero. Here, indeed, the late commentators Rāmānuja and Śrīdhara expressly interpret *jatru* of the two clavicles, using that word in the dual number. Thus Rāmānuja on *Rāmāyaṇa*, I. 1^{12}, says: *Jatruṇī vakṣo-'ṁsa-sandhi-gate asthinī*, i. e. 'The two clavicles are the two bones which constitute the connexion between the breast (sternum) and the shoulder (acromion).' Similarly Śrīdhara, commenting on *Bhagavat Purāṇa*, I. 19^{27}, says: *Kaṇṭhasya adho-bhāgayoḥ sthite asthinī jatruṇī*, i. e. 'The two clavicles are the two bones which are situated on both sides of the lower part of the throat.' But though in these explanations Rāmānuja and Śridhara have obviously in view the traditional medical definition of *jatru*, as above quoted from the commentaries of Ḍallana and Aruṇadatta, they understand that definition in the false sense to which, as we shall see below, the celebrated Indian dictionary, the *Amarakoṣa*, had given currency. Anyhow, in the passages of the Epics and Purānas, commented on by them, the most natural interpretation of *jatru* is that it means the throat or windpipe.

8. In the Non-medical Version (§ 16) of the statement on the skeleton, as found in the Law-book of Yājnavalkya and in the Institutes of Vishnu, *jatru* clearly has the meaning of windpipe, for it explicitly says that there is a single *jatru*. It is true that the text of Yājnavalkya, published by Professor Stenzler (p. 89),

reads *jatrv:ekaikam*, which, of course, can only mean 'one collar-bone on either side', that is, two collar-bones. But, as may be seen from the evidence set out in § 77, the true manuscript reading is *jatrv:ekaṁ ca*, that is 'and one windpipe'. It is unfortunate that the editors and translators of two legal treatises allowed themselves to be misled by the ill-considered explanations of the legal commentators (§ 20) into ascribing to those treatises the doctrine that *jatru* referred to the two clavicles.

9. So far as the matter can be traced at present, the first, and really the sole, authority for interpreting *jatru* of the clavicles is the *Amarakoṣa*, an ancient Sanskrit dictionary written by Amara Siṁha, probably in the seventh century A.D. In that work, after explaining the word *aṁsa* to be a synonym of *bhuja-śiras*, or head of the arm, Amara Siṁha proceeds to say (II. 6^{78}), *Sandhī tasya eva jatruṇī*, i.e. 'The two junctions of that (*aṁsa*, or head of the arm) are the two collar-bones.' Though not very clearly expressed, it is yet clear from the context and the dual number that, in explaining the word *jatru*, he was thinking of the two clavicles. His idea seems to have been that *jatru* was the name of the two bones which run horizontally across the body from one 'head of the arm' (or acromion process) to the other, connecting them with each other and with the base of the neck (Fig. 4). How this idea originated is not exactly known; but the following explanation may be suggested. It seems to be a misunderstanding of the two anatomical terms *aṁsa*, collar-bone, and *sandhi*, joint or articulation. The former, as stated already, is interpreted by Amara Siṁha to mean 'the head of the arm' (*bhuja-śiras*)[1]—a term which evidently is the popular, though inexact, equivalent of the anatomical term *aṁsa-kūṭa*, peak of the shoulder (acromion process, § 55, cl. 5). It is possible that this interpretation was suggested to Amara Siṁha by the peculiar use of the term *aṁsa* in the

[1] Hemachandra (c. 1140 A.D.) in his well-known dictionary called *Abhidhāna Chintāmaṇi*, adopts Amara Siṁha's interpretations. In Section V, verse 588, he says *aṁso bhuja-śiraḥ skandho jatru sandhir-uro-'ṁsagaḥ*, i.e. *aṁsa* or *skandha* is the head of the arm, and *jatru* is the connecting bone between sternum (*uras*) and the head of the arm (*aṁsa*).

osteological summary of Vāgbhaṭa I.[1] In that summary, as shown in §§ 39, cl. 4, and 56, cl. 2, *aṁsa* occurs by the side of *akṣaka*, clavicle, and *aṁsa-phalaka*, shoulder-blade, and therefore, if it has any specialized meaning, it can mean only the peak of the shoulder, or the head of the arm. Having once adopted this interpretation, Amara Siṁha was naturally led, by the traditional medical definition of *jatru*, to the further misinterpretation of the latter term. That definition (as reported by Ḍallana and Aruṇadatta, *ante*, cl. 4) was that *jatru* signified *vakṣo 'ṁsayoḥ sandhi*, that is, the sterno-clavicular articulation. But Amara Siṁha, having taken *aṁsa* to mean the head of the arm, was of necessity driven to interpret the term *sandhi* to signify 'a connecting bone', and the definition in question to mean that *jatru* signified the clavicle, because it was the connecting bone (*sandhi*) between the sternum (*vakṣas*) and the head of the arm (*aṁsa*).[2] But this is not in accordance with anatomical usage: in the latter, *aṁsa* signifies the collar-bone, and *sandhi*, an articulation, that is, the connexion between two contiguous bones. The two terms do not signify, respectively, the summit of the shoulder, and a joint in the sense of a bone that lies between two articulations and connects two other bones. The true anatomical definition of *jatru* is that it is the sterno-clavicular articulation, or, as it is also sometimes, though less technically, expressed, the base of the neck (*grīvā mūla*). Outside the medical schools, the false interpretation of *jatru*, apparently started by the *Amarakoṣa*, that it meant the two clavicles, succeeded in winning general acceptance, so much so that its original and real meaning is, at the present day, practically lost sight of.

10. To sum up: from the foregoing discussion the conclusion

[1] This seems to me the more probable view, though pending the exact determination of the date of Amara Siṁha and Vāgbhaṭa I, the question of priority—assuming that there was any interdependence—must remain uncertain.

[2] The natural corollary of giving to *aṁsa* and *jatru* the meaning of 'head of the arm' and 'collar-bone' respectively is that *aṁsa-kūṭa* and *akṣaka* become superfluous; and, as a fact, both those words are omitted in the *Amarakoṣa*.

suggests itself that the original meaning of the word *jatru* may have been 'immature bone' or cartilage. Originally the word was used to denote the cartilaginous portions of the neck and breast, that is, the windpipe and the costal cartilages. In the Vedas it still has this undefined meaning. In the medical text-books its use is limited to the cartilaginous portion of the neck, i.e. the windpipe (Charaka), and hence, either to the neck generally, or to the sterno-clavicular articulation at the base of the neck (Suśruta). At a comparatively late date (sixth or seventh century A.D.), and in general literature, owing to a misinterpretation of the anatomical terms *sandhi* and *aṁsa*, it was made to mean clavicle.

§ 63. *Cranial Bones*

1. *Śiras*, cranium or brain-case; *śiraḥ-kapāla*, cranial pan-shaped bone. These two terms are employed in all the three lists, which differ only in respect of the number of the bones. While Charaka (§ 4) counts four, Suśruta (§ 27) counts six bones; and Vāgbhaṭa I (§ 37) adopts the count of Suśruta.

2. The brain-case or cranium is a hemispheroidal, oval box, made up of eight bones, namely the frontal, the two parietal, the two temporal, the occipital, the sphenoid and the ethmoid (Figs. 25, 26). Nearly the whole of it, viz. the entire vault and the larger portion of the base, is externally visible: the remainder of the latter lies internally within the skull. The externally visible portion of the cranium comprises six bones, the frontal, the two temporal, the two parietal, and the occipital. The interior, invisible portion comprises two bones, the sphenoid and the ethmoid. These two interior bones, including the small portion of the sphenoid, which shows externally by the side of the frontal (Fig. 25), were not known to the Indian anatomists. As pointed out in § 45, cl. 3, their method of dissection would not enable them to discover them; and so far as the two cranial surfaces of the sphenoid bone (Fig. 32) are concerned, they do not seem to have recognized their existence as separate from the frontal bone and as belonging to the sphenoid. In all probability

they took them to be but continuations of the contiguous frontal bone. As to the temporal bones, they are peculiarly liable to detachment from the rest of the bony case; and it may have been for this reason that they were separately enumerated by the Indian anatomists; they are dealt with

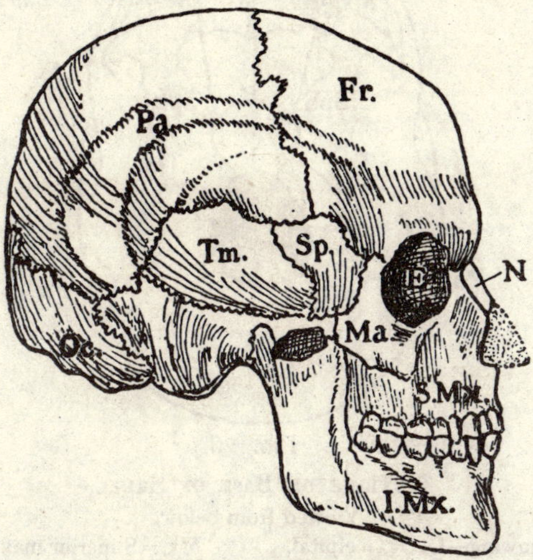

FIG. 25.

PROFILE OF THE SKULL. From the right.

Showing—Fr. = Frontal bone }
Pa. = Parietal ,, } *Śiraḥ-kapāla.*
Oc. = Occipital ,, }
Tm. = Temporal, *Śaṅkhaka.*
Sp. = Sphenoid.
E. = Ethmoid (in inner wall of orbit).
Ma. = Malar, *Gaṇḍakūṭa.*
N. = Nasal, *Nāsikā.*
S. Mx. = Superior maxillary } *Hanu.*
I. Mx. = Inferior maxillary }

in the next paragraph. There remain only four bones, the frontal, the two parietal, and the occipital; and there can be no doubt that it is these four bones which are referred to in the list of Charaka as 'the four pan-shaped bones of the cranium'. They are more or less decidedly concave bones, and therefore are rightly described as pan-shaped (Figs. 27, 28).

3. The list of Suśruta substitutes six pan-shaped bones in the place of the four bones of Charaka. In order to understand this

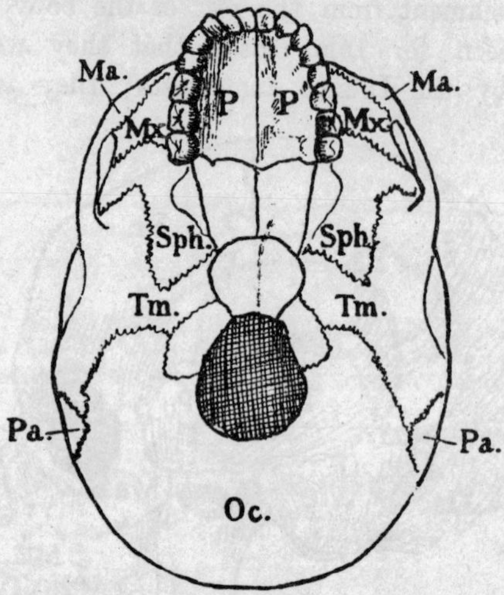

FIG. 26.

OUTLINE OF BASE OF SKULL.

Viewed from below.

Showing—Oc. = Occipital. Pa. = Parietal. Tm. = Temporal. Sph. = Sphenoid. Mx. = Superior maxillary. Ma. = Malar. P. = Palate. E. = Ethmoid (not visible).

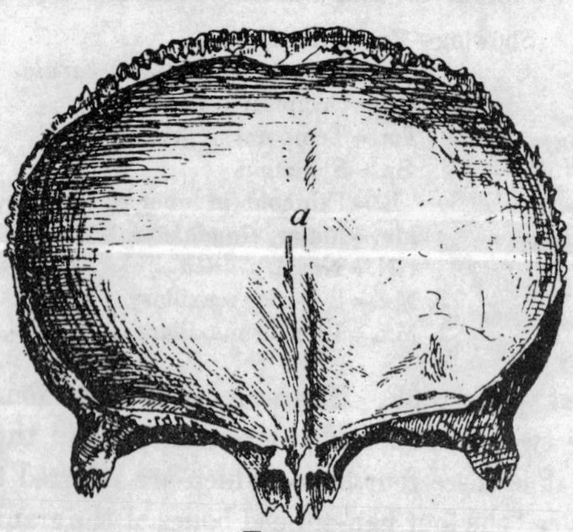

FIG. 27.

FRONTAL BONE, *Śiraḥ-kapāla.*

Internal Surface, showing frontal crest *a*.

difference we must remember that Suśruta's osteological system is strictly dominated by the principle of homology (§ 28), according to which the skeleton is considered as consisting of two lateral halves divided by a mesial plane running through the vertebral column. This plane cuts the frontal and occipital bones into two halves. As a matter of fact, these two bones consist of two halves, indicated by the frontal and occipital crests respectively (Figs. 27 and 28). In the case of the occipital bone, it is true, the two halves coalesce into one from the beginning of

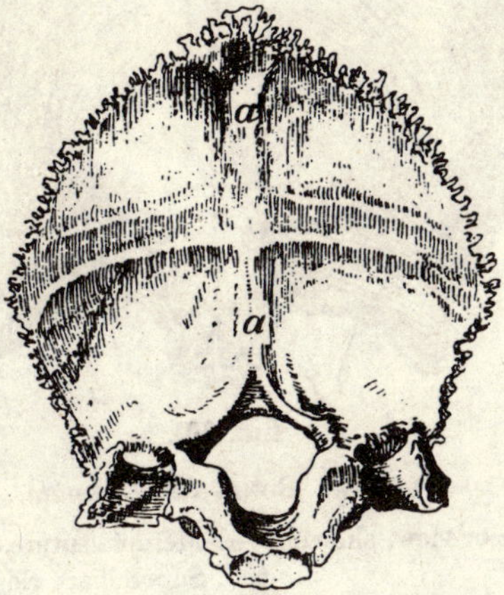

FIG. 28.

THE OCCIPITAL BONE, *Śiraḥ-kapāla.*

Internal Surface, showing occipital crest *a*, *a*.

embryonic development; but in the case of the frontal bone they remain separated by the metopic suture, and do not become fused till about the fifth or sixth year after birth. In fact, traces of the metopic suture persist throughout life between the two superciliary ridges of the frontal bone; and in a certain percentage (about 8 per cent.) of individuals even the whole of it persists in the adult[1] (Figs. 29, 32). Either of the two halves of the frontal and occipital bones forms a separate cavity, divided by their respective crests (Figs. 27 and 28). Thus Suśruta is

[1] I am indebted to Professor Arthur Thomson for the suggestion of this explanation.

justified in counting 'six pan-shaped bones of the cranium', these being, on his principle of division, two frontal, two parietal, and two occipital. In fact in this particular, his system marks an advance on that of Ātreya-Charaka, inasmuch as it shows Suśruta's acquaintance with the existence of the metopic suture. He had, no doubt, observed its surviving traces between the superciliary

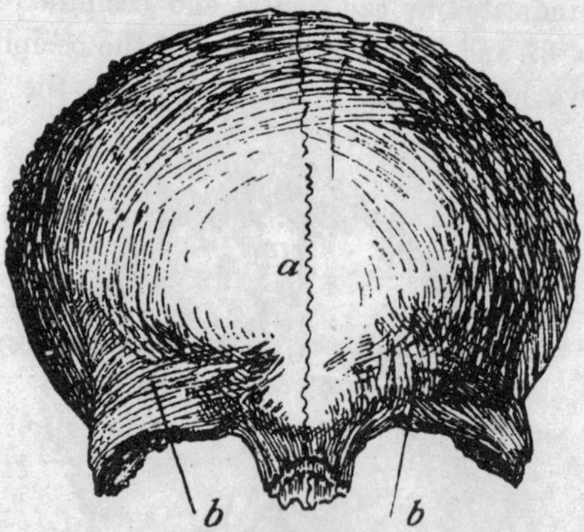

FIG. 29.

FRONTAL BONE, *Siraḥ-kapāla.*

Anterior view, showing—*a.* Metopic suture.
b, b. Superciliary ridges.

ridges, and may even have noticed the exceptional occurrence of a 'metopic skull'. The division of the occipital bone into two halves, however, was the natural resultant of his homological principle.

§ 64. *Continuation: the Temples*

1. *Śaṅkha*, temple; *śaṅkhaka*, temporal bone. The latter form of the term is found only in the Non-medical Version (§ 16), though, of course, there is no real difference of meaning between the two terms.

2. All the three lists give the number of the temporal bones as two. Suśruta, moreover, rightly classes them among the pan-shaped (*kapāla*) bones (§ 30). They are, without any doubt

identical with the two temporal bones which are recognized also by modern Anatomy as bones of the cranium, one on either side (Figs. 25, 26).

§ 65. *Facial Bones: Maxillaries*

1. *Hanu*, jaw; *hanv-asthi*, jaw-bone, or chin; *hanu-mūla-bandhana*, bond, or tie-bone, at the base, or back, of the jaw; *hanu-citya*, pile or structure of the jaws. The term *hanu* properly means simply a jaw, and ordinarily may indicate both, the upper as well as the lower jaw. But it is in the treatment of these bones, as well as of the other bones of the face which are discussed in the next paragraph, that the second of the most striking differences (for the first, see § 59, cl. 3) between the systems of Atreya-Charaka and Suśruta discloses itself. The difference, stated briefly and roughly, is that the system of Ātreya-Charaka (§ 4) recognizes the existence of only one jaw, viz. the lower, while the system of Suśruta includes two jaws, the lower and the upper. Accordingly, in the former system, the term *hanv-asthi* signifies the bone (or 'body') of the lower jaw, and particularly its more prominent portion, the chin, while the term *hanu-mūla-bandhana* signifies the two attachments (or 'rami') at the base, or back, of the lower jaw. In the list of Vāgbhaṭa I (§ 37) there occurs only the term *hanu-bandhana*, jaw-attachment, which is used in a loose way as synonymous with simple *hanu*, jaw (see § 38, cl. 6). The term *hanu-citya* is peculiar to the Atharva Veda (§ 43).

2. Suśruta's way of counting the jaw-bones agrees generally with that of modern Anatomy. The two maxillaries really consist each of two bones, but their two lateral halves are so intimately united by harmonic sutures that they are counted each as a single bone. In the same way Suśruta counts two *hanu* or jaw-bones, which, therefore, practically correspond to the maxillaries. Ātreya-Charaka, on the other hand, does not recognize the existence of a maxillary as a single bone. He divides either of them horizontally into a number of separate bones (Figs. 31 and 32). The superior maxillary (Fig. 30) consists of two parts, the body and certain processes. The chief of the latter are, (1)

the palatine process which forms the hard palate (*tālu* or *tālūṣaka*), and which is counted by both Ātreya-Charaka and Suśruta as a separate bone (§ 67); and (2) the alveolar process which contains sockets of the teeth. This alveolar process, too, is counted as a separate bone, but by Ātreya-Charaka alone, who calls it *dant-olūkhala*, or tooth-socket bone. As to the 'body' of the superior maxillary, it would appear that Ātreya-Charaka looked upon it as being continuous with and forming part of the malar bones (§ 66). In the system of Ātreya-Charaka, therefore, there

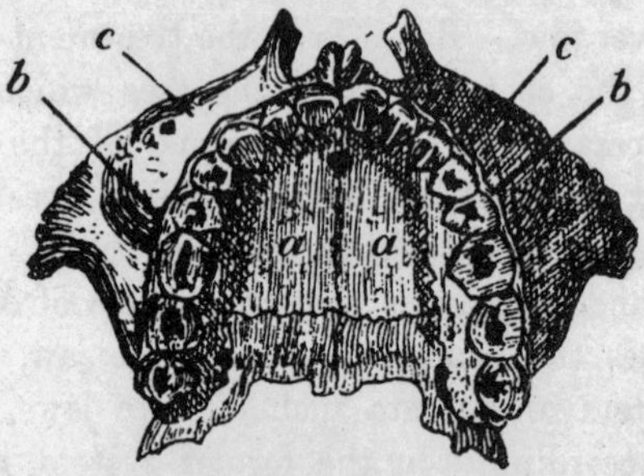

FIG. 30.

SUPERIOR MAXILLARY, *Hanu*. From below.

a, a. Palatine process, or hard palate, *Tālūṣaka*.
b, b. Alveolar process, *Dant-olūkhala*.
c, c. Body of maxillary.

is practically no superior maxillary. It is replaced by three bones, (1) the hard palate (*tālūṣaka*, § 67); (2) superior alveolar process, or tooth-socket bone (*dant-olūkhala*, § 68);[1] (3) the malar bone, of which the 'body' of the maxillary forms a part (Fig. 32). On the other hand, the system of Suśruta, consequent on its recognizing a superior maxillary bone (*hanu*), does not admit any separate tooth-socket bone. At the same time Suśruta's *hanu*, or upper jaw-bone, does not fully correspond to the superior maxillary, because of its excluding the palatine process, which Suśruta (equally with Ātreya-Charaka) counts as a separate bone (*tālu*, § 67).

[1] That is, strictly, the set of thirty-two superior tooth-socket bones.

3. The inferior maxillary (Fig. 31) is a large, strong, horseshoe-shaped bone, which consists of a nearly horizontal body, and two posterior vertical portions, or rami. The body itself consists of three portions, the alveolar process above, the base beneath, and the mental protuberance, or chin, in front. The whole of this inferior maxillary is counted as a single bone by Suśruta, and constitutes his other *hanu*, or jaw-bone. Ātreya-Charaka, on the other hand, treats it as consisting of four bones: (1) the alveolar process (*dant-olūkhala*); (2) the base with the chin, which he calls *hanv-asthi*, or jaw-bone (chin-bone); (3) and

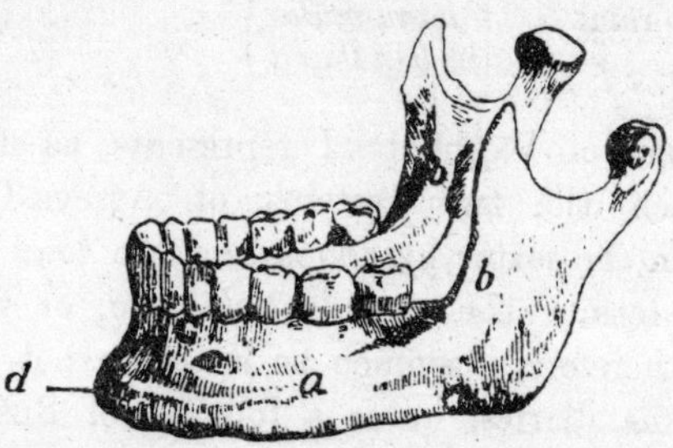

FIG. 31.

INFERIOR MAXILLARY, *Hanu*. Seen from the left.

Showing—*a*. The base of the body, *Hanv-asthi*.
b, *b*. The rami, *Hanu-mūla-bandhana*.
c. Alveolar process, *Dant-olūkhala*.
d. Mental protuberance, or chin, *Hanv-asthi*.

(4) the two rami, which he calls *hanu-mūla-bandhana*, bonds at the root, or back, of the jaw-bone. He calls the rami by this name on account of their being the bones by which the 'body' of the lower jaw is attached to the rest of the skull.

4. To sum up: irrespective of the hard palate, which both Ātreya-Charaka and Suśruta count separately, the list of Suśruta represents the two maxillaries by two *hanu*, or jaw-bones, while the list of Charaka breaks them up into—(1) two alveolar processes (*ulūkhala*), (2) one (lower) jaw-bone (*hanv-asthi*), (3) two rami (*hanu-mūla-bandhana*), and (4) probably a portion of his peculiar central facial bone (§ 66). This is shown in the subjoined tabular statement:

Modern Anatomy.		Ātreya-Charaka.	Suśruta.	Vāgbhaṭa II.
Sup. Max.	1. palatal process	*tālūṣaka*	*tālu*	*tālu*
	2. alveolar process	*ulūkhala*	1st *hanu*	*ulūkhala*
	3. body	facial bone (K, fig. 32)		1st *hanu-bandhana*
Inf. Max.	1. alveolar process	*ulūkhala*	2nd *hanu*	*ulūkhala*
	2. base	*hanvasthi*		2nd *hanu-bandhana*
	3. chin			
	4. rami	*hanu-mūla-bandhana*		

5. The system of Vāgbhaṭa I represents, as usual, a compromise between the two systems of Ātreya-Charaka and Suśruta. From the latter he adopts the two *hanu* or jaw-bones, and from the former the two *dant-olūkhala,* or tooth-sockets. In the main, therefore, inasmuch as he holds not one, but two jaw-bones or maxillaries, he is a follower of Suśruta; but as a concession to the doctrine of Ātreya-Charaka, he divides each maxillary into two separate bones, viz. its alveolar process (*dant-olūkhala*) and its body (*hanu-bandhana*), the latter including, in the case of the inferior maxillary, its two rami. Another concession to that system appears to be Vāgbhaṭa's use of the term *hanu-bandhana,* instead of the simpler Suśrutiyan term *hanu.* It seems probable that Vāgbhaṭa I failed to understand the significance of the word *mūla* in the Charakiyan term *hanu-mūla-bandhana,* bond at the base, or back, of the jaw. That word rrnders the term applicable only to the lower jaw-bone, and signifies its two rami, by which it is attached to the rest of the skull. The omission of the word *mūla* shows that Vāgbhaṭa I understood the term *hanu-bandhana* to be applicable to both jaw-bones, and to indicate that the jaw-bones were attachments of the skull. In his system, therefore, the term *hanu-bandhana* is a mere descriptive synonym of the simpler term *hanu* (§ 38, cl. 6).

6. The system of the Atharva Veda (§ 43) appears to be essentially the same as that of Ātreya-Charaka. This seems to

be indicated by its term *hanvoḥ citya*, or structure (pile) of the two jaws, inasmuch as that term points to the view of the jaw being a composite organ built up, as Ātreya-Charaka holds, of the separate bones which he calls *dant-olūkhala*, alveolar process, *hanv-asthi*, jaw-bone, and *hanu-mūla-bandhana*, two rami.

§ 66. *Continuation: Malar and Nasal Bones, Superciliary Ridges*

1. *Nāsā* or *nāsikā*, nose, nasal bone; *gaṇḍa*, cheek, cheek-bone, malar bone; *gaṇḍa-kūṭa*, or *hanu-kūṭa*, malar prominence; *lalāṭa*, brow or superciliary ridge; *kakāṭikā*, denoting the combined nasal and malar bones. The last term is peculiar to the Atharva Veda. The term *lalāṭa* is only found in the several versions of the system of Atreya (§§ 4, 12, 16), and in the Atharva Veda (§ 43). The term *hanu-kūṭa* is peculiar to the list of Bheḍa (§ 12); Charaka prefers the term *gaṇḍa-kūṭa*, and Suśruta, its shorter alternative *gaṇḍa*.

2. Beside the two maxillary bones which have been discussed in the preceding paragraph, and the palatal bones which will be discussed in the next paragraph, the face of the skeleton (Fig. 32) comprises the following bones: two malar, two nasal, two lachrymal, two inferior turbinated, and one vomer. Of these bones the five last-mentioned are very small, and lie in the interior of the skull. It cannot, therefore, surprise us that they escaped the observation of the ancient Indian anatomists. The only bones which, forming a portion of the external skull, came under their notice, are the malar and nasal bones of the cheek (*gaṇḍa*) and nose (*nāsā* or *nāsikā*) respectively. But regarding the nature of these bones, and, in fact (as already stated in § 65, cl. 1), regarding the structure of the face generally, the opinions of Ātreya-Charaka and Suśruta differ very considerably. It is on this point that the two systems show one of their two most striking divergences (for the other see § 59, cl. 3).

3. In the systems of Ātreya-Charaka (§ 4) those four bones, the two malar (*gaṇḍa-kūṭa*) and the two nasal (*nāsikā*), are considered as forming, together with the two superciliary ridges, or brows (*lalāṭa*), a single continuous central bone which lies across the

middle of the face of the skull, bounded by the frontal bone above, the alveolar process of the superior maxillary below, and the two temporal bones on either side. The configuration of this central bone, and its position in the face, are indicated by dotted

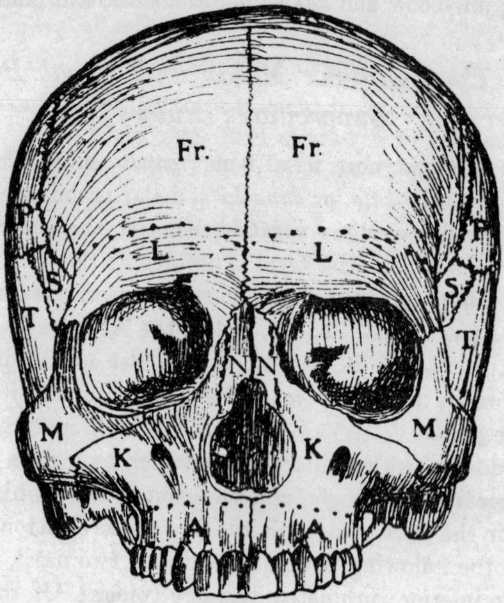

FIG. 32.

ANTERIOR VIEW OF SKULL.

Showing, within dotted lines, the central facial bone (K, L, M, N).

Fr. = Frontal bone, P. = Parietal bone, S. = Sphenoid bone: *Śiraḥ-kapāla.*
T. = Temporal bone, *Śaṅkhaka.*
L. = Superciliary ridges, *Lalāṭa.*
N. = Nasal bones, *Nāsikā.*
M. = Malar bones, *Gaṇḍa-kūṭa.*
K. = Body of superior maxillary, *Kakāṭikā.*
A. = Alveolar process, *dant-olūkhala.*

lines in Fig. 32. It will be seen from it that the central facial bone must include also the 'body' of the superior maxillary, which appears to have been looked upon as forming a continuous whole with the contiguous cheek or malar bones (*gaṇḍa*, or *gaṇḍa-kūṭa*). A more experienced anatomist, such as Suśruta was, could not fail to see that what was supposed to be an undivided central bone was in reality a very composite structure, made up partly of a number of separate small bones, partly of portions of the bones contiguous to the hypothetical central bone. The former are the two malar bones and the two nasal bones, which accordingly Suśruta counted separately in his list (§ 27). The latter are (1) the superciliary ridges which form merely two prominent portions of the frontal bone, and (2) the lower part of the hypothetical central bone which forms really the 'body' of the superior maxillary. Consequently Suśruta altogether omitted the two superciliary ridges, or brows (*lalāṭa*), from his list, while he included (as shown in § 65) the lower part of the central bone in one—the upper—of his two jaw-bones (*hanu*). With regard to the nose, including its cartilaginous portion, Suśruta counted three bones. In accordance with his homological principle, he took the two nasal bones as constituting a single bone in the median line, and added the two lateral cartilages of the external nostrils. That he included the latter is proved by the fact of his enumerating the nose (*ghrāṇa*) among the tender bones (*taruṇa*): see the class-list of the bones in § 30.

4. As to Vāgbhaṭa I, he follows his usual practice of compromise. With Suśruta he holds the separate existence of two nasal, two malar, and two maxillary bones, and with Ātreya-Charaka the separate existence of the superior alveolar process. In the main, therefore, his system agrees with the system of Suśruta, the only difference being that (as already pointed out in § 65, cl. 5) he divides the superior maxillary horizontally into two separate bones, an upper and a lower, the upper being the 'body' (*hanu-bandhana*), and the lower the alveolar process (*dant-olūkhala*), that is, K and A in Fig. 32. It is a difference which indicates a distinct decadence in anatomical knowledge.

5. Ātreya-Charaka's hypothesis of a single, undivided central bone, as reported by Charaka (§ 4), though erroneous, has at least the merit of presenting a consistent view of the structure of the face. In itself, the traditional text of Bheḍa's report (§ 12) of that hypothesis need not necessarily involve an inconsistency. It makes Ātreya hold three central bones, constituting the nose,

the cheeks, and the brows respectively. On referring to Fig. 32, it will be seen that the nasal bones might easily be taken to form a single bone; and the two superciliary ridges, irrespective of the metopic suture, do form a single bone (of the brow, *lalāṭa*). With respect to the two malar bones (including the 'body' of the superior maxillary) there would be some difficulty by reason of the nasal aperture; still, the extension of the bones downwards being undefined, they might, at a pinch, be taken to constitute a single bone. But, as has been shown in § 13, cl. 4, Bheḍa's account of the system of Ātreya cannot be correct, because it works out the incorrect total 362, instead of 360. It is probable, therefore, that the traditional text of that account is corrupted, and that the genuine list of Bheḍa agreed with that of Charaka in counting a single undivided central bone of the face. In confirmation of this view the curious fact should be noted that the traditional text of the list of Bheḍa substitutes the term *hanu-kūṭa*, lit. prominence of the jaw, for the term *gaṇḍa-kūṭa*, prominence of the cheek, in order to indicate the malar bone. It has been pointed out above that in Ātreya's view of the structure of the face the 'body' of the superior maxillary forms an extension of the malar bones. Hence, in itself, the malar prominence might be correctly described by either of the two terms, *gaṇḍa-kūṭa*, prominence of the cheek, or *hanu-kūṭa*, prominence of the (upper) jaw. But the difficulty is that the system of Ātreya knows no more than one *hanu*, and that that *hanu* is the inferior maxillary (see § 65), while the term *hanu-kūṭa* would introduce a reference to the superior maxillary, and thus be inconsistent with the system of Ātreya. For this reason it is practically certain that the word *hanu-kūṭa* in the traditional text of Bheḍa is a false reading for *gaṇḍa-kūṭa*. The case of the Non-medical Version of the system of Ātreya is still more unsatisfactory. That version counts four central bones in the place of the single central bone of Charaka; viz. one each for the nose, brows, cheeks, and eyes (§ 16, also § 17, cl. 4). Referring again to Figure 32, it may be seen that that count represents an impossible view of the structure of the face. The brows, or superciliary ridges, as above explained, do, indeed, form a single bone; so might the two nasal bones, and the two malar bones;

but how the two eyes (or eyeballs) should form but a single bone is not conceivable. This only proves how little the system of Atreya was understood by the author of the Non-medical Version, and how deficient was his knowledge of anatomy—a circumstance, however, hardly surprising in a writer who was not an expert in medicine but in law.

6. The system presented in the Atharva Veda (§ 43) agrees in the main with that of Ātreya-Charaka. The central facial bone of the latter system appears in the Atharva Veda divided into two portions, an upper and a lower. The upper portion consists of the two superciliary ridges, and is called *lalāṭa,* or the brow. The lower portion comprises the body of the superior maxillary together with the malar and nasal bones, and is called *kakāṭikā.*

§ 67. *The Hard Palate*

1. *Tālu*, palate; *tālūṣaka*, palatal cavity. The former term is used by Suśruta (§ 27) and Vāgbhaṭa (37). The latter is peculiar to the system of Ātreya, and is found in the lists of Charaka (§ 4) and Bheḍa (§ 12) as well as in its Non-medical Version (§ 16).

2. Both Ātreya-Charaka and Suśruta enumerate two palate bones in their lists; but these bones are not identical with what are called the palate bones in modern anatomy. The latter being very small bones, situated in the interior of the skull, do not appear to have been observed as separate bones by the ancient Indian anatomists. The two bones which the latter call palate bones are identical with the so-called palatine process, which is a portion of the superior maxillary bone (Fig. 30). This process consists of halves, which, projecting from either side of the junction of the alveolar process and 'body' of the superior maxillary, meet in the median line, in a ridge or raphé, and thus form the roof of the mouth, or what is the major portion of the hard palate.[1] These halves of the hard palate form two shallow concavities; and it is these, no doubt, which Atreya-Charaka appropriately denotes by the term *tālūṣaka*, or palatal cavity, and which Suśruta, in his class-list of the bones (§ 30) describes as being *kapāla*, or pan-shaped. From this point of view those two medical authorities are quite correct in counting,

[1] See Dr. Gerrish's *Textbook of Anatomy*, 2nd ed., pp. 195, 717.

in their lists, two palates (*tālu*) or two palatal concavities (*tālūṣaka*). Vāgbhaṭa I, who ignores the median ridge, counts only one palate (*tālu*).

§ 68. *The Teeth and their Sockets*

1. *Danta*, tooth; *dant-olūkhala*, tooth-socket, or *sthāla*, socket, or *sūkṣma*, minute bone. The term *dant-olūkhala* for the socket of a tooth occurs in the Medical Version of the system of Ātreya, as reported by Charaka (§ 4) and Bheḍa (§ 12), and adopted by Vāgbhaṭa I (§ 37), while the other two terms, *sthāla* and *sūkṣma*, are peculiar to the Non-medical Version (§§ 16, 22, cl. 4).

2. The term *dant-olūkhala*, or tooth-socket, denotes the alveolar processes. These processes are, in reality, only portions of the maxillary bones; but Atreya-Charaka, with whom Vāgbhaṭa I agrees, counts them as separate bones—a procedure which affects his general view of the two maxillaries, fully explained in § 65. Suśruta, in consequence of his counting the maxillaries as a pair of single, undivided bones, discards the socket-bones altogether from his list (§ 27) and counts only the teeth.

3. With reference to the number of the teeth (*danta*) Ātreya-Charaka and Suśruta agree. Both state them correctly to number thirty-two. Ātreya-Charaka goes even so far as to count a corresponding number of sockets. Accordingly he divides either alveolar process into thirty-two alveoli, each of which is counted, in his list (§ 4), as a separate bone.

4. As to the real morphological character of the teeth, the ancient Indian anatomists, of course, were uninformed. They took them to be bone, on account, obviously, of their hardness, and probably also of their white appearance, and because they were found to remain in the skull after every vestige of other tissue had disappeared. As a matter of fact, they 'resemble compact bone in appearance and in composition',[1] yet in reality they are more closely allied to the hair. For both are modifications of a papilla of the outer integument of the body. The tooth, 'though intimately connected with the bony skeleton, is really a calcified papilla of the mucous membrane.'[1]

[1] See Dr. Potter's *Compend of Human Anatomy*, p. 142, and Dr. Gerrish's *Textbook of Anatomy*, 2nd ed., p. 723.

§ 69. *The Nails*

Nakha, nail. The case of the nails is similar to that of the teeth. They, like the teeth, are allied to the hair, being modifications of the cutaneous membrane. The ancient Indian anatomists looked upon the nails as a waste product (*mala*) of the body secreted in the process of growth of the bones. Consistently with this theory, Suśruta excludes the nails from his count of the bones (§ 27). On the other hand, Ātreya, rather inconsistently as the commentator Chakrapāṇidatta indicates (*ante*, p. 35), includes them in his list of bones; and, of course, as all the three versions of his system (Charaka, § 4, Bheḍa, § 12, Non-medical, §§ 16, 22) state, he counts twenty of them, one for each finger and each toe.

§ 70. *The Eyeballs*

1. *Akṣi-koṣa*, eyeball. The organ denoted by this term is included among the bones only in the system of Suśruta. The system of Ātreya, as reported in the Medical Versions of Charaka (§ 4) and Bheḍa (§ 12), does not include them, and in this respect it is followed by Vāgbhaṭa I (§ 37). In the Non-medical Version (§ 16), it is true, the eyeballs are included in Ātreya's system; but its testimony cannot avail against that of the Medical Versions; and the probability is that it adopted the eyeballs under the influence of the system of Suśruta (§ 17, cl. 3). But even as regards the latter system, the eyeballs have experienced strange vicissitudes. For they are absent from Suśruta's list in its Traditional Recension (§ 27), though Suśruta explicitly mentions them in his class-list of the bones as well as in other passages of his Compendium. That his list in its genuine form (§ 34) must have included them has been shown in § 30, cl. 4.

2. Suśruta looked upon the sclerotic coat of the eyeball (Fig. 1) as made of cartilage; and as he counted cartilages as tender, or immature bones (*taruṇa*), he included the two eyeballs among the bones of the skeleton (§ 30). Ātreya-Charaka, on the other hand, excluded them, not because he knew them to be non-cartilaginous, but probably because the prepared skeleton would

ordinarily be deprived of them. As a matter of fact, the sclerotic is not made of cartilage, but of 'connective tissue with elastic fibres';[1] but to the untrained eye the two substances are so nearly alike that the mistake of a primitive anatomist, such as Suśruta, may be easily understood.

§ 71. *The Ears*

1. *Karṇa*, ear. The organ denoted by this term is included among the bones in the systems of Suśruta (§ 27) and Vāgbhaṭa I (§ 37). The system of Ātreya, in all three presentations, by Charaka (§ 4), Bheḍa (§ 12), and the Non-medical Version (§§ 16, 22), does not include it, probably for the same reason as caused the exclusion of the eyeballs (§ 70).

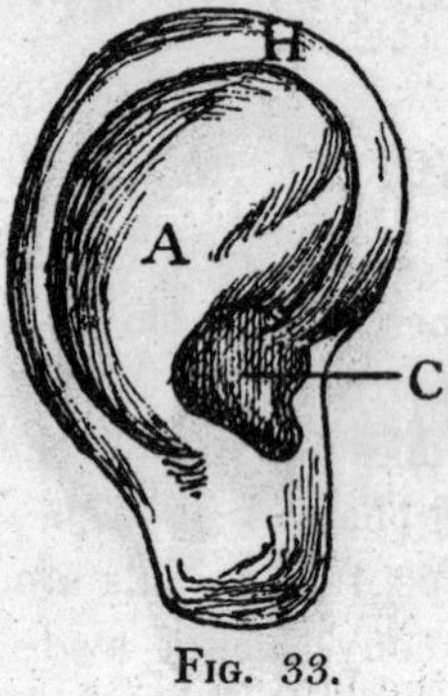

FIG. 33.

PINNA OF THE RIGHT EAR.

Showing—*H.* Helix. *A.* Antihelix. *C.* Concha.

2. Suśruta, who includes the ears among the bones of the skeleton, was doubtless referring to the external ear, the auricle or pinna (Fig. 33), which is 'composed almost entirely of yellow fibro-cartilage'.[2] In his class-list of the bones (§ 30) he explicitly enumerates the ear (*karṇa*) as an organ made of tender bone (*taruṇa*), that is, of cartilage. The other two portions of the ear, the middle or tympanum which contains the three auditory ossicles, and the internal or labyrinth, both lying in the interior of the skull, appear, for that reason, to have escaped the notice of the early Indian anatomists.

[1] Dr. Potter's *Compend of Human Anatomy*, p. 198.

[2] Dr. Gerrish's *Textbook of Anatomy*, 2nd ed., pp. 52, 696.

SECTION IV

APPARATUS CRITICUS

A. The System of Ātreya-Charaka

§ 72. *The Traditional Recension of Charaka*

1. The subjoined Traditional Recension of the Medical Version of the System of Ātreya in the Compendium of Charaka (*Caraka Saṁhitā*), *Śārīra Sthāna*, VIIth *Adhyāya*, is edited from the following materials:

1. A = Alwar Palace Library MS., No. 1624.
2. D¹ = Deccan College MS., No. 368, fl. 30 *b*, l. 4–fl. 31 *a*, l. 3.
3. D² = Deccan College MS., No. 925, fl. 107 *b*, l. 8–fl. 108 *a*, l. 4.
4. IO¹ = India Office MS., No. 338, fl. 225 *b*, l. 2–fl. 226 *a*, l. 1.
5. IO² = India Office MS., No. 851, fl. 71 *b*, ll. 2–13.
6. T¹ = Tübingen University MS., No. 458, fl. 324 *b*, l. 5–fl. 325 *a*, l. 6.
7. T² = Tübingen University MS., No. 459, vol. II, fl. 29 *b*, l. 3–fl. 30 *a*, l. 3.
8. S¹ = Śāradā MS. of Dr. P. Cordier.
9. S² = Śāradā MS. of Jammū Library, No. 3266, fl. 118.
10. EJ = Edition of Jīvānanda, 1877, p. 370, ll. 5–19.

2. It runs as follows:

Tatr=āyaṁ śarīrasy=āṅga-vibhāgaḥ । dvau bāhū dve sakthinī śiro-grīvam=antarādhir=iti ṣaḍ-aṅgam=aṅgam ॥ Trīṇi ṣaṣṭāni[1] śatāny=asthnāṁ saha danta-nakhena । tad=yathā । [1] dvātriṁśad=dan-

[1] So D² T² S² EJ and Chakrapāṇidatta's commentary. IO¹ has ṣaṣṭīni, D¹ T¹ ṣaṣṭyāni, S¹ ṣaṣṭyā, IO² ṣaṣṭy-adhikāni; A om.

tāḥ, [2] dvātriṁśad=dant-olūkhalakāni [1], [3] viṁśatir=nakhāḥ, [4] ṣaṣṭiḥ [2] pāṇi-pād-aṅguly-asthīni, [5] viṁśatiḥ pāṇi-pāda-śalākāḥ, [6] catvāri pāṇi-pāda-śalāk-ādhiṣṭhānāni, [7] dve pārṣṇyor [3]=asthinī, [8] catvāraḥ pādayor=gulphāḥ, [9] dvau maṇikau [4] hastayoḥ, [10] catvāry=aratnyor [5]=asthīni, [11] catvāri jaṅghayoḥ, [12] dve jānunī [6], [13] dve jānu-kapālike, [14] [7] dvāv=ūru-nalakau, [15] [8] dvau bāhu-nalakau, [16 *a*] [9] dvāv=aṁsau, [16 *b*] dve aṁsa-phalake [10], [17] dvāv-akṣakau, [18] ekaṁ [11] jatru, [19] dve tālūṣake [12], [20] dve śroṇi-phalake [13], [21] ekaṁ bhag-āsthi, [22] pañcacatvāriṁśat-pṛṣṭha-gatāny=asthīni, [23] pañca-daśa grīvāyām, [24] caturdaś=orasi, [25 *a*] dvayoḥ pārśvayoś [14]= caturviṁśatiḥ parśukāḥ [15], [25 *b*] tāvanti c=aiva sthālakāni [16], [25 *c*] tāvanti c=aiva sthālak-ārbudāni [17], [26] ekaṁ hanv-asthi, [27] dve hanu-mūla-bandhane, [28] ek-āsthi [18] nāsikā-gaṇḍakūṭa-lalāṭam, [29] dvau śaṅkhau, [30] catvāri śiraḥ-kapālāni [19] । iti trīṇi ṣaṣṭāni [20] śatāny=asthnāṁ saha danta-nakhena ॥

For the translation, see § 4.

[1] So D¹ IO², but T² olūkhalāni, D¹ oḍūkhalāni, IO¹T¹ olūkhakāni, A. S¹·² EJ olūkhala-phalāni.

[2] IO¹ pṛṣṭha-pāda; T¹ ṣaṣṭi-pāda, with pāda cancelled in both MSS., D¹ ṣaṣṭi-pāda; this false reading explains Gangādhar's emendation; S² om.

[3] IO¹ pādayor.

[4] So D¹ IO¹ T¹ S¹·² EJ, but A. D² T² have maṇibandhakau; IO² pāṇikau.

[5] IO² bāhvor.

[6] IO² jānunor=dve.

[7] D¹ T¹ prefix dvāv-ūrū.

[8] A. T¹ S¹ pref. dvau bāhū; IO¹ om. No. 15.

[9] D¹ om. Nos. 16*a*–21.

[10] T² skandha-phalake.

[11] D¹ S¹ EJ evaṁ.

[12] A tāluke, T² tālū-phalake.

[13] T¹ om. No. 20.

[14] T¹ D¹ pārśva-sthayoś.

[15] So T² and Chakrapāṇidatta's commentary; D¹ T¹ paryukāḥ, and IO¹ paryuktāḥ, both obviously corrupt for parśukāḥ; D² pārśvakāḥ; A. S¹ EJ pārśvavaḥ, obviously wrong for parśavaḥ or pārśvakāḥ; IO² panthakāḥ; S² om.

[16] A sthānakā, D² sthānakāni, T² sthānalakāni.

[17] A only arbudāni, IO² sthānak-ārbudāni, D² sthānak-ātmakāni.

[18] From here missing in A.

[19] EJ om. the final clause.

[20] So D²; but D¹ IO¹ T¹ sa-ṣaṣṭi, T² ṣaṣṭa.

§ 73. *Restored Recension of Charaka*

On the grounds explained in the fifth and sixth paragraphs the true form of the Medical Version of Charaka may be restored as follows:

Tatr≠āyaṁ śarīrasy≠āṅga-vibhāgāḥ। dvau bāhū dve sakthinī śiro-grīvam≠antarādhir≠iti ṣaḍ-aṅgam≠aṅgam ॥ Trīṇi ṣaṣṭāni śatāny≠asthnāṁ saha danta-nakhena। tad≠yathā। [1] dvātriṁśad≠dantāḥ, [2] dvātriṁśad≠dant-olūkhalakāni, [3] viṁśatir≠nakhāḥ, [4] ṣaṣṭiḥ pāṇi-pād-āṅguly-asthīni, [5] viṁśatiḥ pāṇi-pāda-śalākāḥ, [6] catvāri pāṇi-pāda-śalāk-ādhiṣṭhānāni, [7] dve pārṣṇyor≠asthinī, [8] catvāraḥ pādayor≠gulphāḥ, [9] *catvāro maṇikāḥ*[1] hastayoḥ, [10] catvāry≠aratnyor≠asthīni, [11] catvāri jaṅghayoḥ, [12] dve jānunī, [13] dve *kapālike*[2], [14] dvāv≠ūru-nalakau, [15] dvau bāhu-nalakau, [16][3] dve aṁsa-phalake, [17] dvāv≠akṣakau, [18][4] dve śroṇi-phalake, [19][4] ekaṁ bhag-āsthi, [20][5] pañca-catvāriṁśat≠pṛṣṭha-gatāny≠asthīni, [21][6] caturdaś≠orasi, [22 *a*][6] dvayoḥ pārśvayoś≠caturviṁśatiḥ pārśvakāḥ, [22 *b*][6] tāvanti c≠aiva sthālakāni, [22 *c*][6] tāvanti c≠aiva sthālak-ārbudāni, [23] pañcadaśa grīvāyām, [24][7] ekaṁ jatru, [25][7] dve tālūṣake, [26] ekaṁ hanv-asthi, [27] dve hanu-mūla-bandhane, [28] ek-āsthi nāsikā-gaṇḍakūṭa-lalāṭam, [29] dvau śaṅkhau, [30] catvāri śiraḥ-kapālāni। iti trīṇi ṣaṣṭāni śatāny≠asthnāṁ saha danta-nakhena ॥

For the translation, see § 7.

§ 74. *Spurious Recension of Charaka*

1. Gangādhar's spurious recension of the Medical Version of Charaka occurs in the Berhampore edition (1877–8), p. 185, l. 26–

[1] Trad. Rec., dvau maṇikau.
[2] Trad. Rec., jānu-kapālike.
[3] Trad. Rec. inserts dvāv≠aṁsau.
[4] Trad. Rec. places Nos. 18, 19, as Nos. 20, 21.
[5] Trad. Rec. places No. 20 as No. 22.
[6] Trad. Rec. places No. 21 and 22 *a b c*, as Nos. 24 and 25 *a b c*.
[7] Trad. Rec. places Nos. 24, 25, as Nos. 18, 19.

186, l. 22. It is reprinted in the edition of Debendranāth and Upendranāth Sen (1897), p. 414, §§ 4, 5, and in the second edition of Jīvānanda (1896), p. 351, §§ 4, 5. It runs as follows:

Tatr≠āyaṁ śarīrasy≠āṅga-vibhāgāḥ। dvau bāhū, dve sakthinī śiro-grīvam≠antarādhir≠iti ṣaḍ-aṅgam≠aṅgam ॥ Trīṇi ṣaṣṭy-adhikāni śatāny≠asthnāṁ saha dant-olūkhala-nakhaiḥ। tad≠yathā। [1] dvātriṁśad≠dant-olūkhalāni, [2] dvātriṁśad≠dantāḥ, [3] viṁśatir≠nakhāḥ, [4] viṁśatiḥ pāṇi-pāda-śalākāḥ, [5 a] catvāry≠adhiṣṭhānāny≠āsāṁ, [5 b] catvāri pāṇi-pāda-pṛṣṭhāni,[1] [6] ṣaṣṭir≠aṅguly-asthīni, [7 a] dve pārṣṇyoḥ, [7 b] dve kūrc-ādhaḥ, [8] catvāraḥ pāṇyor≠maṇikāḥ, [9] catvāraḥ pādayor≠gulphāḥ, [10] catvāry≠aratnyor≠asthīni, [11] catvāri jaṅghayoḥ, [12] dve jānunoḥ, [13] dve kūrparayoḥ, [14] dve ūrvoḥ, [15] dve bāhvoḥ, [16] s-āṁsayoḥ, [17] dvau akṣakau, [18] dve tālunī, [19] dve śroṇi-phalake, [20 a] ekaṁ bhag-āsthi, puṁsāṁ meḍhr-āsthi, [20 b] ekaṁ trika-saṁśritam, [20 c] ekaṁ gud-āsthi, [21] pṛṣṭha-gatāni pañcatriṁśat, [22] pañcadaś≠āsthīni grīvāyāṁ, [23] dve jatruṇī, [24] ekaṁ hanv-asthi, [25] dve hanu-mūla-bandhane, [26 a] dve lalāṭe, [26 b] dve akṣṇoḥ, [26 c] dve gaṇḍayoḥ, [26 d] nāsikāyāṁ trīṇi ghoṇ-ākhyāni, [27 a] dvayoḥ pārśvayoś≠caturviṁśatiḥ, [27 b] caturviṁśatiḥ pañjar-āsthīni ca pārśvakāni, [27 c] tāvanti c≠aiṣāṁ sthālikāny≠arbud-ākārāṇi, tāni dvisaptatiḥ, [28] dvau śaṅkhakau, [29] catvāri śiraḥ-kapālāni, [30] vakṣasi saptadaśa। iti trīṇi ṣaṣṭy-adhikāni śatāny≠asthnām≠iti ॥

For the translation, see § 8.

2. The commentary of Gangādhar on the above recension runs as follows, *ibidem*, pp. 185–7:

Dvau bāhū iti dve aṅge। dve sakthinī iti dve aṅge। śiro-grīvam≠ity≠ekam≠aṅgam। śiraś≠ca grīvā c≠eti tayoḥ samāhāra ity≠ekavad-bhāvam। antarādhir≠iti ekam≠aṅgam। antar≠madhyam≠ādadhāt≠īti utpattyā madhya-deha iti। ity≠evaṁ ṣaḍ-aṅgam≠aṅgaṁ śarīram। Suśrute 'py≠uktaṁ śarīra-saṁkhyā-vyākaraṇaṁ Śārīre। tac≠ca ṣaḍ-aṅgaṁ śākhāś≠catasro, madhyaṁ pañcamaṁ, ṣaṣṭhaṁ śira iti atra grīvā-paryantaṁ śiraḥ-saṁjñam≠iti ॥

[1] This clause seems to be based on some false reading like that noticed in § 72, note 2.

Trīṇ≠īty-ādi । asthnāṁ ṣaṣṭy-adhikāni śaṭāni nṛṇām≠iti । nanu śalya-tantre trīṇi śatāny≠asthnām≠ity≠uktam । katham≠iha ṣaṣṭy-adhikāni ity≠ata āha । sah≠ety-ādi । śalya-tantre Suśrute 'py≠uktam । trīṇi sa-ṣaṣṭāny≠asthi-śatāni veda-vādino bhāṣante । śalya-tantreṣu yeṣām≠asthnāṁ viśeṣeṇa śastra-kriyā cikitsite n≠āsti, tāni ṣaṣṭy-asthīni n≠opadiśyante । na tu 'na santi' iti kṛtvā n≠opadiśyante । tāni ca ṣaṣṭir≠asthnām≠eṣā । dant-olūkhala-nakha-jatrv-asthīni śaṣṭis[1]≠taiḥ saha trīṇi śatāni bhavanty≠asthnām≠iti । tāni vivṛṇoti ॥

Dvātriṁśad≠ity-ādi । dantānāṁ dvātriṁśat । ekaikasy≠aikaikam≠ulūkhal-ākṛti-sthiti-sthānam≠iti dvātriṁśad≠eva dant-olūkhalāni । śalya-tantre n≠oktāni । dvātriṁśad≠dantās≠t≠ūktās≠tad-grahaṇena tāny≠api gṛhyante । viṁśatir≠nakhā iti śalya-tantre n≠oktam । viṁśatiḥ pāṇi-pāda-śalākā iti dvayoḥ pāṇyoḥ pādayoś≠ca dvayos≠taleṣu caturṣu sthāneṣv≠aṅguli-viṁśater≠mūleṣu sthitā viṁśatiḥ śalākāḥ । ṣaṣṭir≠aṅguly-asthīni । pāṇi-pāda-catuṣṭaye viṁśater≠aṅgulīnām≠ekaikasyām≠aṅgulyāṁ trīṇi trīṇy≠asthīni, tāny≠ekaikasmin pāṇi-pāde pañcadaśa, caturṣu ṣaṣṭiḥ । dve asthinī pārṣṇoḥ pādayor≠mūle śalākābhyo 'dhaḥstham≠ekaikam≠iti dve । dve kūrcādha iti pāṇyoḥ śalākābhyo 'dhastāt≠tac≠chalākā-bandha ekaikam≠iti dvayoḥ pāṇyor≠mūle dve asthinī । pārṣṇyor≠asthi-vat । tato 'dhastāc≠catvāraḥ pāṇyor≠maṇikā maṇibandha-sthāne ekaikasmin pāṇau dve asthinī dvayoś≠catvāri । evam≠eva pādayoś≠catvāro gulphā iti । tato 'dhastāc≠catvāry≠aratnyor≠asthīni । hastayoḥ koṣṭhe tv≠ekaikasmin dve dve asthinī, tataś≠catvāri aratnyor≠iti । evaṁ catvāri jaṅghayor≠asthīni gulph-ādhastāj≠jānu-paryante । dve jānunor≠iti pṛthu-guḍik-ākāre । evam≠eva kūrparayor≠dve asthinī । prakoṣṭha-bāhvoḥ sandhau kṣudra-guḍik-ākāre dve । dve ūrvor≠ity≠ekaikasmin ūrāv≠ekaikam≠iti dve । evam≠eva s-āṁsayor≠bāhvor≠dve, ekaikasmin bāhāv≠ekaikam≠iti dve । ity≠evaṁ catasṛṣu pāṇi-pāda-rupāsu śākhāsu khalv≠ekaikasyāṁ śākhāyāṁ nakhaiḥ saha dvātriṁśad≠asthīni, catasṛṣu tāny≠aṣṭāviṁśaty-uttaraṁ śataṁ bhavanti । śalya-tantreṣu Suśrut-ādiṣu nakh-ānuktatvād≠ekaikasyāṁ śākhāyāṁ saptaviṁ-

[1] There appears to be an error here in the print of the commentary. The three items which are mentioned, *dant-olūkhala* (32), *nakha* (20), and *jatru* (2), work out a total, not of 60, but only of 54.

śatiḥ, tāny≠aṣṭ-ottara-śatam≠uktāni । iti dantolūkhala-danta-sahitāni tāny≠aṣṭāviṁśaty-uttara-śat-āsthīni dvinavaty-adhika-śataṁ bhavanti । dvāv≠akṣakāv≠ity-ādi । atra dvitva-prasaṅgād≠dve tālunī ity≠uktam । tālu-gata-dvaya-varjam≠akṣak-ādiṣu khalv≠akṣaka-śroṇi-bhaga-meḍhra-trika-guda-pṛṣṭheṣu dvācatvāriṁśat । tad-yathā । dvāv≠akṣakau kaṇṭh≠ādho 'ṁsakau dvau । dve śroṇi-phalake iti nitambe dve । strīṇāṁ ekaṁ bhag-āsthi, puṁsāṁ meḍhr-āsthi, trikaṁ saṁsṛtam ≠ekaṁ, gude c≠aikam≠iti pañca śroṇyām≠akṣakau dvāv≠iti sapta, pṛṣṭha-gatāni pañcatriṁśad≠iti dvācatvāriṁśat । atha grīvāṁ praty≠ūrdhvaṁ saptatriṁśad≠iti । tad-yathā । dve tālunī ity≠uktam । pañcadaśa grīvāyām≠iti । teṣām≠ekādaśa grīvāyāṁ, kaṇṭhanāḍyāṁ catvāri । dve jatruṇī । Nemeḥ śalya-tantre varṇite । hanv-asthi c≠aikaṁ na varṇitam≠iti । dve hanu-mūla-bandhane । dve lalāṭe । dve akṣṇoḥ । dve gaṇḍayoḥ । nāsikāyāṁ trīṇ≠īti ghana-rūpa-vat । iti vakṣyati । śiraḥ-kapālāni catvāri, dvau śaṅkhakāv≠iti jatru-gata-dvaya-varjaṁ pañcatriṁśad≠grīvāṁ praty≠ūrdhvam । atha madhya-dehe । dvayoḥ pārśvayor≠ity-ādi । dvayoḥ pārśvayor≠ekaikasmin pārśvaka-mūle vakṣasi lagnāni dvādaśa dvādaśa iti caturviṁśatiḥ । caturviṁśatiḥ pañjar-āsthīni pārśvakāni । tāny≠ekaikasmin pārśve dvādaśa dvādaś≠eti caturviṁśatiḥ । tāvanti c≠aiṣāṁ sthālikāni pṛṣṭhe tv≠arbud-ākārāṇi dvādaśa dvādaś≠eti caturviṁśatis≠tāni militvā dvisaptatiḥ । vakṣasi saptadaś≠eti । pūrvaṁ dve jatruṇī ity≠uktam≠ity≠ek-ādhika-navatir≠madhya-dehe ॥ dvau śaṅkhakau catvāri śiraḥ-kapālān≠īti grīvāṁ praty≠ūrdhvaṁ ṣaḍ vyākhyātāni iti militvā ṣaṣṭy-adhikāṇi trīṇi śatāny≠asthnāṁ bhavanti । tatra śalya-tantreṣu dantolūkhalāni dvātriṁśad≠viṁśatir≠nakhā jatruṇī dve hanv-asthi c≠aikam≠iti pṛthaṅ≠n≠ocyante[1] । danta-grahaṇena dantolūkhalānāṁ grahaṇāt । nakhānāṁ bāhyatvāt । jatruṇi dvayor≠vakṣaso 'sthi-grahaṇena grahaṇāt । hanv-asthnaś≠ca yauvane pṛthaktvābhād≠dvitvam≠iti na virodhaḥ ॥

§ 75. *The Glosses of Chakrapāṇidatta*

The glosses of Chakrapāṇidatta are edited from the following materials:

[1] See the preceding note. This clause seems to involve a similar error; for the four items 32 + 20 + 2 + 1 give a total 55, but not 60.

1. T = Tübingen MS., No. 463 (vol. II), fls. 284 *b*, 285 *a*.

2. C = Copy of the osteological statement, as contained in the manuscript in Dr. P. Cordier's possession (see § 11, footnote 1), kindly supplied by him to me.

They run as follows:

Tatra ayam=ity-ādi ı śiro-grīvam=etad=ekam=eva śiro-vivakṣāyām ı antarādhir=madhye ı ṣaṣṭāni iti ṣaṣṭy-adhikāni ı dant-olūkhalakaṁ yatr=āśrito dantaḥ[1] ı yadyapi nakhā Vividhāśitapītīyena mala-bhoga-poṣyatvena mala eva[2] prakṣiptās=tathāp=īh=āsthitā[3]-rūpa-yogasy=āpi vidyamānatvād=asthi-gaṇanāyāṁ paṭhitāḥ[4] ı pratyaṅguli-parva-trayaṁ tena viṁśaty-aṅguli-gatam=asthnāṁ viṁśati-trayaṁ[5] bhavati ı vṛddh-āṅguṣṭhe ca hasta-pāda-praviṣṭaṁ tṛtīyaṁ[6] parva jñeyam ı vṛddh-āṅguṣṭha-śalākā api svalpa-pramāṇā jñeyā ı aṅgulīnāṁ śalākā yatra saṁlagnāḥ tac=chalāk-ādhiṣṭhānam[7] ı jānu jānukaṁ[8] jaṅgh-orvoḥ sandhiḥ ı akṣakau koṣṭh-āvāk aṁsa-jatru-sandheḥ kīlakau[9] ı tālūṣake tālv-asthinī ı

[1] T dant-olūkhalako, C danteṣ=ūlūkhalaṁ yatr=āśritā dantāḥ ı

[2] T vividhāśītapītīyena mana-bhoga-poṣyatvena mana eva; C vividhāśitapītīye mala-bhāga-poṣyatvena male eva ı

[3] T āstitā ıı [4] So T; C has patitāḥ ı

[5] So C; T reads annāṁ viṁśatiyaṁ ı

[6] So T, except that it has va for ca. C reads yad=dhasta=pāda-praviṣṭaṁ tat tṛtīyam ı

[7] C tatra śalāk-āṅguṣṭh-ādhiṣṭhānam ı

[8] T om. jānu, C om. jānukam ı

[9] Conjectural; T has akṣakāṣ-koṣṭāṁvāṁkaśayattu sandhe kīlakau; C reads akṣāv=iv=ākṣakau jatru-sandheḥ kīlakau ı The reading of C conveys the impression of being a conjectural emendation of a corrupt text, perhaps made by the person who copied C for Dr. P. Cordier. It is clearly not the original reading; for (1) it is so simple and easy that it seems difficult to conceive how a copyist, however ignorant he might be, should transmogrify it into the reading of the Tübingen MS., from which it widely differs; and (2) it involves for the terms *jatru* and *sandhi* the meanings 'collar-bone' and 'connecting-link', which are quite unknown to the older Indian medical science (see § 62). Literally that reading may be translated: 'The two axle-like *akṣaka* are the pegs of the clavicular connexion'; i. e. the two clavicles (*jatru*) which connect (*sandhi*) the neck with the shoulder are pegs (*kīlaka*) resembling the axle of a car which connects its wheels with one another, and hence are called 'little axles' (*akṣaka*, diminutive of *ákṣa*). In the older Indian Medicine, *jatru* means the windpipe or neck, and *sandhi* denotes an articulation. See my article in the *Journal of the Royal Asiatic Society* for 1906, pp. 922 ff.

bhag-āsthi abhimukhaṁ kaṭi-sandhāna-kārakaṁ[1] tiryag-asthi । sthālakāni iti parśukānāṁ mūla-sthānāni nimnāni[2] । sthālak-ārbudāni tu parśuk-āsthiṣu nimneṣu madhye sthitāny[3]≈arbud-ākārāṇy≈asthīni । nāsikā-gaṇḍakūṭa-lalāṭair≈militvā[4] ekaṁ≈eva asthi gaṇanīyam । ye[5] tu pṛthag-aṅgāni[6]≈paṭhanti teṣāṁ nāsā-gaṇḍakūṭa-lalāṭānāṁ trayāṇāṁ trīṇy≈eva asthīni iti na[7] saṅkhyā-pūraṇam ॥

For the translation, see § 11.

§ 76. *The Traditional Recension of Bheḍa*

The traditional recension of the Medical Version of Ātreya's system in the Compendium of Bheḍa (*Śārīra Sthāna*, VII *adhyāya*) is edited from the following sources:

1. The copy of the Tanjore Manuscript which, as stated in § 12, is my possession. It is a beautifully written copy in Telugu characters, carefully collated with the original manuscript by Mr. C. Krishnayya, the Tanjore Palace Librarian.

2. A copy, in Roman characters, of the osteological statement, kindly made for me by Professor Jolly, from the copy of the Tanjore manuscript in the possession of Dr. P. Cordier (marked J).

3. An edited copy, in Roman, of the same statement, kindly supplied to me by Dr. P. Cordier from his copy of the Tanjore manuscript (marked C).

Seeing that the Bheḍa manuscript is unique and very difficult of access, the osteological statement is first reproduced exactly as it stands in my excellent copy. This reproduction is followed by an amended copy, edited from the sources mentioned above. A translation of it is given in § 12.

[1] So C; but T reads atisukhaṁ kāya-sandhāna-kārakaṁ ।
[2] So T; but C reads mūla-sthāna-lagnāni ।
[3] So T; but C reads only parśuka-mūlāny ।
[4] So T; but C has lalāṭānām-eka-mūlatvād, which reading yields exactly the same sense.
[5] T om. ye । [6] So C; but T pṛthag-gaṇanāt ।
[7] So T; but C has ekatvena tu for iti na, which yields the same meaning.

1. *Reproduction.*

Trīṇi ṣaṣṭīṇi[1] śavāny[2]≠asthāṁ[3] tad-yathā ı dvātriṁśad≠daṁtāḥ ı dvātriṁśad≠daṁt-olūkhalakāni[4] ı viṁśati pāṇi-pāda-śalānāny≠aṁguḷy-asthīni viṁśatiḥ ı pāṇi-pāda-śalākā catvāri ı pāṇi-pāda-śalāk-ādhiṣṭhānāni dve[5] ı pārṣor[6]≠asthīni catvāraḥ ı pādayor≠gulbaḥ[7] dvau māṇikau pāṇike dve hastayoḥ catvāry≠aṁśayor[8] ≠asthīni dve jaṁghayor≠dve jānuni[9] dve jānu-kapāṇike[10] dvāv≠ūrū dvāv≠ūru-naśakau[11] dvāv≠asau[12] dve ansa-phalake[13] dvāv≠aṁkṣaṇau[14] ekaṁ jatṛu (जत्रु)[15] dve tālū[16] dve cubuke dve śroṇi-phalake ı ekaṁ bhag-āsthi ı paṁcacatvāriṁśat≠pṛṣṭha-gat-odhṛṣ-ṭhiti[17] paṁcadaśa grīvāyāṁ ı caturdaś≠orasi ı catūrviṁśati[18] pār-śakā[19] ı pārśvayor[20]≠yāvaṁti c≠aiva sthālakāni tāvaṁti c≠aiva sthālak-ārbudakāni[21] ı ekaṁ hanv-asthi dve hanu-baṁdhane[22] ı ekaṁ nās-āsthi tathā hanukūṭa-lātī[23] ı catvāri śīrṣa-kapālāni ıı

2. *Edition.*

Trīṇi ṣaṣṭīni śatāny≠asthnām ı tad-yathā ı [1] dvātriṁśad≠dantāḥ, [2] dvātriṁśad≠dant-olūkhalakāni, [3] viṁśatir≠nakhāḥ[24], [4] ṣaṣṭy[24]≠aṅguly-asthīni, [5] viṁśatiḥ pāṇi-pāda-śalākāḥ, [6]

[1] J.C ṣaṣṭīni.

[2] So also J, but C śatāny.

[3] J.C asthnāṁ.

[4] So also C, but J olūkhalāni.

[5] So the three preceding clauses also in J, but C edits them as follows: '..... viṁśatiḥ pāṇi-pāda-śalākāḥ ı...... aṅguly-asthīni ı catvāri pāṇi-pāda-śalāk-ādhiṣṭhānāni ı'

[6] C pārṣṇyor.

[7] C gulphāḥ.

[8] C aratnyor.

[9] C jānunī.

[10] C kapālike.

[11] So also J, but C nalakau.

[12] J dvau nasau; but C dvāv≠aṁsau.

[13] J anna-phalake; but C aṁsa-phalake.

[14] J vaṁkṣaṇau; but C akṣakāv≠.

[15] J jatru; C jatrū.

[16] J tālu.

[17] So also J; but C gatāny≠asthīni.

[18] J.C caturviṁśati.

[19] So also J; but C pārśvakāni.

[20] J pārśvayo.

[21] So also C; but J ārbudāni.

[22] So also J; but C hanu-mūla-bandhane.

[23] J lāṭ; but C lalāṭaṁ.

[24] These two words are omitted in the original by a confused blunder of the scribe.

catvāri pāṇi-pāda-śalāk-ādhiṣṭhānāni, [7] dve pārṣṇyor⸗asthinī, [8] catvāraḥ pādayor⸗gulphāḥ, [9] dvau maṇikau[1] hastayoḥ, [10] catvāry⸗aratnyor⸗asthīni, [11] dve jaṅghayoḥ, [12] dve jānunī, [13] dve jānu-kapālike, [14] [2]dvāv⸗ūru-nalakau, [15] deest, [16 *a*] dvāv⸗aṁsau, [16 *b*] dve aṁsa-phalake, [17] dvāv⸗akṣakau[3], [18] ekaṁ jatru, [19] dve tālunī[1], [20] dve śvroṇi-phalake, [21] ekaṁ bhag-āsthi, [22] pañcacatvāriṁśat⸗pṛṣṭha-gatāny⸗asthīni[3], [23] pañcadaśa grīvāyām, [24] caturdaś⸗orasi, [25 *a*] caturviṁśatiḥ pārśvakāḥ, [25 *b*] pārśvayor⸗yāvanti c⸗aiva sthālakāni, [25 *c*] tāvanti c⸗aiva sthālak-ārbudāni, [26] ekaṁ hanv-asthi, [27] dve hanu-mūla-bandhane, [28 *a*] ekaṁ nās-āsthi, [28 *b*] tathā hanukūṭa-lalāṭe, [29] deest, [30] catvāri śīrṣa-kapālāni ||

§ 77. *The Non-medical Version of Yājnavalkya*

The traditional recension of the Non-medical Version of Ātreya's System in the Law-book of Yājnavalkya is edited from the following sources:

1. ASB¹ = Asiatic Society of Bengal, No. I B 51.
2. ASB² = „ „ „ No. II A 10.
3. ASB³ = „ „ „ No. II A 11.
4. Bd. = Bodleian MS., No. 65.
5. Bl. = Berlin MS., No. 340 (Prof. Stenzler's A, p. 132).
6. IO¹ = India Office, No. 1079.
7. IO² = „ „ No. 1176.
8. IO³ = „ „ No. 1278.
9. IO⁴ = „ „ No. 1786.
10. IO⁵ = „ „ No. 2035.
11. IO⁶ = „ „ No. 2060.
12. IO⁷ = „ „ No. 2074.
13. IO⁸ = „ „ No. 2167.

[1] *Pāṇike dve* and *dve cubuke*, in the original, are marginal glosses which have got into the text.

[2] *Dvāv⸗ūrū*, in the original, is an obvious false duplication.

[3] *Aṁkṣaṇau* and *odhṛṣṭhiti*, in the original, are obvious clerical errors.

14. IO^{9} = India Office, No. 2823.
15. IO^{10} = „ „ No. 3022.
16. IO^{11} = „ „ No. 23 (50).
17. St. = Prof. Stenzler's edition, pp. 89, 90.

It runs as follows:

Ṣaḍ≠aṅgāni tath≠āsthnāṁ ca saha ṣaṣṭyā śata-trayam ‖ 84 ‖
Sthālaiḥ saha catuḥṣaṣṭir≠dantā vai, viṁśatir≠nakhāḥ ।
pāṇi-pāda-śalākāś≠ca, tāsāṁ sthāna-catuṣṭayam ‖ 85 ‖
Ṣaṣṭy≠aṅgulīnāṁ, dve pārṣṇyor≠gulpheṣu ca catuṣṭayam ।
catvāry≠aratnik-āsthīni, jaṅghayos≠tāvad≠eva tu ‖ 86 ‖
Dve dve jānu-kapol-oruphalak-āṁsasamudbhave ।
akṣa-tālūṣake śroṇiphalake ca vinirdiśet ‖ 87 ‖
Bhagāsthy≠ekaṁ, tathā pṛṣṭhe catvāriṁśac≠ca pañca ।
grīvā pañcadaś-āsthiḥ syāj≠jatrv≠ekaṁ[1] ca, tathā hanuḥ ‖ 88 ‖
Tan-mūle dve lalāṭ-ākṣi-gaṇḍe, nāsā ghan-āsthikā[2] ।
pārśvakāḥ sthālakaiḥ sārdham≠arbudaiś≠ca dvisaptatiḥ ‖ 89 ‖
Dvau śaṅkhakau, kapālāni catvāri śirasas≠tathā ।
uraḥ saptadaś-āsth≠īti puruṣasy≠āsthi-saṁgrahaḥ ‖ 90 ‖

For the translation, see § 16.

§ 78. *Gangādhar's Recension of the Non-medical Version*

Gangādhar's recension of the Non-medical Version, reprinted from his Berhampore edition, pp. 187–8, runs as follows, his emendations being shown in italics. (Translation in § 18.):

Sthālaiḥ saha catuḥṣaṣṭir≠daśanā, viṁśatir≠nakhāḥ ।
pāṇi-pāda-śalākāś≠ca, tāsāṁ sthāna-catuṣṭayam ‖ 85 or 28 ‖
Ṣaṣṭy≠aṅgulīnāṁ, dve pārṣṇyoḥ, *kūrc-ādho maṇi-gulphayoḥ* ।
catvāry≠aratnyoś≠c≠āsthīni, jaṅghāyāṁ tad-vad≠eva ca ‖ 86 or 29 ‖

[1] So Bd., Bl., $IO^{4.5.6.7.9.10.11}$; but ASB^{2}, $IO^{1.2}$, St. jatrv≠ekaikaṁ; IO^{5} originally had jatrv≠ekaikaṁ, but corrected by the same hand to jatrv≠ekaṁ ca; ASB^{3} jatruṇy≠ekaṁ; ASB^{1} jatrāv≠ekaṁ; IO^{8} jālikaṁ ca; IO^{3} om.

[2] ASB^{1} nānāṁghriṇāsthikā.

Dve dve jānu-*kūrpar*-oruphalak-āṁsasamudbhave ı
akṣa-tālūṣake śroṇiphalake c=aivam=ādiśet ıı 87 or 30 ıı
Bhagāsthy=ekaṁ, *trike*, *pāyau*, *pṛṣṭhe triṁśac=ca pañca ca* ı
grīvā pañcadaś-āsthiṁ syāj=*jatrv=ekaikaṁ*, tathā hanoḥ ıı 88 or 31 ıı
Tan-mūle dve, lalāṭ-ākṣi-gaṇḍe, nāsā ghan-āsthikā ı
pārśvaka-sthālikaiḥ sārdham=arbudāni dvisaptatiḥ ıı 89 or 32 ıı
Dvau śaṅkhakau, kapālāni catvāry=eva śirasy=atha ı
uraḥ pañcadaś-āsthi syāt, puruṣasy=āsthi-saṁgrahaḥ ıı 90 or 33 ıı

Ity=etad=eva Agneya-purāṇe Yājñavalkya-Saṁhitāyāṁ ca smṛtāv=uktam ıı

This recension is not quite easy to construe so as to work out the required total of 360. The main difficulty lies in the second verse. There may be an error in the text; but taking it as it stands, it would seem that the numeral which is meant to be construed with *maṇi-gulphayoḥ* is the subsequent *catvāri*, four, which likewise governs *aratni* and *jaṅgha*. That is to say, 'of wrist-bones and ankle-bones there are four, also in the fore-arms, and likewise in the legs.' It would also seem that the dual *pārṣṇyoḥ* is meant to indicate, not the two heels of the feet, but the heels (supposed to be) in the hands as well as in the feet (see §§ 32, 50). The meaning of *dve pārṣṇyoḥ*, therefore, is 'there are two bones in either of the two sets of heels', that is, there are two heels in the hands and two in the feet, or altogether four heels. This, no doubt, gives the impression of a rather forced interpretation: the more obvious meaning would seem to be, 'there are two bones in the heels (of the feet), and two in the wrists as well as in the ankles'; that is to say, there are only two heels, two wrist-bones, and two ankle-bones. But with this, apparently more natural, interpretation, it is impossible to work out satisfactorily the total of Gangādhar's recension. That (as shown in § 19) is only possible with the alternative interpretation. And there is this to be said for the latter interpretation, that, as shown by his reconstruction of Charaka's Medical Version (§§ 8, 23), Gangādhar certainly held the existence of four wrist-bones, as well as four ankle-bones.

As to his doctrine of four heels, he was, no doubt, guided by the Traditional Recension of Suśruta's system (§ 27), and by the system of Vāgbhaṭa I (§ 37).

§ 79. *The Commentary of Aparārka*

The commentary of Aparārka on the Non-medical Version, edited from the India Office MS., No. 3022, runs as follows:

[Verse 84.] Ṣaḍ≠aṅgāni ity-ādinā manuṣya-śarīram≠eva nirūpayati I . . . . . . I śiraḥ pāṇī pādau madhya-kāya iti ṣaḍ≠aṅgāni I asthīni ca ṣaṣṭy-adhika-śata-traya-saṁkhyakāni manuṣya-śarīraṁ dhārayanti II

[Verse 85.] uktām≠asthi-saṁkhyām≠upapādayitum≠āha I dantā dvātriṁśat I dvātriṁśad≠eva teṣāṁ sthāla-saṁkhyakāny≠āyatan-āsthīni I evaṁ sa-sthālā[1] dantāś≠catuḥṣaṣṭir≠bhavanti I . . . . I nakhāś≠ca viṁśatiḥ I pāṇyoḥ pādayoś≠c≠āṅguli-mūlāni śalākāḥ tāś≠ca viṁśatiḥ I tāsāṁ ca śalākānāṁ sthānam≠asthi-catuṣṭayam I evam≠aṣṭ-ottar-āsthi-śatam II

[Verse 86.] ekaikasyām≠aṅgulyām≠asthi-trayaṁ tataś≠ca sarvāsām≠aṅgulīnāṁ ṣaṣṭir≠asthīni I pādayoḥ paścimau bhāgau pārṣṇī, tayor≠asthi-dvayam I jaṅgha-pārṣṇyoḥ sandhi-pradeśatvaṁ tad-bahir-avasthitau ekatra pāde gulphau, tataś≠ca pādayor≠gulpheṣu catvāry≠asthīni I aratnir≠eva aratnikāḥ, yady-apy≠aratni-śabdo bāhv-agraha eva vartate tath-āpy≠atra asthi-catuṣṭaya-saṁkhyā-saṁpatty-arthaṁ prayujyamānaḥ, samagram≠eva hastam≠āha, evam≠aratnik-āsthīni bhavanti I jaṅgha-śabdo 'pi tath≠aiva samagra-pāda-vacano[2] 'tra, tataś≠ca jaṅghayor≠api catvāry≠eva asthīni I eṣāṁ catussaptatiḥ I pūrveṇa aṣṭ-ottara-śatena saha dvyaśītaṁ śatam II kiṁ ca II

[Verse 87.] jānunī jaṅgh-oru-sandhī I kapolau gallau I ūrū sakthinī, te ca phalak-ākārau I aṁśau bāhu-mūle, tat-samudbhave I tathā akṣa-tālūṣake netra-prānt-āsthinī I śroṇi-phalake jaṅghā-pṛṣṭha-madhya-deśau I praty-abhidhānaṁ dve dve asthinī I evaṁvidhayā saṁkhyayā saha caturnavaty-adhikaṁ śatam II kiṁ ca II

[1] MS. sa-sthālaṁ.

[2] MS. pāde vacano.

[Verse 88.] bhag-āsthi upasth-āsthy≠ekam I pṛṣṭhe pañcacatvāriṁśat I grīvāyāṁ pañcadaśa I jatruṇi uro-'ṁsayos≠sandhāv≠ekam I hanuś≠cibukaṁ, tad≠apy≠ek-āsthi I s≠aiṣā triṣaṣṭiḥ I pūrvayā saṁkhyayā saha śata-dvayaṁ saptapañcāśad-adhikam II kiṁ cā II

[Verse 89.] tan-mūle dve asthinī I tathā lalāṭ-āsthy≠ekam I tath≠ākṣayor≠dve I gaṇḍayor≠dve I kapol-ākṣi-madhya-pradeśau gaṇḍau I nāsā ghana-saṁjñaken≠āsthn≠āpy≠uktā [1] veditavyā I tena tad≠asthy≠ekam II parśukā vaṅkrayaḥ, tāḥ sthālakair≠arbuda-saṁjñakaiś≠ca asthibhis≠sārdhaṁ dvāsaptatiḥ I pūrvair≠aṣṭābhis≠sārdham≠aśītiḥ I pūrva-saṁkhyayā saha sapta-triṁśad-adhika-śata-trayam II kiṁ ca II

[Verse 90.] bhrū-karṇa-madhya-pradeśau śaṅkhau I asthīni śiras-saṁbandhīni kapāl-ākārāṇi catvāri I . . . . . . I uro vakṣas≠tasya saptadaśa I tataḥ trayoviṁśatiḥ I pūrva-saṁkhy-opetā ṣaṣṭy-adhikaṁ śata-trayam I eṣa puruṣasya manuṣya-śarīrasya asthi-saṁkhyā-saṁgrahaḥ II

Translation.

[Verse 84.] With the words 'six parts, &c.' the author describes the human body . . . . . the head, the two hands, the two feet, and the trunk: these are the six parts; and the bones, which number three hundred and sixty, support the body of man.

[Verse 85.] Detailing the said number of bones the author says: the teeth (*danta*) are thirty-two; thirty-two are also their socket-bones, termed *sthāla*; hence the teeth, together with their sockets, amount to sixty-four . . . . . The nails (*nakha*) number twenty. The long bones (*śalākā*) form the bases of the fingers of the hands and feet; they also number twenty. The bases (*sthāna*) of the long bones number four [2]. Thus we have altogether one hundred and eight bones.

[Verse 86.] In each digit (*aṅguli*) there are three bones; hence in all the digits together there are sixty bones. The heels (*pārṣṇi*) are the posterior parts of the two feet. They contain two bones. At the place where the leg and heel join there are, externally, in each foot, two ankle-bones (*gulpha*); and hence the

[1] MS. saṁjñakenāsthāpukra.
[2] See the Exegetical Note in § 83.

ankle-bones of the two feet number four. *Aratnikā* is a synonym of *aratni*, forearm : though the word 'forearm' (*aratni*) does not really include the arm (*bāhu*), yet here, for the sake of obtaining the number four of the bones, it is employed in that sense [i.e. as including the arms]. The author is speaking really of the whole upper limb; hence the bones of the 'forearms' (*aratni*) number four. Similarly the word 'leg' (*jaṅgha*) here signifies the whole lower limb; and hence the bones of the two legs also number four. These items together number seventy; and these, together with the aforementioned one hundred and eight, amount to one hundred and eighty-two bones. Further:

[Verse 87.] The two knees (*jānu*) are the two joints between the leg and the thigh. By the two *kapola* the two cheeks are meant; and by the two *ūru* the two thighs, which are shaped like boards. The two shoulders (or shoulder-summits, *aṁsa*) are the bases from which the arms spring. Next, by the two *akṣa-tālūṣaka*, the two bones are meant which lie on the edge of the eye. The two hip-blades (*śroṇi-phalaka*) are the two places between the two lower limbs and the back. Each item consists of two bones. Together with the number (twelve) thus obtained, the total of the bones amounts to one hundred and ninety-four. Further:

[Verse 88.] The pubic (*bhagāsthi*) or private bone is one. In the back (*pṛṣṭha*) there are forty-five bones; in the neck (*grīvā*) fifteen; in the windpipe (*jatru*), at the joint of the breast and shoulder, one. *Hanu* signifies the chin; that also consists of one bone. This makes sixty-three bones; and with the aforesaid number (194) the total amounts to two hundred and fifty-seven. Further:

[Verse 89.] At the back of that bone [i.e. of the chin] there are two bones. Next, the brow contains one bone. Next, in the two eyes, there are two bones; so also there are two in the two *gaṇḍa*, by which term the two places intermediate between the cheeks and the eyes are meant. The nose must be understood to be expressed also by the term *ghana*-bone. *Parśuka* denotes the ribs; these, together with their sockets (*sthālaka*) and the so-called tubercles (*arbuda*), number seventy-two. With the previous eight bones they amount to eighty; and these, together with the previously stated number (257), amount to three hundred and thirty-seven. Further:

[Verse 90.] The two temples (*śaṅkha*) are the two places intermediate between the eyebrows and the ears. The pan-shaped bones (*kapāla*) which constitute the cranium number four . . . . *Uras* signifies the breast; it contains seventeen bones. Hence we have altogether twenty-three; and these, together with the previously numbered (337), amount to a total of three hundred and sixty. This makes up the aggregate number of bones of the human skeleton.

§ 80. *The Commentary of Vijnāneśvara*

In the Mitākshară commentary of Vijnāneśvara, the passages on the Non-medical Version, edited from the India Office MSS., Nos. 1079, 2035, 2060, run as follows:

[Verse 84.] Tath≠āṅgāni ṣaḍ≠eva kara-yugmaṁ caraṇa-yugalam≠uttamāṅgaṁ gātram≠iti । asthnāṁ tu ṣaṣṭi-sahitaṁ śata-trayam≠uparitana-ṣaṭ-śloka-vakṣyamāṇam≠avagantavyam ॥ kiṁ ca ॥

[Verse 85.] sthālāni danta-mūla-pradeśa-sthāny≠asthīni dvātriṁśat । tais≠saha dvātriṁśad≠dantāś≠catuḥṣaṣṭir≠bhavanti । nakhāḥ kara-ruhā viṁśatiḥ । hasta-pāda-sthitāni śalāk-ākārāṇy≠asthīni maṇibandhasy≠opari-vartīny≠aṅguli-mūla-sthāni viṁśatir≠eva । teṣāṁ nakhānāṁ śalāk-āsthnāṁ ca sthāna-catuṣṭayaṁ dvau caraṇau karau ca । ity≠evam≠asthnāṁ catur-uttara-śatam ॥ kiṁ ca ॥

[Verse 86.] viṁśatir≠aṅgulayas≠tāsām≠ekaikasya trīṇi trīṇi, ity≠evam≠aṅguli-saṁbaddhāny≠asthīni ṣaṣṭir≠bhavanti । pādayoḥ paścimau bhāgau pārṣṇī, tayor≠asthinī dve । ekaikasmin pāde gulphau dvāv≠ity≠evaṁ caturṣu gulpheṣu catvāry≠asthīni । bāhvor≠aratni-pramāṇāni catvāry≠asthīni । jaṅghayoś≠ca tāvad≠eva catvāri । ity≠evaṁ catuḥsaptatiḥ ॥ kiṁ ca ॥

[Verse 87.] jaṅgh-oru-sandhir≠jānuḥ । kapolo gallaḥ । ūruḥ sakthi, tat phalakam । aṁso bhuja-śiraḥ । akṣaḥ karṇa-netrayor≠madhye śaṅkhād≠adhobhāgaḥ । tālūṣakaṁ kākudam । śroṇiḥ kakudminī, tat phalakam ı teṣām≠ekaikaśo 'sthinī dve dve vinirdiśet ı ity≠evaṁ caturdaś≠āsthīni bhavanti ıı kiṁ ca ıı

[Verse 88.] guhy-āsthy≠ekam ı pṛṣṭhe paścima-bhāge pañca-catvāriṁśad≠asthīni bhavanti ı grīvā kandharā, sā pañcadaś-āsthiḥ syāt ı vakṣo-'ṁsayoḥ sandhir≠jatru, prati-jatrv≠ekaikam ı hanuś≠cibukaṁ, tatr≠āpy≠ekam≠asthi ı ity≠evaṁ catuḥṣaṣṭiḥ ıı kiṁ ca ıı

[Verse 89.] tasya hanor≠mūle 'sthinī dve ı lalāṭaṁ bhālam ı akṣi cakṣuḥ ı gaṇḍaḥ kapol-ākṣayor≠madhya-pradeśaḥ ı teṣāṁ samāhāro lalāṭ-ākṣi-gaṇḍaṁ, tatra pratyekam≠asthi-yugalam ı nāsā ghana-saṁjñak-āsthimatī ı pārśvakāḥ kakṣ-ādhaḥpradeśa-saṁbaddhāny≠asthīni, tad-ādhāra-bhūtāni sthālakāni, taiḥ sthālakaiḥ arbudaiś≠c≠āsthi-viśeṣaiḥ saha pārśvakā dvisaptatiḥ ı pūrv-oktaiś≠ca navabhiḥ sārdham≠ekāśītir≠bhavanti ıı kiṁ ca ıı

[Verse 90.] bhrū-karṇayor≠madhya-pradeśāv≠asthi-viśeṣau śaṅkhakau ı śirasaḥ saṁbandhīni catvāri kapālāni ı uro vakṣaḥ, tat≠saptadaś-āsthikam ı ity≠evaṁ trayoviṁśatiḥ ı pūrv-oktaiś≠ca saha ṣaṣṭy-adhikaṁ śata-trayam≠ity≠evaṁ puruṣasy≠āsthi-saṁgrahaḥ kathitaḥ ıı

Translation.

[Verse 84.] The six parts of the body are the following: the pair of hands, the pair of feet, the head, and the trunk. As to the three hundred and sixty bones, they must be understood to be detailed in the ensuing six verses; as thus:

[Verse 85.] The sockets (*sthāla*), i. e. the bones which hold the roots of the teeth, number thirty-two. Together with them the thirty-two teeth (*danta*) amount to sixty-four. The nails (*nakha*) which grow on the hands [and feet] number twenty. The pencil-like (*śalākā*) bones, occurring in the hands and feet, situated above the wrist-bones [and ankle-bones] and at the roots of the digits, number also twenty. These nails and long bones have four places (*sthāna*), namely, the two feet and the two hands.[1] So far, the bones amount to one hundred and four. Further,

[Verse 86.] The digits (*aṅguli*) number twenty; in each of them there are three bones; thus the bones which make up the digits amount to sixty. The heels (*pārṣṇi*) are the posterior parts

[1] See the Exegetical Note in § 83.

of the two feet; their bones number two. In each foot there are two ankle-bones (*gulpha*); thus in the four ankles there are four bones. The bones of the two arms (*bāhu*), being implied in the term forearm (*aratni*), number four. Those of the two legs (*jaṅgha*) likewise number four. Further,

[Verse 87.] The knee (*jānu*) is the joint of the leg and thigh. The term *kapola* signifies the cheek. The thigh (*ūru*) is the broad bone (*phalaka*) of the lower limb. The shoulder (*aṁsa*) signifies the head of the arm (i. e. the summit of the shoulder). By the term *akṣa* is meant that part which lies below the temple between the ear and the eye. The term *tālūṣaka* denotes the hard palate. The hip (*śroṇi*) is the broad bone (*phalaka*) in the loins. In each of these organs one should recognize two bones. Thus we have altogether fourteen bones. Further,

[Verse 88.] The private part (*guhya*) consists of one bone. In the back (*pṛṣṭha*), or posterior part of the body, there are forty-five bones. The term *grīvā* signifies the neck; it consists of fifteen bones. The collar-bone (*jatru*) is the junction of breast and shoulder [i.e. head of the arm, or summit of the shoulder: see verse 87]; either collar-bone contains one bone. The term *hanu* signifies the chin; it also contains one bone. Thus we have altogether sixty-four bones. Further,

[Verse 89.] At the back of the chin (*hanu*) there are two bones. The term *lalāṭa* signifies the brow; *akṣi*, the eye; *gaṇḍa*, the spot between the cheek and the eye. The aggregate of these (three organs) is indicated by the compound of the three terms *lalāṭa*, *akṣi*, *gaṇḍa*; each of the three component parts consists of a pair of bones. The nose (*nāsā*) is the bone termed *ghana*. The ribs (*pārśvaka*) are the bones which make up the part of the body situated below the armpits; the sockets (*sthālaka*) are their supporters; with these supporters, and with the peculiar bones termed tubercles (*arbuda*), the ribs number seventy-two. Thus, together with the previously mentioned nine, we have eighty-one bones. Further,

[Verse 90.] In the space intermediate between the eyebrow and the ear there are the two peculiar bones termed temples (*śaṅkha*). The pan-shaped bones which constitute the cranium (*śiraḥ-kapāla*) number four. The term *uras* denotes the breast;

it contains seventeen bones. Thus we have altogether twenty-three bones; and these, together with all the afore-mentioned, make up the total of three hundred and sixty bones which constitute the skeleton of man.

§ 81. *The Commentary of Śūlapāṇi*

The commentary of Śūlapāṇi, called Dīpakālikā, on the Non-medical Version, edited from the India Office MS., No. 1278, runs as follows:

[Verse 84.] Asthnām≠api ṣaṣṭy-adhikaṁ śata-trayam । tad-vibhāgam≠āha.

[Verse 85.] sthālair≠ity-ādi । sthālāni danta-bandha[1]-sthānāni, taiḥ saha dantāś≠catuḥṣaṣṭiḥ । nakhāś≠ca viṁśatiḥ । pāṇi-pāda-śalākāś≠ca viṁśatiḥ । teṣāṁ hasta-dvayena pāda-dvayena ca sthāna-catuṣṭayam । evaṁ ca catur-uttara-śatam≠asthīni ॥

[Verse 86.] ṣaṣṭy≠ity-ādi । aṅgulīnāṁ pratyekaṁ trīṇi trīṇi ity≠evaṁ ṣaṣṭir≠asthīni । aratnik-āsthīni bāhvoḥ । evaṁ ca catuḥsaptatir≠asthīni ॥

[Verse 87.] dve dve ity-ādi । akṣa-saṁjñe dve । jānu-saṁjñe dve । evaṁ ca caturdaś≠āsthīni ॥

[Verse 88.] bhag-āsthi ity-ādi । hanuś[2]≠cibukam । evāṁ catuḥṣaṣṭir≠asthīni ॥

[Verse 89.] tan-mūla ity-ādi । tan-mūle hanu-mūle, dve la-lāṭe । akṣi-gaṇḍe dve । nāsāyāṁ ca ghan-āsthikāyām≠ekam । pārśvakāḥ pañjar-āsthīni, tad-ādhāraiḥ sthālair≠arbudaiś≠ca saha dvisaptatir≠bhavati । evam≠ekāśītir≠asthīni ॥

[Verse 90.] dvāv≠ity-ādi । karṇa-bhruvor≠madhye dvau śaṅkha-kau । śirasaḥ kapālāni catvāri । uraḥ saptadaśa । evaṁ trayoviṁ-śatiḥ । evaṁ puruṣasya asthi-saṁgrahaḥ kathitaḥ ॥

Translation.

[Verse 84.] The number of bones is three hundred and sixty. The author states their details.

[Verse 85.] 'With the sockets,' &c. The sockets (*sthāla*) are the fixing places of the teeth. Together with these, the teeth number sixty-four. The nails (*nakha*) number twenty.

[1] MS. buddha. [2] MS. hanu.

The long bones (*śalākā*) of the hands and feet also number twenty. The bases (*sthāna*) of them [i.e. of the nails], by reason of there being a pair of hands and a pair of feet, are four.[1] Thus (in this verse) the bones amount to one hundred and four.

[Verse 86.] 'Sixty,' &c. Each digit (*aṅguli*) has three bones; thus there are altogether sixty bones. The bones of the forearms (*aratnikā*) signify those of the two arms (*bāhu*). Thus (in this verse) there are altogether sixty-four bones.

[Verse 87.] 'Two each,' &c. The so-called collar-bones (*akṣa*) number two. The so-called knees (*jānu*) number two. Thus (in this verse) there are altogether fourteen bones.

[Verse 88.] 'The pubic bone,' &c. By *hanu* is meant the chin. Thus (in this verse) there are altogether sixty-four bones.

[Verse 89.] 'At the base of it,' &c. The two bases of it (*tan-mūle*) refer to the bases of the chin. There are two brows (*lalāṭa*); also two each of eyes (*akṣi*) and cheeks (*gaṇḍa*). In the *ghana*-bone, that is, in the nose (*nāsā*), there is one bone. The ribs (*pārśvaka*) are the bones of the (thoracic) cage; together with their sockets (*sthāla*) and tubercles (*arbuda*) they number seventy-two. Thus (in this verse) there are altogether eighty-one bones.

[Verse 90.] 'Two,' &c. Between the ears and the eyebrows there are the two temples (*śaṅkha*). The pan-shaped bones (*kapāla*) of the cranium number four. The breast (*uras*) has seventeen bones. Thus (in this verse) the total is twenty-three. Herewith the bones of the skeleton of man have been explained.

§ 82. *The Commentary of Mitramiśra*

The commentary of Mitramiśra on the Non-medical Version, edited from the India Office MS., No. 1176, runs as follows:

[Verse 84.] Karadvaya-caraṇadvaya-śiro-gātrāṇi ṣaḍ-aṅgāni ı asthnāṁ ṣaṣṭi-sahitaṁ śata-trayaṁ ṣaṭ-śloka[2]-vakṣyamāṇaprakāreṇa dhārayanti ı . . . ıı

[1] See the Exegetical Note in § 83.

[2] MS. ślokyā.

[Verse 85.] dvātriṁśatā sthālair⸗danta-mūla-pradeśā-sthair⸗asthibhiḥ sahitā dvātriṁśad⸗dantāś⸗catuḥṣaṣṭir⸗bhavati । pāṇi-pāda-nakhā viṁśatiḥ । pāṇi-pāda-stāḥ śalākās⸗tad-ākārāṇy⸗asthīni ca viṁśatir⸗maṇibandhasya gulphasya ca puro-vartīni । teṣāṁ nakhānāṁ śalākānāṁ ca mūla-pradeśa-rūpaṁ sthāna-catuṣṭayaṁ kara-dvayaṁ caraṇa-dvayaṁ[1] ca । ity⸗evam⸗atra catur-adhikaṁ śatam⸗asthnām ॥ uktaṁ sthāna-catuṣṭayaṁ sv-āsthi-bhinnasya prasaṅgato 'bhidhānāt ; yad⸗vā nakhānāṁ sthānaṁ śalākā ity⸗abhed-ānvayaḥ, catuṣṭayatvaṁ[2] c⸗aikaika-hast-ādi-śalākānāṁ samudāyam⸗abhipretya uktam⸗ity⸗avirodhaḥ ॥

[Verse 86.] aṅgulīnāṁ ṣaṣṭir⸗asthīni, ekaikasyā aṅguler⸗asthi-traya-saṁbandhāt । pārṣṇyoḥ pāda-paścima-bhāgayor⸗asthīni dve । ekaikasmin pāde gulphau vāma-dakṣiṇa-sthau dvau dvāv⸗iti caturṣu gulpheṣu asthi-catuṣṭayam । bāhavo 'ratni-pramāṇāni catvāry⸗asthīni । iti catuḥsaptatiḥ ॥

[Verse 87.] jānunī jaṅgh-oru-sandhī[3] । kapolau gallau । ūru-phalake sakthinī । aṁsau bāhu-mūla etat-samudbhave । pratyekaṁ dve dve asthinī । akṣe karṇa-netr-āntarāla-deśe । tālūṣake tālu-mūle । śroṇi-phalake kaṭī । pratyekaṁ dve dve asthinī । iti caturdaś⸗āsthīni ॥

[Verse 88.] bhaga-padena śiśnasya apy⸗upalakṣaṇaṁ, tad-asthi ekam । pṛṣṭhe pañcacatvāriṁśad⸗asthīni । grīvā kandharā pañcadaś-āsthi-yuktā bhavati । ekam⸗asthim⸗āśritya jatru, vakṣo-'ṁsa-sandhi[4]-dvayam । hanuś⸗cibukam syāt । ity⸗evaṁ catuḥṣaṣṭir⸗asthīni ॥

[Verse 89.] tasya hanor⸗mūle dve asthinī lalāṭe ākṣiṇī[5], gaṇḍe ca kapol-ākṣi[6]-madhya-pradeśe, pratyekaṁ dve । nāsā vā ghan-aikāsthimatī[7] । parśukāḥ pañjar-āsthīni, sthālais⸗tad-ādhāra-bhūtair⸗asthibhir⸗arbuda-nāmakair⸗asthi-viśeṣaiś⸗ca saha dvisaptatiḥ । ity⸗evam⸗ekāśītir⸗asthnāṁ bhavati ॥

[Verse 90.] śaṅkhakau bhrū-karṇ-āntarāl-āsthinī dvau । śirasaḥ kapālāni catvāri । uraḥ prati saptadaś⸗āsthīni । ity⸗evaṁ trayoviṁśatiḥ । evaṁ militvā ṣaṣṭy-adhikaṁ śata-trayam⸗iti puruṣasya manuṣasya asthi-parimāṇam ॥

[1] MS. vara-dvayaṁ, om. caraṇa-dvayaṁ. [2] MS. catuṣṭaye tvaṁ.
[3] MS. sandhiḥ. [4] MS. vakṣo saṁdhi. [5] MS. akṣṇi.
[6] MS. akṣa. [7] MS. nāsāvadhānaikāsthimatī.

Translation.

[Verse 84.] The pair of hands, the pair of feet, the head, and the trunk—these are the six parts of the body. They contain the three hundred and sixty bones which are detailed in the following six verses:

[Verse 85.] The thirty-two teeth (*danta*), together with their thirty-two sockets (*sthāla*), that is, with the bones which form the basements of the teeth, number sixty-four. The nails (*nakha*) of the hands and feet number twenty. Also the pencil-like long bones (*śalākā*) which are in the hands and feet, and which are situated in front of the wrist and ankle, number twenty. With regard to the nails and long bones, there are four places (*sthāna*) which form their foundations, viz. the pair of hands and the pair of feet. Thus, here (in this verse), the total of the bones is one hundred and four. The 'four places' are named as considered apart from their component bones; on the other hand, since the bases of the nails are identical with the long bones, the fourfoldness of the latter is also mentioned in order to indicate their forming sets in each hand and foot; there is therefore here no incongruity.[1]

[Verse 86.] In the digits (*aṅguli*) there are sixty bones, on account of each digit being composed of three bones. In the heels (*pārṣṇi*), that is, the posterior part of the two feet, there are two bones. In either foot there are two ankle-bones (*gulpha*), two on the right and two on the left sides; thus there are four bones in the four ankles. The two arms (*bāhu*), being implied in the term 'forearms' (*aratni*), make up four bones. Thus we have a total of seventy-four bones.

[Verse 87.] The two knees (*jānu*) are the two joints between the leg and the thigh. By the two *kapola* are meant the two cheeks. The two broad bones of the thigh (*ūru-phalaka*) refer to the lower limbs. The two shoulders (*aṁsa*) are the two bases whence the arms spring. Each of these items consists of two bones. By the two *akṣa* are meant the spaces intermediate between the ear and the eye. By the two *tālūṣaka* are meant the

[1] See the Exegetical Note in § 83.

two bases of the palate. The two broad bones (*phalaka*) of *śroṇi* are the two hips. Each of these items consists of two bones. This makes altogether fourteen bones.

[Verse 88.] The word 'vulva' (*bhaga*) indicates also the penis; it consists of one bone. In the back (*pṛṣṭha*) there are forty-five bones; *grīvā*, or the neck, is made up of fifteen bones. By *jatru* are meant the two junctions of breast and shoulder, each consisting of one bone. *Hanu* signifies the chin. This makes a total of sixty-four bones.

[Verse 89.] At the back of that chin there are two bones. As to the forehead, eye, and *gaṇḍa*, that is, the space intermediate between the cheek and the eye, there are two bones in each. The nose (*nāsā*) consists of one bone, called also *ghana*. The ribs (*parśuka*) are the bones of the (thoracic) cage; together with their sockets (*sthālaka*) or supporting bones, and with the peculiar bones called tubercles (*arbuda*), they number seventy-two. This makes a total of eighty-one bones.

[Verse 90.] The temples (*śaṅkha*), that is, the bones lying between the eyebrow and the ear, number two. The pan-shaped bones (*kapāla*) of the cranium number four. In the breast (*uraḥ*) there are seventeen bones. This makes a total of twenty-three bones. Adding up all these we obtain three hundred and sixty as the grand total of the bones of the human body.

§ 83. *Exegetical Note*

Comparing the commentaries quoted in the preceding paragraphs 79–82, it will be seen that, in verse 85, Aparārka counts a total of 108, while Vijnāneśvara, who is followed by Śūlapāṇi and Mitramiśra, counts only 104. The cause of this difference is that in the text of that verse Aparārka read *tāsām*, of them (feminine), while Vijnāneśvara read *teṣām*, of them (masculine). The former form, being the feminine genitive plural, can refer only to the preceding feminine noun *śalākā*, long bone, while the latter form, being the masculine genitive plural, must refer to the preceding masculine noun *nakha*, nail. Accordingly, Aparārka understands the text to mean: 'The nails number twenty; so also the long bones of the hands and feet (*scl.* number twenty); the bases of them (i.e. of the long bones) are four.' This interpretation enumerates three different items: (1) nails, (2) long bones, (3) bases of long bones. On the other hand, Vijnāneśvara understands the text to mean: 'The nails number twenty; so also the long bones of the hands and feet (*scl.* number twenty); the bases of them (i.e. of the nails) are four.' Seeing that the nails are fixed in the digits, and that the bases of the digits are the long bones of the hands and feet, it follows that the bases of the nails are identical with the long bones of the hands and feet. Hence Vijnāneśvara's interpretation admits only two items, namely: (1) nails, (2) long bones or bases of nails. The second item, as Mitramiśra explains, may be considered in two ways—either distributively, or in the aggregate. Considered distributively, the long bones number twenty; but considered as aggregates (*samudāya*), they number only four, that is, two hands and two feet. On the other hand, if, with Aparārka, we translate 'bases of the long bones', we obtain, of course, a third item, namely, the carpus and tarsus. The question arises: Which is the correct reading of the text; is it *tāsām* or *teṣām*; feminine or masculine? The answer cannot be doubtful: obviously the correct reading is the feminine *tāsām*, referring to *śalākā,* or the long bones. It is correct for two quite sufficient reasons: (1) with the reading *teṣām*, the bones of the carpus and tarsus drop out altogether; (2) with the same reading, the four aggregates of the long bones, that is, really the long bones themselves, are declared to be the bases of the nails; but obviously that is an incongruous view: the nails are fixed on the digits, and the digits are fixed on the long bones. As Aparārka rightly says, 'The long bones are the bases of the digits; and the bases of the long bones are four,' namely, the two carpi of the hands and the two tarsi of the feet. Hence the total of the bones, enumerated in verse 85, is 108, but not 104.

§ 84. *The Non-medical Version in the Institutes of Vishnu*

The recension of the Non-medical Version in the Institutes of Vishnu is edited from the following sources:

1. ASB[1] = Asiatic Society of Bengal, MS. No. II A 10.
2. ASB[2] = „ „ „ MS. No. II A 11.
3. ASB[3] = „ „ „ MS. No. I B 25.
4. C[1] = Calcutta, Sanskrit College, MS. No. 5.
5. C[2] = „ „ „ MS. No. 62.
6. D[1] = Deccan College, MS. No. 19.
7. D[2] = „ „ MS. No. 20.
8. D[3] = „ „ MS. No. 155.
9. E[1] = Elphinstone College, Bombay, MS. No. 162.
10. E[2] = „ „ „ MS. No. 174.
11. IO[1] = India Office, MS. No. 200.
12. IO[2] = „ „ MS. No. 540.
13. IO[3] = „ „ MS. No. 913.
14. IO[4] = „ „ MS. No. 915.
15. IO[5] = „ „ MS. No. 1545.
16. IO[6] = „ „ MS. No. 1247.
17. M = Madras, Oriental Library, MS. No. 87.
18. Y = Professor Jolly's Edition, pp. 196, 197.

It runs as follows:

॥ 55 । Asthnāṁ tribhiḥ śataiḥ ṣaṣṭy-adhikair≠dharyamāṇam । 56 । teṣāṁ vibhāgaḥ । 57 sūkṣmaiḥ saha catuḥṣaṣṭir≠daśanāḥ । 58 । viṁśatir≠nakhāḥ । 59 ।[1] pāṇi-pāda-śalākāś≠ca । 60 । ṣaṣṭir≠aṅgulīnāṁ parvāṇi । 61 । dve pārṣṇyoḥ । 62 । catuṣṭayaṁ gulpheṣu । 63 । catvāry≠aratnyoḥ । 64 । catvāry≠jaṅghayoḥ । 65 । dve dve jānu-kapolayoḥ [2] । 66 [1] । ūrv-aṁsayoḥ । 67 । akṣa-tālūṣaka-śroṇiphalakeṣu । 68[3] । bhag-āsthy≠ekam । 69 । pṛṣṭh-āsthi pañcacatvāriṁśad-bhāgam

[1] C[1] IO[3] read No. 59, dvau bāhūḍaka (or ṭaka) -dvayam; IO[2] M, dve bāhū dve prabāhū ūru-dvayam. Also all four omit No. 66. ASB[1] also omits No. 66, though it has No. 59.

[2] IO[2] kapālayoḥ.

[3] C[1] IO[2.3] read No. 68 evaṁ adhaḥ; E[1] reads bhagākhekaṁ pṛṣṭhākhekam.

। 70 । pañcadaś≠āsthīni grīvā । 71 [1] । jatrv≠ekam । 72 । tathā hanuḥ । 73 । tan-mūle ca dve । 74 [2] । dve lalāṭ-ākṣi-gaṇḍe । 75 [3] । nāsā ghan-āsthikā । 76 । arbudaiḥ sthālakaiś≠ca sārdhaṁ dvāsaptatiḥ pārśvakāḥ । 77 [4] । uraḥ saptadaśa । 78 । dvau śaṅkhakau । 79 । catvāri kapālāni śirasaś≠c≠eti ॥

Translation.

। 55 । The body is sustained by three hundred and sixty bones. । 56 । Their detail is as follows. । 57 । Together with the minute (sockets) there are sixty-four teeth (*daśana*). । 58 । The nails number twenty. । 59 । So also the long bones of the hands and feet (number twenty). । 60 । In the digits there are sixty joints. । 61 । There are two bones in the two heels; 62 । Four, in the ankles; । 63 । Four, in the two forearms; । 64 । Four, in the two legs; । 65 । Two each, in the knees and elbows; । 66 । And in the thighs and shoulders; । 67 । And in the collar-bones, palate, and hip-blades. । 68 । There is one pubic bone. । 69 । The backbone consists of forty-five parts. । 70 । The neck has fifteen bones. । 71 । The windpipe has one bone; । 72 । So also the chin. । 73 । Its bases number two. । 74 । So do the brows, eyes, and cheeks. । 75 । The nose consists of the *ghana*-bone. । 76 । Together with the tubercles and sockets the ribs number seventy-two. । 77 । The breast has seventeen bones. । 78 । There are two temples. । 79 । And there are four pan-shaped bones in the cranium.

§ 85. *The Commentary of Nanda Paṇḍita*

The commentary of Nanda Paṇḍita, called *Vaijayantī*, is edited from the following manuscripts:

1. ASB[3] = Asiatic Society of Bengal, No. I B 25.
2. C[2] = Calcutta Sanskrit College, No. 62.
3. E[2] = Elphinstone College, Bombay, No. 174.

[1] ASB[1.3] jānv≠ekam; C[1] jānukam; IO[3] jatrukam.

[2] C[1] lalāṭākṣiṇī mate; IO[2] lalakṣiṭāṇigate; IO[3] lalāṭākṣiṇīgate; M lalakṣiyaṇigate.

[3] ASB[3] nāsā sthānāsthikā; C[1] nāsāyām≠asthikā; IO[2] nāsā gramasthikā; IO[3] nāsā vāmasthikā; M nāsā gnamasthikā.

[4] C[1] etakāḍakyaḥ; IO[2] M kā uraḥ; IO[3] eḍakāḍakyaḥ.

4. IO[1] = India Office, No. 200.
5. IO[4] = „ „ No. 915.
6. IO[5] = „ „ No. 1545.

It runs as follows:

[55] Aṅga-pratyaṅga-saṁsthitānāṁ sthūla-sūkṣmāṇām≠asthnāṁ trīṇi śatāni ṣaṣṭiś≠ca saṁkhyā । taiḥ śarīraṁ dhāryate । nanv≠anyāny≠apy≠agre gaṇanīyāni, tat≠katham≠iyaṁ saṁkhyā, ity≠atra āha ॥

[56] vakṣyamāṇo vibhāgas≠teṣām≠eva avadheyo n≠ātiriktānām ॥

[57] Sūkṣmāṇi danta-mūla-bhūtāny≠asthīni sthāl-ākhyāni dvātriṁśat । tavanta eva tad-utpannā dantās≠taiḥ saha catuḥṣaṣṭir≠bhavanti । sthālaiḥ saha catuḥṣaṣṭir≠dantā iti Yogi-smaraṇāt ॥

[58] hasta-pāda-sthā nakhā viṁśatiḥ ॥

[59] kara-pādayoḥ pṛṣṭhe śalāk-ākārāṇy≠aṅguli-mūla-bhūtāni viṁśatir≠eva asthīni ॥

[60] pratyekaṁ viṁśaty≠aṅgulīnāṁ trīṇi trīṇi parvāṇi । ity≠evaṁ ṣaṣṭiḥ parv-āsthīni ॥

[61] pārṣṇiḥ pāṇi-pāda-paścādbhāgas≠tayor≠asthinī dve ॥

[62] gulphau ghuṭike, jaṅghā-pāda-granthitau ca । pratyekaṁ pādayor≠dvau dvāv≠ity≠evaṁ catvāro gulphās≠teṣu catvāry≠asthīni ॥

[63] aratnir≠aratnimān bāhus≠tatra pratyekaṁ dve dve ity≠evaṁ catvāri ॥

[64] jaṅghā jaṅghāvān pādaḥ । tayoḥ pratyekaṁ dve dve ity≠evaṁ catvāri ॥

[65] jaṅgh-oru-sandhir≠jānuḥ । kapolo gaṇḍas≠tayoḥ pratyekaṁ dve dve ity≠evaṁ catvāri ॥

[66] ūrū sakthinī । aṁsau bhuja-śirasī । tayoḥ pratyekaṁ dve dve ity≠evaṁ catvāri ॥

[67] akṣaḥ karṇa-netrayor≠madhya-bhavaḥ śaṅkh-ādhobhāgaḥ । tālūṣakaṁ kākudam । śroṇiphalakaṁ kaṭiḥ । eteṣu triṣv≠api pratyekaṁ dve dve ity≠evaṁ ṣaṭ ॥

[68] bhaga upasthas≠tatr≠aikam≠asthi ॥

[69] pṛṣṭha-āsthi pṛṣṭha-vaṁśo 'pi pañcacatvāriṁśad-asthikaḥ ॥

[70] grīvā śiro-dharā । tasyāṁ pañcadaś≠āsthīni ॥

[71] vakṣo-'ṁsayoḥ sandhir⸗jatru । tayoḥ pratyekam⸗ekaikam⸗ evaṁ dve jatruṇī ॥

[72] hanuś⸗cibukam । tatr⸗aikam⸗asthi ॥

[73] tasyā hanor⸗mūla-bhūte dve asthinī ॥

[74] lalāṭaṁ bhālam । akṣi cakṣuḥ । gaṇḍaḥ kapol-ākṣayor⸗ madhya-bhāgas⸗teṣāṁ samāhāro lalāṭ-ākṣi-gaṇḍam । tatra pratyekaṁ dve dve asthinī ity⸗evaṁ ṣaṭ ॥

[75] nāsā nāsikā । sā ca ghana-saṁjñ⸗aik-āsthimatī ॥

[76] pārśvakāḥ vaṅkrayaḥ । pratyekaṁ pārśvayos⸗trayodaśa trayodaśa iti ṣaḍviṁśatiḥ । tāsāṁ vakṣasi sandhy-asthīny⸗arbudāny⸗ubhayato daśa daśa iti viṁśatiḥ । saṇṇāṁ pārśvakāṇāṁ paraspar-ādhāratayā ev⸗āvasthānen⸗ārbud-ānapekṣatvāt । tāsām⸗ eva pṛṣṭhataḥ sandhy-asthīni sthālakā ubhayatas⸗trayodaśa iti ṣaḍviṁśatir⸗ity⸗evaṁ sthālak-ārbuda-saṁhitāḥ pārśvakā dvisaptatiḥ ॥

[77] uro vakṣas⸗tat⸗saptadaś-āsthikam ॥

[78] bhrū-karṇayor⸗antarvartinī asthinī śaṅkhakau dvau ॥

[79] śirasaś⸗catvāri kapālāni । ca-kāraḥ samuccitānām⸗uktasaṁkhyā-pūrakatva-dyotan-ārthaḥ । iti vibhāga-samāsau ॥

Translation.

[55] The number of the bones, large and minute, which constitute the major and minor limbs, is three hundred and sixty. They uphold the body. In the following clauses the author shows how they are to be counted.

[56] The details given below refer to them only, and not to any others.

[57] The minute bones (*sūkṣma*) which form the bases of the teeth, and which are called sockets (*sthāla*), number thirty-two. The teeth (*danta*), set in them, number as many. Both together number sixty-four. 'Together with the sockets the teeth number sixty-four'—such is the traditional teaching of the Yogin[1] (see § 77).

[58] The nails (*nakha*), set in the hands and feet, number twenty.

[59] The pencil-like (*śalākā*) bones in the back of the hands and feet, which form the bases of the digits, number twenty.

[1] Yogin is one of the names of Yājnavalkya.

[60] In each of the twenty digits (*aṅguli*) there are three joints; thus we have sixty joint-bones.

[61] The heel (*pārṣṇi*) is the posterior portion of the hands and feet. Their bones number two.

[62] *Gulpha* signifies the two ankles which knit together the leg and the foot. In each foot there are two of these. Thus there are four ankles, and in them there are four bones.

[63] *Aratni* signifies the whole arm (*bāhu*) or upper limb, inclusive of the forearm. In each of these there are two bones; hence there are altogether four bones.

[64] *Jaṅghā* signifies the whole foot (*pāda*), or lower limb. In each of these there are two bones; hence there are altogether four bones.

[65] The knee (*jānu*) is the joint of the leg and thigh. *Kapola* signifies the cheek. In each there are two bones. Hence there are altogether four bones.

[66] *Ūru* signifies the thigh; the shoulder (*aṁsa*) is the head of the arm. In each of these there are two bones. Hence there are altogether four bones.

[67] *Akṣa* signifies the lower portion of the temples, situated between the ear and the eye. *Tālūṣaka* signifies the hard palate, and *śroṇiphalaka*, the hip. In each of these three there are two bones. Hence there are altogether six bones.

[68] *Bhaga* signifies the generative organ. In this there is one bone.

[69] The back (*pṛṣṭha*) or vertebral column is composed of forty-five bones.

[70] The neck (*grīvā*) is the organ which supports the head. In it there are fifteen bones.

[71] *Jatru* signifies the junction of the breast and the shoulder. In either of the two (junctions) there is one bone. Hence there are two *jatru*, or collar-bones.

[72] *Hanu* signifies the chin. In it there is one bone.

[73] At the base of the chin (*hanu-mūla*) there are two bones.

[74] *Lalāṭa* signifies the forehead or brow; *akṣi*, the eye; and *gaṇḍa*, the part intermediate between the cheek and the eye. Their combination is expressed by the compound term *lalāṭ-*

ākṣi-gaṇḍa. In each of them there are two bones. Hence there are altogether six bones.

[75] *Nāsā* signifies the nose. It is also termed the *ghana*-bone, and it contains one bone.

[76] *Pārśvaka* signifies the ribs. On either of the two sides of the body there are thirteen ribs, that is, altogether twenty-six. On either side are ten *arbuda*, or bones which join them to the breast-bone, that is, altogether twenty. As to six ribs, they mutually support one another without any reference to any *arbuda*. On either side, also, there are thirteen *sthālaka*, or bones which connect the ribs with the back-bone, that is, altogether twenty-six. In this way, the ribs, together with the *sthālaka* and *arbuda*, number seventy-two.

[77] *Uras* signifies the breast; that consists of seventeen bones.

[78] The temples (*śaṅkhaka*), or the bones which are situated between the eyebrows and the ears, number two.

[79] In the cranium there are four pan-shaped (*kapāla*) bones. The object of the word 'and' is to make clear that the bones, when added together, make up the total number (360) previously stated. Thus the bones have now been stated both in detail and in the aggregate.

§ 86. *The Non-medical Version in the Purānas*

The recensions of the Non-medical Version in the Agni Purāna, and in the Vishnu Dharmottara Purāna are identical. The former is edited from (1) IO = India Office MS., No. 5 (7) of the Surindra Mohun Collection; (2) RM = Rajendra Mitra's edition, vol. III, pp. 308–9. The latter is edited from T = Tübingen University Library MS., M. a. I. 483.

They run as follows:

Asthnām≠atra śatāni syus≠trīṇi ṣaṣṭy-adhikāni ca [1] ॥ 27 ॥
Sūkṣmaiḥ saha catuḥṣaṣṭir≠daśanā viṁśatir≠nakhāḥ ।
pāṇi-pāda-śalākāś≠ca tāsāṁ sthāna-catuṣṭayam ॥ 28 ॥
Ṣaṣṭy≠aṅgulīnāṁ dve pārṣṇyor≠gulpheṣu ca catuṣṭayam ।

[1] IO, RM read only a half-verse: asthi-ṣaṣṭi-śata-trayam.

catvāry≠aratnyor≠asthīni jaṅghayos≠tāvad≠eva tu ‖ 29 ‖
Dve dve jānu-kapol-oruphalak-āṁsasamudbhave ।
akṣa-tālūṣake[1] śroṇiphalake c≠aivam≠ādiśet ‖ 30 ‖
Bhag-āsthy≠ekaṁ[2] tathā pṛṣṭhe catvāriṁśac≠ca pañcakam ।
grīvā pañcadaś≠āsthīni[3] jatrv≠ekaṁ ca[4] tathā hanuḥ[5] ‖ 31 ‖
Tan-mūle dve lalāṭ-ākṣi-gaṇḍe nāsā ghan-āsthikā[6] ।
parśukāḥ sthālakaiḥ sārdham≠arbudaiś≠ca dvisaptatiḥ ‖ 32 ‖
Dve śaṅkhake[7] kapālāni catvāry≠eva śiras≠tathā ।
uraḥ saptadaś≠āsthīni puruṣasy≠āsthi-saṁgrahaḥ[8] ‖ 33 ‖

Translation.

[Verse 27.] There are three hundred and sixty bones.

[Verse 28.] Together with the minute bones (*sūkṣma*), the teeth (*daśana*) number sixty-four ; the nails (*nakha*) twenty ; so also the long bones (*śalākā*) of the hands and feet ; their bases (*sthāna*) are four.

[Verse 29.] In the digits (*aṅguli*) there are sixty bones ; in the two heels (*pārṣṇi*) two ; in the ankles (*gulpha*) four ; in the two forearms (*aratni*) four ; also as many in the two legs (*jaṅgha*).

[Verse 30.] There are two bones each in the knees (*jānu*), cheeks (*kapola*), thighs (*ūruphalaka*), and shoulder-blades (*aṁsa-samudbhava*). Also as many are indicated in the collar-bones (*akṣa*), palatal cavities (*tālūṣaka*), and hips (*śroṇi-phalaka*).

[Verse 31.] There is one pubic bone (*bhagāsthi*), and there are forty-five bones in the back (*pṛṣṭha*). The neck (*grīvā*) contains fifteen bones, the windpipe (*jatru*) one ; so also the chin (*hanu*).

[Verse 32.] At the base of the chin (*hanu-mūla*) there are two bones ; so also in the brows (*lalāṭa*), eyes (*akṣi*) and cheeks (*gaṇḍa*). The nose (*nāsā*) consists of the *ghana*-bone. The ribs,

[1] IO sthānopakā, RM sthānāṁsake ; T akṣi-sthāne kaṭī yoni-phalake.

[2] T bhage tv≠ekam.

[3] IO grīvā pañca tath≠āsthīni ; RM grīvāyāṁ ca tath≠asthīni ; T grīvāyāṁ ca daś-āsthīni.

[4] IO, RM jatrukaṁ ca ; T jatrv≠asthy≠ekam.

[5] T hanoḥ.

[6] IO, RM nās≠āṅghry-avasthitāḥ ; T nāsā-samāsthitā.

[7] T dvau śaṅkhakau.

[8] IO, RM om. puruṣasy≠āsthi-saṁgrahaḥ.

together with their sockets (*sthālaka*) and tubercles (*arbuda*), number seventy-two.

[Verse 33.] There are two temples (*śaṅkhaka*); there are also four pan-shaped bones (*kapāla*) in the cranium. The breast (*uras*) contains seventeen bones. These are the bones of the human skeleton.

§ 87. *The Non-medical Version in the 'Anatomy'*

The recension of the Non-medical Version in the anonymous 'Anatomy' (§ 23), edited from the Tübingen (T) University Library MS., M. a. I. 483 (Catalogue No. 167), fol. 5 *b*, runs as follows:—

Ṣaḍ≠aṅgāni śarīrāṇi । . . . . । \
ṣaṣṭiḥ śata-trayaṁ c≠āsthnām । . . . . [1] ॥ 127 ॥

Tad-yathā । dvau bāhū dve sakthinī, śiro madhyam≠iti ṣaḍ-aṅgam ॥ ṣaṣṭiḥ śata-trayaṁ c≠āsthnām≠iti [2] ॥

Dantā dvātriṁśad≠ākhyātāḥ s-olūkā, viṁśatir≠nakhāḥ । \
pāṇi-pāda-śalākāś≠ca, tāsāṁ sthāna-catuṣṭayam ॥ 128 ॥

Ṣaṣṭy≠aṅgulīnāṁ, dve pārṣṇyor≠gulpheṣu ca catuṣṭayam । \
catvāry≠aratnik-āsthīni, jaṅghāyās≠tāvad≠eva tu ॥ 129 ॥

Dvāv≠aṁsāv≠aṁsaphalake dve, hasta-maṇikāv≠ubhau । \
dvau bāhu-nalakāv≠ūru-nalakau, dve ca tāluni [3] ॥ 130 ॥

Netre dve, jānunī dve ca, dve ca jānu-kapālike । \
dve śroṇiphalake, dve ca hanu-mūlasya bandhane [3] ॥ 131 ॥

Bhage tv≠ekaṁ, tathā pṛṣṭhe catvāriṁśac≠ca pañcakam । \
grīvāyāṁ ca daś≠āsthīni, jatrv≠ekaṁ tu, tathā hanuḥ ॥ 132 ॥

Tadvan≠mukhe mataṁ nāsā-gaṇḍakūṭa-lalāṭakam । \
pārśvakāḥ kaulakaiḥ sārdhaṁ arbudaiś≠ca [4] dvisaptatiḥ ॥ 133 ॥

Dvau śaṅkhakau, kapālāni catvāri śirasas≠tathā । \
uraḥ saptadaś-āsth≠īti [5] puraṣasy≠āsthi-saṁgrahaḥ ॥ 134 ॥

[1] Two half-verses of the text, respecting the number of skins and muscles, are omitted.

[2] This clause is a commentary in prose on the preceding verse.

[3] Verses 130 and 131 are a recast of verse 87 of the recension of Yājnavalkya (§ 77).

[4] MS. arbudais≠tu.

[5] MS. āsthīni.

Translation.

[Verse 127.] The bodies consist of six parts . . . . . ; the number of bones is three hundred and sixty. . . . . .

[Commentary.] As thus: the two upper extremities, the two lower extremities, the head, and the trunk,—these are the six parts. The three hundred and sixty bones are as follows:

[Verse 128.] The thirty-two teeth (*danta*) are enumerated along with their sockets (*ulūka*); the nails (*nakha*) number twenty; so also the long bones (*śalākā*) of the hands and feet; their bases (*sthāna*) are four.

[Verse 129.] There are sixty bones in the digits (*aṅguli*); two in the heels (*pārṣṇi*), and four in the ankles (*gulpha*). There are four bones in the forearms (*aratnikā*), and there are as many in the legs (*jaṅghā*).

[Verse 130.] There are two collar-bones (*aṁsa*), two shoulder-blades (*aṁsa-phalaka*), two wrist-bones (*maṇika*) in either hand, two hollow bones of the arm (*bāhu*), two hollow bones of the thigh (*ūru*), and two palates (*tālu*).

[Verse 131.] There are two eyes (*netra*), two knee-caps (*jānu*), as well as two elbow-pans (*kapālikā*), two hip-blades (*śroṇiphalaka*), and two tie-bones at the base of the (lower) jaw (*hanu-mūla*).

[Verse 132.] There is one bone in the pubes (*bhaga*); also there are forty and five bones in the back (*pṛṣṭha*), as well as ten in the neck (*grīvā*). The windpipe (*jatru*) consists of one bone; so also the (lower) jaw (*hanu*).

[Verse 133.] Likewise in the face there is considered to be one bone consisting of the nose (*nāsā*), the prominences of the cheeks (*gaṇḍakūṭa*), and the brows (*lalāṭa*). The ribs (*pārśvaka*), together with their sockets (*kaulaka*[1]) and tubercles (*arbuda*), number seventy-two.

[Verse 134.] There are two temples (*śaṅkhaka*); also there are four pan-shaped (*kapāla*) bones of the cranium. The breast (*uras*) consists of seventeen bones. This is the aggregate of the bones of man.

[1] Probably false reading for *kolaka*, diminutive of *kola*, flank. *Kolaka* would mean a small flank, or side-bone, and would be a good term for the transverse process of a vertebra.

B. The System of Suśruta

§ 88. *The Traditional Recension of Suśruta's System*

The traditional recension of the System of Suśruta is edited from the following materials:

1. A = Alwar Palace Library MS., No. 1703.
2. B = Benares Sanskrit College MS., No. 23 (old No. 64).
3. Bd[1] = Bodleian MS., No. 1092 (Hultzsch 349).
4. Bd[2] = " MS., No. 739 (Wilson 290).
5. D[1] = Deccan College MS., No. 224.
6. D[2] = " " MS., No. 466.
7. D[3] = " " MS., No. 948.
8. D[4] = " " MS., No. 949.
9. D[5] = " " MS., No. 956.
10. IO[1] = India Office MS., No. 72 *b* (Cat. No. 2645).
11. IO[2] = " " MS., No. 1842 (Cat. No. 2646).
12. EG = Edition of Madhusudan Gupta (Calcutta).
13. EJ = " of Jīvānanda (Calcutta).
14. EM = " of Madras.
15. EP = " of Prabhuram Jivanaram (Bombay).
16. CD = Commentary of Dallana.
17. CG = " of Gayadāsa.

It runs as follows:

Trīṇi sa-ṣaṣṭiny[1]≠asthi-śatāni veda-vādino bhāṣante ı śalya-tantre tu [2] trīṇy≠eva śatāni [3] ı teṣāṁ sa-viṁśam[4]≠asthi-śataṁ śākhāsu ı saptadaś≠ottaraṁ śataṁ śroṇi-pārśva-pṛṣṭh-odar-orassu [5] ı grīvāṁ [6] praty-ūrdhvaṁ triṣaṣṭiḥ ı [7] evam≠asthnāṁ trīṇi śatāni pūryante ıı [8] Ekaikasyāṁ tu pād-āṅgulyāṁ trīṇi trīṇi, tāni pañcadaśa ı tala-kūrca-gulpha[9]-saṁśritāni daśa ı pārṣṇyāṁ≠

[1] So Bd[2], EJ, EM, EP; but A, EG sa-ṣaṣṭāny; B sa-ṣaṣṭyāny; D[5] IO[2] ṣaṣṭy-adhikāni; Bd[1] D[4] IO[1] only ṣaṣṭāny; D[2.3] only ṣaṣṭy.

[2] D[2.3.4.6] om. tu; D[5] IO[2] tantreṣu.

[3] B, D[1], D[2.3.4] asthi-śatāni.

[4] Bd[1] viṁśottaram.

[5] B odarossu; so also originally IO[1]; IO[2] reads śroṇi-pṛṣṭha-pārśv-oro-kṣassu for °oro-'kṣeṣu or °pārśv-ākṣ-orassu.

[6] A grīvāyāṁ.

[7] B, Bd[2], D[1.5], IO[1.2] om. this clause.

[8] A prefixes pṛthak-pṛthag-gaṇanā.

[9] D[2.3.4.5], IO[1] tala-gulpha-kūrca; Bd[1] tala-tāla-kūrca-gulpha.

ekam[1] | jaṅghāyāṁ dve[2] | jānuny=ekam | ekam=ūrāv=iti triṁśat | evam[3]=ekasmin sakthni bhavanti | eten=etara-sakthi[4] bāhū ca vyākhyātau | śroṇyāṁ pañca, teṣāṁ bhaga-guda[5]-nitambeṣu catvāri, trika-saṁśritam=ekam | pārśve ṣaṭtriṁśat | evam[6]=ekasmin, dvitīye 'py=evam | pṛṣṭhe triṁśat | aṣṭāv=urasi | dve akṣaka-saṁjñe[7] | grīvāyāṁ nava[8] | kaṇṭhanāḍyāṁ catvāri | dve hanvoḥ[9] | dantā[10] dvātriṁśat | nāsāyāṁ trīṇi | ekaṁ tāluṇi | gaṇḍa-karṇa-śaṅkheṣv=ekaikam | ṣaṭ=śirasi ||

Immediately after the above-given Number-list follows the Class-list as follows:

Etāny=asthīni pañca-vidhāni bhavanti | tad=yathā | kapāla-rucaka-taruṇa-valaya-nalaka-saṁjñāni | teṣāṁ jānu-kūrpara[11]-nitamb-āṁsa=gaṇḍa-tālu-śaṅkha-vaṅkṣaṇamadhya[12]-śirassu kapālāni | daśanās=tu rucakāḥ | ghrāṇa-karṇa-grīv-ākṣikośeṣu taruṇāni | pāṇi-pāda-pārśva-pṛṣṭhodar-orassu[13] valayāni | śeṣāṇi nalaka-saṁjñāni ||

For the translation, see §§ 27 and 30.

§ 89. *Restored Recension*

The original form of the osteological summary of Suśruta may be restored as follows, differences from the traditional recension being shown in *italics*:—

Trīṇi sa-ṣaṣṭiny=asthi-śatāni vedavādino bhāṣante | śalya-tantre tu trīṇy=eva śatāni | teṣāṁ *ṣaḍ-uttaram*=asthi-śataṁ śākhāsu | *aṣṭāviṁśaty*-uttaraṁ śataṁ śroṇi-pārsva-pṛṣṭh-*āṁs*-orassu | grīvāṁ praty-ūrdhvaṁ *ṣaṭṣaṣṭiḥ* | evam=asthnāṁ trīṇi śatāni pūryante || Ekaikasyāṁ tu pād-aṅgulyāṁ trīṇi trīṇi, tāni pañca | tala-gulpha-kūrca-saṁśritāni *sapta* | pārṣṇyām=ekam | jaṅghā-

[1] D[5] ekaikam. [2] D[2] dve dve, D[1] jaṅghayor=dve.
[3] A eva. [4] A etara-sakthni, Bd[1] etare sakthni.
[5] A, EG, EJ, EP, CD, CG guda-bhaga.
[6] B, D[3.4] om. evam. [7] B akṣa-saṁjñe.
[8] A, IO[1], EG, EJ, EM, EP navakam.
[9] B hane, IO[2] hano. [10] Bd[1] dantanteṣu.
[11] So B, IO[2]; but Bd[1.2] D[1.2.3.4.5] IO[1], EG, EJ, EM, EP om. kūrpara.
[12] So B, D[1]; but IO[1.2] om. vaṅkṣaṇa, while A, Bd[1.2], D[2.3.4.5], EG, EJ, EM, EP om. vaṅkṣaṇamadhya.
[13] So B, Bd[1.2], D[3], IO[1], EG, EJ, EM, EP; but D[1.2] pṛṣṭh-odaraḥsu; D[4] IO[2] pṛṣṭh-odareṣu; D[5] pṛṣṭh-odarissu.

yāṁ dve । jānuny⸗ekam । ekam⸗ūrāv⸗iti *saptaviṁśatiḥ* । evam⸗ekasmin⸗sakthni bhavanti । eten⸗etara-sakthi, bāhū ca vyākhyātau । śroṇyāṁ pañca, teṣāṁ bhāga-guda-nitambeṣu catvāri, trika-saṁśritam⸗ekam । pārśve ṣaṭtriṁśat । evam⸗ekasmin⸗dvitīye 'py⸗evam । pṛṣṭhe triṁśat । *saptadaś*⸗orasi । dve *akṣak-āṁsaje* । grīvāyāṁ nava । kaṇṭhanāḍyāṁ catvāri । dve hanvoḥ । dantā dvātriṁśat । nāsāyāṁ trīṇi । *dve* tāluni । gaṇḍ-ākṣikoṣa-karṇa-śaṅkheṣv⸗ekaikam । ṣaṭ⸗śirasi ॥

Etāny⸗asthīni pañcā-vidhāni bhavanti । tad-yathā । kapāla-rucaka-taruṇa-valaya-nalaka-saṁjñāni । teṣāṁ jānu-kūrpara-nitamb-*āṁsaja*-gaṇḍa-tālu-śaṅkha-vaṅkṣaṇamadhya-śirassu kapālāni । daśanās⸗tu rucakāḥ । ghrāṇa-karṇa-grīv-ākṣikośeṣu taruṇāni । pāṇi-pāda-pārśva-pṛṣṭh-odar-orassu valayāni । śeṣāṇi nalaka-saṁjñāni bhavanti ॥

For the translation, see §§ 30 and 34.

§ 90. *The Recension of Gangādhar*

Gangādhar's recension of the osteological summary of Suśruta, extracted from his Berhampore edition of the *Caraka Saṁhitā*, p. 188, ll. 5–14, runs as follows, differences from the traditional recension being shown in *italics* :—

Atha punaḥ Sauśrute śalya-tantre tu trīṇy⸗eva śatāni । teṣām⸗*aṣṭottara*-śataṁ śākhāsu । *ṣaḍviṁśaty*-uttara-śataṁ śroṇi-pārśva-pṛṣṭh-*ākṣ*-oraḥsu । grīvāṁ praty-ūrdhvaṁ *ṣaṭṣaṣṭiḥ* । evam⸗asthnāṁ trīṇi śatāni pūryante ॥ Ekaikasyāṁ tu pād-āṅgulyāṁ trīṇi trīṇi, tāni pañcadaśa । tala-kūrca-gulpha-saṁśritāni *sapta* । pārṣṇāv⸗ekam । jaṅghāyāṁ dve । jānuny⸗ekam । ekam⸗ūrāv⸗iti *saptaviṁśatir*⸗ekasmin sakthni bhavanti । eten⸗etara-sakthi, bāhū ca vyākhyātau । *tāny⸗aṣṭ-ottara-śatam⸗asthnām* । śroṇyāṁ pañca, teṣāṁ dve nitambe, guda-bhaga-trika-saṁśritam⸗ekaikaṁ । pārśve ṣaṭtriṁśat । evam⸗ekasmin⸗dvitīye 'py⸗evam । pṛṣṭhe triṁśat । dve akṣa-saṁjñe । *saptadaś*⸗orasi । grīvāyām⸗*ekādaśa* । kaṇṭhanāḍyāṁ catvāri । dve hanvoḥ । dantā dvātriṁśat । nāsāyāṁ trīṇi । *dve* tāluni । gaṇḍa-karṇa-śaṅkheṣv⸗ekaikaṁ, tāni ṣaṭ । ṣaṭ⸗śirasi ॥

For the translation, see § 35.

§ 91. *The Systems of Suśruta in the Śārīra Padminī*

1. The statement of the system of Suśruta in the *Śārīra Padminī*, and its commentary, edited from a manuscript in the possession of Dr. P. Cordier, runs as follows:

Kīkasaṁ tri-śata-saṁkhyam≠ath≠ādyaiś≠śalya-tantra upayuktam≠ ih≠oktam ।
viṁśatiś≠ca śatam≠apy≠adhi-śākhaṁ śroṇi-pārśva udar-orasi pṛṣṭhe ॥ 70 ॥
Sapta-yukta-daśa-śataṁ syāt [1] try-uttar-opari śirodhiṣu ṣaṣṭiḥ ।
aṅka-saṁkalanatas≠triśat≠ītthaṁ pañcadh≠ākṛti-bhidā punar≠ etat ॥ 71 ॥

For the translation, see § 36.

2. The commentary of Vaidyanātha, called *Padminī Prabodha*, on the above-given statement runs as follows:

Śarīre 'sthnāṁ sāra-bhūtatayā tad-vivaraṇam≠āha 'kīkasam' ity≠ādi । 'kīkasam'≠asthi 'tri-śata-saṁkhyam' āhuḥ 'śalya-tantra' upayoga-vaśena śalya-tantra upayuktatvād≠ity≠arthaḥ । tad-upayuktatā tu granth-āntarāj≠jñeyā । kathaṁ tri-śata-saṁkhyaṁ bhavati ity≠āha 'viṁśatir' ity-ādi । 'adhi-śākhaṁ' sarva-śākhāsu 'viṁśatiś≠ca śatam≠api' । yathā । pratyekaṁ pād-āṅgulyāṁ trīṇi trīṇi iti pañcadaśa । 30 । tala[2]-gulpha-kūrca-saṁśritāni daśa । 20 । 50 । jaṅghayor≠dve । 4 । 54 । pārṣṇāv≠ekam । 2 । 56 । jānuny≠ekam । 2 । 58 । ūrāv≠ekam । 2 । 60 । sakthnoḥ ṣaṣṭiḥ । 120 [3] ॥ 'śroṇi-pārśva udar-orasi pṛṣṭhe sapta-yukta-daśa-śatam' । yathā । guda-bhagayor≠ dve । 2 । nitambayor≠dve । 2 । trika-saṁśritam≠ekam । 1 । śroṇyāṁ pañca । 5 । pārśvayor≠dvisaptatiḥ । 72 । 77 । pṛṣṭhe triṁśat । 30 । 107 । dve akṣa-saṁsakte । 2 । 109 । aṣṭāv≠urasi । 8 । 117 ॥ evam 'upari śirodhiṣu' । grīvāṁ praty-ūrdhvaṁ 'try≠uttarā ṣaṣṭiḥ' । yathā । grīvāyāṁ nava । 9 । kaṇṭhanāḍyāṁ catvāri । 4 । 13 । dve hanvoḥ । 2 । 15 । nāsāyāṁ trīṇi । 3 । 18 । ekaṁ tāluni । 1 । 19 । gaṇḍa-karṇa-śaṅkheṣv≠ekaikaṁ । 6 । 25 । ṣaṭ śirasi । 6 । 31 । dvātriṁśad≠ dantāḥ । 32 । 63 । 'Ittham≠aṅka≠saṁkalanatas≠triśatī' । yathā । 120 । 117 । 63 । 300 ॥

[1] Short by two instants.
[2] MS. om. tala.
[3] See Note below.

Note: In the original manuscript, the clauses, which refer to the first aggregate 120, run as follows:

yathā । pratyekaṁ pād-āṅgulyāṁ trīṇi trīṇi iti pañcadaśa । 30 । gulpha-kūrca=saṁśritāni daśa । 10 । 50 । jaṅghayor=dve । 2 । 52 । pārṣṇāv=ekaṁ । 1 । 53 । jānuny=ekaṁ । 1 । 54 । ūrāv=ekaṁ । 55 । sakthnoḥ ṣaṣṭiḥ । 60 । 115 । guda-bhagayor=dve । 2 । 117 । nitambayor=dve । 2 । 119 । trika-saṁśritam=ekam । 1 । 120 ॥

Obviously this reading is quite absurd, and must be due to some ignorant copyist who failed to recognize the accidental misplacement of the three clauses: *guda-bhagayor=dve*, *nitambayor=dve*, and *trika-saṁśritam=ekam*, which should not precede, but follow the clause *śroṇi-pārśva*, &c.

Translation.

Because of the conciseness of the statement of the bones of the body, he makes the comment which begins with *kīkasa*, &c. '*Kīkasa*, or the bones of the skeleton, number three hundred'; this is said on the authority of the count in surgical text-books; for this is meant by the phrase 'in accordance with the count in the Surgical Text-book'. But that count itself must be learned from treatises other (than the *Śārīra Padminī*). In order to explain how the number three hundred arises, he goes on to say '*viṁśati*, or twenty, &c.' '*Adhiśākham*, or in all the limbs together,' there are one hundred and twenty bones. As thus: in each digit of the foot there are three, making fifteen (i. e. 30 in both feet); in the sole, ankle, and cluster there are altogether ten (i. e. 20 in both feet; hence together 50). In the legs there are two (i. e. 4 in both legs; hence together 54). In the heel there is one (i. e. 2 in both heels; hence together 56). In the knee there is one (i. e. 2 in both knees; hence together 58). In the thigh there is one (i. e. 2 in both thighs; hence together 60). In either of the lower limbs there are sixty (i. e. altogether 120). 'In the hips, sides, abdomen, breast, and back, there are one hundred and seventeen bones.' As thus: In the anus and pubes there are two; in the hips, two; in the sacrum, one; hence in the pelvis there are together five. In the two sides there are seventy-two (i. e. together 77); in the back there are thirty (i. e. together 107); two are contained in the collar-bones

(i. e. together 109); in the breast there are eight (i. e. together 117). Further, 'above in the *śirodhi*, or head-holders,' that is, from the neck upwards, there are sixty-three bones. As thus: in the neck there are nine; in the windpipe, four (i. e. together 13); in the jaws, two (i. e. together 15); in the nose, three (i. e. together 18); in the palate, one (i. e. together 19); in either cheek, ear, and temple, one (i. e. 6, or altogether 25); in the cranium, six (i. e. together 31). The teeth number thirty-two (i. e. altogether 63). By adding up all these items we obtain three hundred; as thus, 120 + 117 + 63 = 300.

§ 92. *The Osteological Summary in the Bhāva Prakāṣa*

The statement of the osteological system of Suśruta in the *Bhāva Prakāśa*, extracted from the edition of Jīvānanda of 1875 (pp. 40, 41), runs as follows:

Śalya-tantre 'sthi-khaṇḍānāṁ śata-trayam≠udāhṛtam ı
tāny≠ev≠ātra nigadyante, teṣāṁ sthānāni yāni ca ıı
Sa-viṁśati-śataṁ tv≠asthnāṁ śākhāsu kathitaṁ budhaiḥ ı
pārśvayoḥ śroṇi-phalake vakṣaḥ-pṛṣṭh-odareṣu ca ıı
Jāniyād≠bhiṣag≠eteṣu śataṁ saptadaś-ottaram ı
grīvāyām≠ūrdhvagāṁ vidyād≠asthnāṁ ṣaṣṭiṁ tri-saṁyutām ıı

For the translation, see § 36.

C. The System of Vāgbhaṭa I

§ 93. *The Osteological System of Vāgbhaṭa I*

1. The statement of the osteological system of Vāgbhaṭa I, extracted from the *Aṣṭāṅga Saṁgraha* (Bombay edition, vol. I, p. 224, ll. 3–13), runs as follows:

Trīṇi ṣaṣṭy-adhikāny≠asthi-śatāni ı teṣāṁ catvāriṁśac≠chataṁ śākhāsu, sa-viṁśa-śatam≠antarādhau, śataṁ mūrdhani iti ıı Tatr≠aikaikasmin sakthini pañca pāda-nakhāḥ ı pratyekam≠aṅgulyāṁ trīṇy≠asthīni, tāni pañcadaśa ı pañca pāda-śalākāḥ ı tat-pratibandhakam≠ekam ı dve dve kūrca-gulpha-jaṅghāsu ı ekaikaṁ pārṣṇijān-ūruṣu ı sarvāṇi ca nakh-āsthy-ādīni sakthi-vad≠bāhvoś≠ca ı caturviṁśatiḥ parśukāḥ, tāvanty=eva tat-sthālakāny=arbudāni ca । triṁśat=pṛṣṭhe । aṣṭāv=urasi । ekaikaṁ bhage trike । nitambayoś=ca dve । tad-vad=akṣak-āṁs-āṁsaphalakeṣu । tathā gaṇḍa-karṇa-śaṅkheṣu jatru-tālunoś=ca । trayodaśa grīvāyām । catvāri kaṇṭhanāḍyām । dve hanu-bandhane । dvātriṁśad=dantāḥ । tad-vad=ulūkhalāni ca । trīṇi nāsāyām । ṣaṭ=śirasi ॥

2. Immediately after the above-given Number-list follows the Class-list (*ibidem*, ll. 13–16), which runs as follows:

Tāni jānu-kūrpara[1]-nitamb-āṁsa-gaṇḍa-tālu-śaṅkha-vaṅkṣaṇa-madhya-śirassu kapāla-saṁjñāni । daśanās=tu rucakāḥ । ghrāṇa-karṇa-grīv-akṣikośeṣu taruṇāni । pāṇi-pāda-pārśva-pṛṣṭh-odar-orassu [1] valayāni । śeṣāni nalakāni । iti nām-ānugat-ākṛtīni pañca-vidhāny=asthīni ॥

3. For the translation of the Number-list, see § 37. The Class-list may be translated as follows:

Those bones which occur in the knees, elbows, hips, shoulders, cheeks, palate, temples, interiliac space (i. e. sacrum), and cranium are termed pan-shaped. The teeth are sharp bones. Tender bones occur in the nose, ears, neck, and eye-balls. The bones in the hands, feet, sides, back, abdomen, and breast are ornament-shaped. The remaining bones are reed-shaped. These are the five classes of bones which take their names from their shapes.

D. Miscellaneous Texts

§ 94. *Suśruta and Vāgbhaṭa on the Muscles*

1. The statement of Suśruta on the number of the muscles, in *Śārīra Sthāna*, ch. V, cl. 33, referred to in § 40, and edited from Bd[1] (fol. 21 *b*), Bd[2] (fol. 20 *b*), IO[2] (fol. 24 *a*)[2], and EJ (p. 334), runs as follows:

[1] The Bombay edition omits *kūrpara*, as well as *udara* and *uras*; probably owing to defective manuscripts. The missing items are required by the context, as well as by the fact that the whole passage is obviously a copy from the statement (§ 88) in the Compendium of Suśruta.

[2] Unfortunately MS. IO[1] (fl. 18 *b*) is defective at this point, omitting the whole of the text from JE, p. 333, l. 11, to p. 334, l. 11.

Pañca peśī-śatāni bhavanti ı tāsāṁ catvāri śatāni śākhāsu ı koṣṭhe ṣaṭṣaṣṭiḥ ı grīvāṁ praty-ūrdhvaṁ catustriṁśat ॥

Translation.

There are five hundred muscles. Four hundred of them are in the (four) extremities. In the trunk there are sixty-six. Upwards from the neck there are thirty-four.

2. The statement in the commentary of Ḍallana, extracted from Jīvānanda's edition, p. 578, runs as follows:

'Pañca peśī-śatāni' ity-ādi ı māṁs-āvayava-saṁghātaḥ paras-paraṁ vibhaktaḥ peśī ity≠ucyate ı Gayī tu 'koṣṭhe ṣaṣṭiḥ ı grīvāṁ praty-ūrdhvaṁ catvāriṁśad'≠iti paṭhati ı . . . . . . ı vṛddha-Vāgbhaṭo 'pi koṣṭhe ṣaṣṭim≠ev≠āha ॥

Translation.

With reference to 'the five hundred muscles', the compact mass of flesh, when separated into its several strands, is called muscle. Gayī (or Gayadāsa), however, reads: 'in the trunk there are sixty; from the neck upwards there are forty.' . . . . . Vāgbhaṭa the elder, also, says that there are sixty in the trunk.

3. The statement of Vāgbhaṭa I, on the same subject, extracted from the Bombay edition, vol. I, p. 225, ll. 20, 21, runs as follows:

Pañca peśī-śatāni ı tāsāṁ catvāri śatāni śākhāsu ı ṣaṣṭir≠antar-ādhau ı catvāriṁśad≠ūrdhvam ॥

Translation.

There are five hundred muscles. Four hundred of them are in the (four) extremities. Sixty there are in the trunk; forty there are upwards (of it).

§ 95. *Statement of Suśruta on Dissection*

The statement on dissection in the Compendium of Suśruta, referred to in § 45, is edited from the following materials:

1. Bd[1] = Bodleian MS., No. 1092 (Hultzsch 349).
2. Bd[2] = „ MS., No. 739 (Wilson 290).

3. IO¹ = India Office MS., No. 72 *b* (Cat. No. 2645).
4. IO² = " " MS., No. 1842 (Cat. No. 2646).
5. EG = Edition of Mudhusudana Gupta (Calcutta).
6. EJ = " of Jīvānanda (1889, pp. 335–6).
7. EP = " of Prabhuram Jivanaram (Bombay).

It is translated in § 45, and runs as follows:

Tvak-paryantasya dehasya yo 'yam≠aṅga-viniścayaḥ ।
[1] śalya-jñānād≠ṛte [2] n≠aiṣa varṇyate 'ṅgeṣu keṣu-cit ॥ 43 ॥
Tasmān≠niḥsaṁśayaṁ jñānaṁ hartrā śalyasya vāñchatā [3] ।
śodhayitvā [4] mṛtaṁ samyag≠draṣṭavyo 'ṅga-viniścayaḥ ॥ 44 ॥
Pratyakṣato hi yad≠dṛṣṭaṁ śāstra-dṛṣṭaṁ ca yad≠bhavet ।
[5] samāsatas≠tad≠ubhayaṁ bhūyo jñāna-vivardhanam ॥ 45 ॥

Tasmāt≠samasta-gātram≠a-viṣ-opahatam≠[6]a-dīrgha-vyādhi-pīḍitam[7]≠a-varṣa-śatikaṁ niṣkṛṣṭ-āntra[8]-purīṣaṁ puruṣam≠a-vahantyām≠āpagāyāṁ nibaddhaṁ pañjara-sthaṁ [9] muñja-vaikala-kuśa-śaṇ-ādīnām≠anyatamena āveṣṭit-āṅgam[10]≠a-prakāśe deśe kothayet । samyak-prakuthitaṁ c≠oddhṛtya tato dehaṁ saptarātrād≠usīra-bāla-veṇu-valkala[11]-kūrcānām[12]≠anyatamena śanaiḥ śanair≠avaghṛṣya [13] tvag-ādīn≠sarvān≠eva vāhy-ābhyantar-āṅga-pratyaṅga-viśeṣān≠yath-oktān lakṣayec≠cakṣuṣā ॥

§ 96. *Suśruta on Homology*

1. The statement of Suśruta on homology in *Śārīra Sthāna*, ch. VI, cl. 29, referred to in § 28, and edited from Bd¹ (fol. 26 *a*), Bd² (fol. 25 *a*), IO¹ (fol. 22 *b*), IO² (fol. 30 *a*), and EJ (p. 341), runs as follows:

[1] IO¹ (fl. 19 *b*) om. verses 43*b*, 44*a*, *b*.
[2] IO² (fl. 25 *b*) jñān-oddhṛte.
[3] Bd², IO² jñānam≠icchatā śalya-jīvinā.
[4] Bd², IO² dhāvayitvā.
[5] IO¹ samāsena dvayaṁ tat≠tu tayor≠jñāna-vivardhanam; IO² samāgataṁ dvayaṁ cakṣu bhūyo-jñāna-vivardhanam.
[6] IO¹ adīrgham≠avyādhikaṁ, om. avarṣaśatikam.
[7] IO² inserts ahīnam after pīḍitam.
[8] So Bd², IO²; but EJ, EG niḥsṛṣṭāntra; IO¹ niḥkṛṣyāmbu, om. purīṣaṁ; EP niḥsṛṣṭa-mūtra.
[9] IO¹ pañjar-ākhyam.
[10] Bd² veṣṭit-āṅga-pratyaṅgam.
[11] Bd² valkaja.
[12] So IO¹·², but EG, EJ, EP kūcīnām.
[13] So IO¹·²; but BD² gharṣayan; EG, EJ, EP avagharṣayan.

Viśeṣatas≠tu yāni sakthni gulpha-jānu-viṭapāni, tāni bāhau maṇibandha-kūrpara-kakṣadharāṇi ı yathā vaṅkṣaṇa-vṛṣaṇayor[1]≠ antare viṭapam≠evaṁ vakṣaḥ-kakṣayor≠madhye kakṣadharam ıı

Translation.

In particular, just as there are in the leg (the three vital spots) ankle-bone, knee-cap, and ischio-pubic arch, so there are in the arm (the three) wrist-bone, elbow-pan, and collar-bone. Just as between the hip-bone and scrotum there is the ischio-pubic arch, so between the breast-bone and the arm-pit there is the clavicular arch.

Suśruta and Vāgbhaṭa on the Eyeball

2. The statement of Suśruta on the eyeball, in the *Uttara Tantra*, ch. I, verses 16 *b*, 17 *a*, referred to in § 30, and edited from IO[2] (fol. 3 *a*, v. 19 *b*, 20 *a*) and EJ (p. 659), runs as follows:

Tejojal-āśritaṁ bāhyaṁ teṣv≠anyat≠piśit-āśritam ı
Medas≠tṛtīyaṁ paṭalam≠aśritaṁ tv≠asthi c≠āparam ıı

Translation.

The outer-one of the protective covers of the pupil consists of a luminous fluid, and the next-one, of flesh. The third is made of fat, and the farther-one, of bone.

In the Summary of Vāgbhaṭa I (*Aṣṭāṅga Saṁgraha, Śārīra Sthāna*, ch. V, vol. I, p. 223, l. 10) the statement is as follows:

Bāhyaṁ c≠āśritam≠agny-ambhasī, dvitīyaṁ māṁsaṁ, tṛtīyaṁ medaś≠caturtham≠asthi ıı

Translation.

The outer-one consists of fire and water; the second, of flesh; the third, of fat; the fourth, of bone.

Bhoja on the Nalaka bones

3. The doctrine of Bhoja on the *nalaka*, or reed-like bones, as reported by Ḍallana (Jīv., p. 576) and Gayadāsa (Cambridge

[1] IO[2] vṛṣaṇa-vaṁkṣaṇayor.

MS., Add. 2491, fol. 49 *a*, l. 3), and referred to on p. 80, runs as follows:

Tad-uktaṁ Bhoje ।

Hasta-pād-āṅguli-tale kūrceṣu maṇi-gulphayoḥ ।
bāhu-jaṅghā-dvaye c≠āpi jānīyān≠nalakāni tu ॥

Translation.

In Bhoja's (treatise) this is said: 'The bones which are in the digits and flats of the hands and feet, in the clusters, in the wrists and ankles, and also in both the upper and lower limbs,—these one should know to be reed-like.'

The manuscripts read *maṇibandhayoḥ*; the reading *maṇi-gulphayoḥ* is a conjectural emendation, which is suggested by the fact that otherwise the statement of Bhoja would entirely ignore the ankle-bones (*gulpha*), which, as homologues of the wrist-bones (*maṇi* or *maṇibandha*), should by parity of reasoning be included in it. The dual of the MS. reading would have to be made to refer, not to the two wrists of the hands, but to the couple of organs consisting of the wrists and their homologues, the ankles, respectively—a very forced interpretation. In the term *bāhu-jaṅghā-dvaya*, *bāhu* denotes the whole upper limb, and *jaṅghā*, the whole lower limb, either of which consists of a couple (*dvaya*) of organs: arm, forearm, and thigh, leg.

Ḍallana on the Aggregate Ten

4. The statement of Ḍallana on the aggregate ten, referred to in § 31, and edited from D[4] (= Deccan College MS., No. 949, fol. 54 *a*), and Jīvānanda's edition, p. 576, runs as follows:

Tala-kūrca[1]-gulph-etyādi । kara-pāda-tale[2] pañca śalākāḥ । tat-prabandhanam≠ekam≠asthi । dve dve kūrca-gulphayor≠iti daśa ॥

Translation.

As to the phrase 'sole-cluster-ankle', &c., there are five long bones in the sole of the hand and of the foot, and there is a single bone which interlocks them. In each of the clusters

[1] D[4] om. kūrca. [2] So D[4]; Jīv. tale pāda-tale.

and ankles there are two bones. This makes altogether ten bones.

Suśruta and Vāgbhaṭa on the Number of Kūrca

5. The statement of Suśruta on the number of *kūrca*, cluster, in the *Śārīra Sthāna*, ch. V, cl. 10, referred to in § 31, and edited from Bd[1] (fol. 18 *b*), Bd[2] (fol. 18 *a*), IO[1] (fol. 17 *a*), IO[2] (fol. 21 *a*), and EJ (p. 330), runs as follows:

Ṣaṭ⸗kūrcāḥ ı te hasta-pāda-grīvā-meḍhreṣu ı [1]hastayor⸗dvau, pādayor dvau, grīvā[2]-meḍhrayor⸗ekaikaḥ ıı

Translation.

There are six clusters. They occur in the hands, feet, neck, and penis. In the two hands there are two; in the two feet there are two; there is one each in the neck and penis.

In the Summary of Vāgbhaṭa I (*Śārīra Sthāna*, ch. V, vol. I, p. 223, l. 21) the statement is as follows:

Ṣaṭ⸗kūrcā, hasta-pāda-grīvā-meḍhreṣu ıı

Suśruta and Vāgbhaṭa on the Number of Ankles, &c.

6. The statement of Suśruta on the number of ankle-bones, wrist-bones, and cluster-heads, in the *Śārīra Sthāna*, ch. VI, verse 19, referred to in § 31, and edited from Bd[1] (fol. 24 *a*), Bd[2] (fol. 23 *b*), IO[1] (fol. 21 *a*), IO[2] (fol. 28 *a*), and EJ (p. 338), runs as follows:

Gulphau dvau, maṇibandhau dvau, dve dve kūrca-śiraṁsi ca ı
ruja-karāṇi jānīyād⸗aṣṭāv⸗etāni buddhimān ıı 19 ıı

Translation.

There are two ankle-bones, two wrist-bones, and also two cluster-heads each (in the hands and feet). These eight an experienced (physician) should know to be exciters of disease.

In the Summary of Vāgbhaṭa I (*Śārīra Sthāna*, ch. VIII, vol. I, p. 236, l. 11) there is the following statement:

Gulphau maṇibandhau stana-mūle ca ṣaḍ⸗dvy-aṅgulāni ıı

[1] Bd[1], BD[2], IO[1] om. whole of third clause. [2] IO[2] om. grīvā.

Translation.

The two ankle-bones, the two wrist-bones, and the two areolae (lit., bases of the nipples)—these six are of the size of two *aṅgula*, or finger-breadths.

§ 97. *Suśruta on the Position of Cluster and Cluster-head*

1. The statement of Suśruta on the position of the cluster and of the cluster-head, in the *Śārīra Sthāna*, ch. VI, cl. 28, referred to in § 49, and edited from Bd[1] (fol. 25 *b*), Bd[2] (fol. 24 *b*), IO[1] (fol. 22 *a*), IO[2] (fol. 29 *b*), and EJ (p. 340), runs as follows:

Pādasy=āṅguṣṭh-āṅgulyor=madhye kṣipram=iti marma । kṣiprasy=opariṣṭād=ubhayataḥ kūrcaḥ [1] । gulpha-sandher=adho 'nubhayataḥ [2] kūrca-śiraḥ [1] ॥

Translation.

Between the great toe and the toe next to it, there lies the vital spot, called *kṣipra*. Upwards of this *kṣipra*, both ways (i.e. externally and internally), there lies the *kūrca*, or cluster. Below the ankle-joint, but not both ways, there lies the *kūrca-śiras*, or cluster-head (astragalus).

Ḍallana, Gangādhar and Nanda Paṇḍita on the Collar-bone

2. The statement of Ḍallana on the collar-bone, in his Commentary on Suśruta's Compendium, referred to in § 55, extracted from Jīvānanda's edition, pp. 663, 665, runs as follows:

Akṣakaḥ aṁsa-sandher=upariṣṭād=bhavati ॥ Akṣakaḥ aṁsa-sandher=uparibhāgaḥ ॥

Translation.

The *akṣaka*, or collar-bone, is located above the shoulder-joint. It is the upper part of the shoulder-joint.

Gangādhar's statement, in his commentary on the Compendium of Charaka, p. 187, l. 14, is as follows:

[1] Bd[1], Bd[2], EJ kūrco nāma, and kūrcaśiro nāma.

[2] So IO[1]; but IO[2] adhaḥ ubhayataḥ, Bd[1], Bd[2] only ubhayataḥ.

Dvāv⸗akṣakau kaṇṭhād⸗adho 'ṁsakau dvau ॥

Translation.

The two *akṣaka*, or collar-bones, are the shoulder-bones (which lie) below the throat.

Nanda Paṇḍita, in his commentary on the Institutes of Vishnu (Professor Jolly's ed., p. 197), has the following statement:

Akṣaḥ karṇa-netrayor⸗madhya-bhavaḥ śaṅkh-ādhobhāgaḥ.

Translation.

Akṣa is the lower portion of the temple which lies between the eye and the ear.

Suśruta and Vāgbhaṭa on the Position of the Scapula and Clavicle

3. The statement of Suśruta on the position of the shoulder-blade and collar-bone, in the *Śārīra Sthāna*, ch. VI, cl. 31, referred to in § 55, and edited from Bd[1] (fol. 26 *b*), Bd[2] (fol. 26 *a*), IO[1] (fol. 23 *a*), IO[2] (fol. 32 *b*), and EJ (p. 342), runs as follows:

Pṛṣṭh-opari pṛṣṭhavaṁśam⸗ubhayatas⸗trika-saṁbaddhe aṁsa-phalake nāma । bāhumūrdha-grīvā-madhye 'ṁsapīṭha-skandha-[1] nibandhanāv⸗aṁsau nāma ॥

Translation.

In the upper part of the back, on both sides of the vertebral column, there lie the two so-called shoulder-blades, being of triangular form. Between the head of the arms and the neck, there lie the two so-called collar-bones, connecting the shoulder-seat, or glenoid cavity, with the nape of the neck.

The comment of Ḍallana on the preceding statement, referred to in § 56, and extracted from Jīvānanda's edition, p. 588, runs as follows:

'Trika-saṁbaddhe' iti । grīvāyā aṁsa-dvayasya ca yaḥ saṁyogaḥ sa trikaḥ । tatra saṁbaddhe aṁsaphalake ॥

Translation.

Regarding the phrase *trika-saṁbaddha*, trebly joined, the place

[1] Bd[1] bandha.

where the two collar-bones connect with the neck, that is the *trika*, and in that place the (two) shoulder-blades are joined.

The same statement, as given in the Summary of Vāgbhaṭa I, *Śārīra Sthāna*, ch. VII, vol. I, p. 234, l. 9, referred to in § 56, runs as follows:

Pṛṣṭhavaṁsam≠ubhayato bāhumūla-saṁbaddhe aṁsaphalake ı grīvā-bāhuśiro-madhye 'ṁsapīṭha-skandha-bandhanāv≠aṁsau ıı

Translation.

On both sides of the vertebral column there are the two shoulder-blades, joined on to the base of the arms. Between the neck and the head of the arms there lie the two collar-bones, connecting the shoulder-seat, or glenoid cavity, with the nape of the neck.

Suśruta on the Number of the Scapula and Clavicle

4. The statements of Suśruta on the number of the shoulder-blades and collar-bones, in the *Śārīra Sthāna*, ch. V, cl. 34 and ch. VI, cl. 3, 11, 18, referred to in §§ 55 and 56, and edited from Bd[1] (fols. 21 *a*, 23 *a*, 23 *b*, 24 *a*), Bd[2] (fols. 20*b*, 22 *a*, 22 *b*, 23 *b*), IO[1] (fols. 18 *b*, 21 *a*), IO[2] (fols. 24 *a*, 26 *b*, 27 *a*, 28 *a*), and EJ (pp. 334, 336–8), runs as follows:

(1) Akṣak-āṁsau [1] prati samantāt≠sapta ıı 34 ıı

(2) [2]Aṣṭāv≠asthi-marmāṇi ıı 3 ıı kaṭīka-taruṇa-nitamb-āṁsa-phalaka-śaṅkhāsv≠asthi-marmāṇi ıı 11 ıı

(3) Aṁs-āṁsaphalak-āpāṅga-nīla-manye [3] phaṇau [4] tathā ıı 18 ıı

Translation.

(1) All round about the collar-bones and shoulder-blades there are seven (muscles).

(2) There are eight vital spots in the bones. These are, two each in the *kaṭīka-taruṇa*, the hips, the shoulder-blades, and the temples [5].

[1] Read akṣak-āṁsajau. [2] Bd[2] om. this clause.
[3] Bd[1], Bd[2], EJ nīle manye. [4] IO[2] phaṇe.
[5] The places referred to appear to be the attachment areas of the

(3) There are two (vital spots) each in the collar-bones, shoulder-blades, *apāṅga*, *nīla*, *manya*, and *phaṇa*.

Suśruta on Aṁsakūṭa

5. The statement of Suśruta on *aṁsakūṭa*, in the *Śārīra Sthāna*, ch. VI, cl. 30, referred to in § 55, and edited from Bd[1] (fol. 26 *b*), Bd[2] (fol. 26 *b*), IO[1] (fol. 23 *a*), IO[2] (fol. 31 *a*), and EJ (p. 341), runs as follows:

Aṁsakūṭayor=adhastāt=pārśv-oparibhāgayor=apalāpau nāma[1] ॥

Translation.

Below the two summits of the shoulder, in the upper part of the two sides (of the thoracic cage) there are two (vital spots) called *Apalāpa*.

Suśruta on Aṁsapīṭha

6. The statement of Suśruta on *aṁsapīṭha*, in the *Śārīra Sthāna*, ch. V, cl. 23, referred to in § 55, and edited from Bd[1] (fol. 20 *b*), Bd[2] (fol. 19 *b*), IO[1] (fol. 18 *a*), IO[2] (fol. 23 *a*), and EJ (p. 332), runs as follows:

Aṁsapīṭha-guda-bhaga[2]-nitambeṣu sāmudgāḥ ॥

Translation.

There are (two) casket-shaped (joints): (one is) the shoulder-seat (glenoid cavity), (the other is formed by) the anal, pubic, and hip-bones (acetabulum).

Rājanighaṇṭu and Amarakoṣa on Bhaga

7. The definition of *bhaga* in the *Rājanighaṇṭu*, referred to in p. 153, footnote 1, occurs in the Supplement (*pariśiṣṭa*) of that work, chap. xviii, verses 43 and 44 (Ānandāśrama ed., p. 399), runs as follows:

rotator muscles of the thighs about the ischio-pubic arch, of their flexor muscles in the ilium, of the rotator muscles of the arms, and of the temporal muscles of mastication.

[1] IO[1,2] apālāpau, om. nāma.

[2] Bd[2] pāda-guda-bhaga; Bd[1] pāda-guda and IO[1] guda-pāda, om. bhaga.

Guda-muṣkadvayor≠madhye puṁsām≠aṅgaṁ bhagaḥ smṛtaḥ
॥ . . . . . . 43 ॥

. . . . . । yonir≠bhago varāṅgaṁ syād≠upasthaṁ smara-mandiram ॥ 44 ॥

Translation.

[Verse 43.] The member of the male between the anus and the bipartite scrotum is known as *bhaga*.

[Verse 44.] The vulva is (called) *bhaga*, or *varāṅga* (lit. choice part), or *upastha* (underlying), or *smara-mandira* (lit. Cupid's shrine).

In the edition published by Ashu Bodha and Nitya Bodha Bhattacharjya (Calcutta, 1899), verse 43 (there numbered 72, p. 389) runs as follows:

Guda-muṣkadvayor≠madhye yo bhāgaḥ sa bhagaḥ smṛtaḥ ॥ 72 ॥

That is, That part which lies between the anus and the bipartite scrotum is known as *bhaga*.

In this reading there is no explicit mention of the male, but, of course, the reference to it is implied in the mention of the scrotum. The reading of the Ānandāśrama edition is supported by the Bodleian MS., No. 765 (Wilson, 297), fl. 106 *a*, l. 2.

The teaching of the *Amarakoṣa* on the subject occurs in its Section II, Chapter vi, verse 76 (in Dr. R. G. Bhandarkar's 5th ed., p. 150, Bombay, 1896), and runs as follows:

Bhagaṁ yonir≠dvayoḥ, śiśno meḍhro mehana-śephasī ॥

Translation.

The vulva (*yoni*) has also the other name *bhaga*, and the penis (*śephas*) or urinary organ (*mehana*) is (also called) urethra (*meḍhra*), and the 'piercer' (*śiśna*).

The manner in which the two words are contrasted is significant.

§ 98. *Suśruta and Vāgbhaṭa on Jatru and Grīvā*

1. The statements of Suśruta on *jatru*, windpipe, and *grīvā*, neck, in the *Śārīra Sthāna*, ch. VI, cl. 4, 32, referred to in § 62

(p. 160), and edited from IO[1] (fols. 20 *a*, 23 *b*, 24 *a*), IO[2] (fols. 26 *b*, 33 *a*, 34 *b*), and EJ (pp. 336, 342, 343), are as follows:

(1) Grīvāyāṁ [1] praty-ūrdhvaṁ saptatriṁśat ॥ 4 ॥

(2) Ata ūrdhvam[2]⸗ūrdhvajatru-gatāny⸗anuvyākhyāsyāmaḥ [3] । tatra kaṇṭhanāḍīm⸗ubhayataś⸗catasro dhamanyaḥ . . . . । grīvāyām⸗ubhayataś⸗catasraḥ sirāḥ . . . . . . evam⸗etāni saptatriṁśad⸗ūrdhvajatru-gatāni marmāṇi vyākhyātāni ॥ 32 ॥

Translation.

(1) In the neck and upwards there are thirty-seven (vital spots).

(2) Now, further on, we shall describe in detail (the vital spots) occurring from the neck upwards. In that region, in the windpipe there are four *dhamanī*, &c., and in the cervical column there are four blood-vessels, &c. . . . . . Thus, these thirty-seven vital spots which occur from the neck upwards have been described.

In the Compendium of Vāgbhaṭa II (*Aṣṭāṅga Hṛdaya*, *Śārīra Sthāna*, ch. IV, verse 2 *a*, in 1st ed., vol. I, p. 592) the first-quoted statement runs as follows:

Pṛṣṭhe caturdaś⸗ordhvaṁ tu jatros⸗triṁśac⸗ca sapta ca ॥

Translation.

In the back there are fourteen (vital spots); but from the neck upwards there are thirty and seven.

Suśruta, Vāgbhaṭa, and Mādhava on the Valmīka Disease

2. The statement of Suśruta on the *Valmīka* disease, in the *Nidāna Sthāna*, ch. XIII, verses 7, 8, referred to in § 62 (p. 161), and edited from IO[2] (fol. 48 *b*) and EJ (p. 286), runs as follows:

Pāṇi-pāda-tale sandhau grīvāyām⸗ūrdhva-jatruṇi ।
grantthir⸗valmīkavad⸗yaś⸗ca śanaiḥ samupacīyate ॥ 7 ॥

[1] EJ grīvām. [2] IO[1] om. ūrdhvam.
[3] EJ vyākhyāsyāmaḥ.

Toda-kleda-parīdāha-kaṇḍūmadbhir≠vraṇair≠vṛtaḥ ।
vyādhir≠Valmīka ity≠eṣa kapha-pitt-ānil-odbhavaḥ ॥ 8 ॥

Translation.

An anthill-like swelling which gradually grows up in the palm of the hand, in the sole of the foot, in a joint, in the neck, or anywhere above the windpipe, and which turns into pricking, running, burning, and itching ulcers—such a disease is called *Valmīka*, and is caused by disorders in the phlegm, bile, and air humours.

The same statement in the Summary of Vāgbhaṭa I, *Uttara Sthāna*, ch. XXXVII, vol. II, p. 316, l. 2, runs as follows:

Pāṇi-pāda-tale sandhau jatrūrdhvaṁ c≠opacīyate ।
valmīkavac≠chhanair≠granthis≠tad-vad≠bahv-aṇubhir≠mukhaiḥ ॥
Rug≠dāha-kaṇḍū-kled-āḍhyair≠Valmīko 'sau samasta-jaḥ ॥

Translation.

An anthill-like swelling with numerous minute apertures, which gradually grows up in the palm of the hand, in the sole of the foot, in a joint, or anywhere above the neck, and is full of burning and itching discharges—such a disease is called *Valmīka*, and is caused by all (the three) humours.

The same statement in the Pathology of Mādhava (*Nidāna*, ch. LV, cl. 6, ed. Jīv., 1901, p. 276) runs as follows:

Grīv-āṁsa-kakṣā-kara-pāda-deśe sandhau gale vā tribhir≠eva doṣaiḥ ।
Granthiḥ sa valmīka-vad≠akriyāṇāṁ jātaḥ krameṇ≠aiva gataḥ pravṛddhim ॥
Mukhair≠anekaiḥ sruti-toda-vadbhir≠visarpa-vat≠sarpati c≠onnat-āgraiḥ ।
Valmīkam≠āhur≠bhiṣajo vikāraṁ niṣpratyanīkaṁ cira-jaṁ viśeṣāt ॥ 6 ॥

Translation.

An anthill-like swelling, which has arisen from all the three humours (when disordered) in the neck, shoulder, armpit, and flat of the hand or foot, or in a joint, or in the throat, and which has gradually grown to a size, with numerous raised orifices running and pricking, and which spreads like erysipelas —such a disease the physicians call *Valmīka*, especially if it has been neglected and is of long standing.

Suśruta on Ūrdhvajatru and Jatrūrdhva

3. The use by Suśruta of the terms *ūrdhvajatru* and *jatrūrdhva*, referred to in § 62 (p. 162), is further illustrated by the following two passages. The first occurs in *Sūtra Sthāna*, ch. I, cl. 5, and, extracted from EJ (p. 2), runs as follows:

Śālākyaṁ nāma ūrdhvajatru-gatānāṁ rogāṇāṁ śravaṇa-nayana-vadana-ghrāṇ-ādi-saṁśritānāṁ vyādhīnām≠upaśamanārtham ‖

Translation.

(The branch of medical science) called Minor Surgery is concerned with the cure of the diseases seated in the body from the neck upwards, that is, of the maladies affecting the ears, eyes, mouth, nose, and other organs.

Chakrapāṇidatta's comment on this passage in the *Bhānumatī* (Calcutta edition, p. 20) runs as follows:

(1) Jatru grīvā-mūlam । jatruṇa ūrdhvam≠ūrdhvajatru ‖

The comment of Ḍallana, in Jīvānanda's edition, p. 7, is:

(2) Jatru grīvā-mūlam । anye vakṣo-'ṁsa-sandhim≠āhuḥ ‖

Translation.

(1) The term *jatru* signifies the base of the neck; hence the term *ūrdhvajatru* denotes the body from the neck upwards.

(2) The term *jatru* signifies the base of the neck. Others explain it as the joint of breast-bone and collar-bone.

The second passage occurs in the *Nidāna Sthāna*, ch. I, verse 14, and, edited from IO² (fol. 3 *a*, l. 3) and EJ (p. 244), runs as follows:

Tena bhāṣita-gīt-ādi-viśeṣo 'bhipravartate ।
ūrdhvajatru-gatān≠rogān≠karoti ca viśeṣataḥ ‖ 14 ‖

Translation.

By means of it (i. e. the *udāna* or uprising air humour) speaking, singing, and other functions (such as breathing) are performed; and in particular (when disordered) it causes the diseases which are seated in the body from the neck upwards.

The comment of Dallana on the term *ūrdhvajatru* in this passage (Jīv. ed., p. 459) runs as follows:

'Ūrdhvajatru-gatān' iti nayana-vadana-ghrāṇa-śravaṇa-śiraḥ-saṁśrayān ॥

Translation.

The phrase 'seated in the *ūrdhvajatru*' refers to those diseases which have their seat in the eyes, mouth, nose, ears, and the cranium.

The similar comment of Aruṇadatta, also referred to in § 62, occurs in the *Aṣṭāṅga Hṛdaya, Sūtra Sthāna*, ch. I, verse 1 (1st ed., vol. I, p. 368), and runs as follows:

Ūrdhvajatru-vikāreṣu śiro-rog-ādiṣu.

Translation.

The phrase 'in diseases of the *ūrdhvajatru*' means 'in diseases which affect the cranium and other parts of the head'.

§ 99. *The Śatapatha Brāhmaṇa on the Total Number of Bones*

1. The statement in the *Śatapatha Brāhmaṇa*, X, 5, 4, 12 (Weber's ed., p. 801), on the total number of the bones of the human body, referred to in § 42, cl. 1, runs as follows:

Ātmā ha tv⸗ev⸗aiṣo 'gniś⸗citaḥ । tasy⸗āsthīny⸗eva pariśritās⸗tāḥ ṣaṣṭiś⸗ca trīṇi ca śatāni bhavanti, ṣaṣṭiś⸗ca ha vai trīṇi ca śatāni puruṣasy⸗āsthīni; majjāno yajuṣmatya iṣṭakās⸗tāḥ ṣaṣṭis⸗c⸗aiva trīṇi ca śatāni bhavanti, ṣaṣṭiś⸗ca ha vai trīṇi ca śatāni puruṣasya majjāno 'tha ॥ 12 ॥

A similar statement occurs, *ibidem*, XII, 3, 2, 3 and 4 (Weber's ed., p. 912), and is as follows:

Trīṇi ca vai śatāni ṣaṣṭiś⸗ca saṁvatsarasya rātrayas,⸗trīṇi ca śatāni ṣaṣṭiś⸗ca puruṣasy⸗āsthīny,⸗atra tat-samam । trīṇi ca śatāni ṣaṣṭiś=ca saṁvatsarasy=āhāni, trīṇi ca śatāni ṣaṣṭiś=ca puruṣasya majjāno 'tra tat-samam ॥ 3 ॥ sapta ca vai śatāni viṁśatiś=ca saṁvatsarasy=āho-rātrāṇi, sapta ca śatāni viṁśatiś=ca puruṣasy=āsthīni ca majjānaś,=c=ātra tat-samam ॥ 4 ॥

For a translation of the above two passages, see § 42, cl. 2.

Suśruta on Marrow

2. The statement of Suśruta on marrow, in *Sūtra Sthāna*, XIV, verse 6 (Jīv., p. 48), referred to in § 42, cl. 6, runs as follows:

Rasād=raktaṁ, tato māṁsaṁ, māṁsān=medaḥ prajāyate ।
medaso 'sthi, tato majjā, majñaḥ śukrasya sambhavaḥ ॥ 6 ॥

Translation.

From chyle originates blood; from the latter, flesh (muscle); from flesh, fat; from fat, bone; from the latter, marrow: from marrow is the origin of semen.

There is nothing like this statement in that portion of Charaka's text-book, which was composed by Charaka himself. In the complement of that work made by Dṛiḍhabala, however, there occurs, in the *Chikitsita Sthāna*, ch. XIX, verse 14 (Jīv. ed., 1896, p. 656), a similar statement, which is based on Vāgbhaṭa I's account of the subject in his *Aṣṭāṅga Saṁgraha, Śārīra Sthāna*, ch. VI (ed., vol. I, p. 231, l. 12), and which is quoted by Aruṇadatta, as Dṛiḍhabala's statement, in his commentary on Vāgbhaṭa II's *Aṣṭāṅga Hṛdaya, Śārīra Sthāna*, ch. III, verses 62 *a* and 63 *b* (1st ed., vol. I, p. 569). This statement runs as follows:

Rasād=raktaṁ, tato māṁsaṁ, māṁsān=medas, tato 'sthi ca ।
asthno majjā, tataḥ śukraṁ, śukrād=garbhaḥ prajāyate ॥ 14 ॥

Translation.

From chyle originates blood; from the latter, flesh; from flesh, fat; and from the latter, bone: from bone, marrow; from the latter, semen; from semen, the foetus.

The further statement of Suśruta, in *Śārīra Sthāna*, ch. IV, cl. 9 and 10 (Jīv. p. 319), also referred to in § 42, cl. 6, and edited from Bd[1] (fol. 11 *a*), Bd[2] (fol. 11 *a*), IO[1] (fol. 11 *b*), IO[2] (fol. 14 *a*), runs as follows:

Tritīyā medodharā nāma; medo hi sarva-bhūtānām≠udara-stham, aṇv-asthiṣu ca mahatsu ca majjā bhavati ॥ 9 ॥

Sthūl-āsthiṣu viśeṣeṇa majjā tv≠abhyantar-āsthitaḥ ।
tath≠etareṣu sarveṣu sa-raktaṁ meda ucyate ॥
Śuddha-māṁsasya yaḥ snehaḥ sā vasā parikīrtitā ।
[1] ath≠etareṣu sarveṣu sneho medo vibhāvitā ॥ 10 ॥

Translation.

The third stratum (*kalā*) is called the fat-bearing; fat exists in the abdomen of all creatures; it also occurs in the small and large bones as marrow. In the large bones particularly, in the cavity of which it is found, it is called marrow: in all other bones it is called bloody fat. The grease which attaches to clean flesh (in the abdomen) is known as suet: in all other cases the fat is denoted simply grease.

The Śatapatha Brāhmaṇa on the Number of Bones in the Head and Trunk

3. The statement in the *Śatapatha Brāhmaṇa*, XII, 2, 4, 9–14 (Weber's ed., p. 910), on the number of bones, or portions, of the head and trunk, referred to in § 42, cl. 3, and § 62, cl. 6, runs as follows:

Śira ev≠āsya trivṛt । tasmāt≠tat≠tri-vidhaṁ bhavati, tvag≠asthi mastiṣkaḥ ॥ 9 ॥ grīvāḥ pañcadaśaḥ । caturdaśa vā etāsāṁ karūkarāṇi, vīryaṁ pañcadaśaṁ, tasmād≠etābhir≠aṇvībhiḥ satībhir≠gurum bhāraṁ harati, tasmād≠grīvāḥ pañcadaśaḥ ॥ 10 ॥ uraḥ saptadaśaḥ । aṣṭāv≠anye jatravo 'ṣṭāv≠anya, uraḥ saptadaśaṁ, tasmād≠uraḥ saptadaśaḥ ॥ 11 ॥ udaram≠ekaviṁśaḥ । viṁśatir≠vā antar≠udare kuntāpāny≠udaram≠ekaviṁśaṁ, tasmād≠udaram≠ekaviṁśaḥ ॥ 12 ॥ pārśve triṇavaḥ । trayodaś≠ānyāḥ parśavas≠trayodaś≠ānyāḥ, pārśve triṇave, tasmāt≠pārśve triṇavaḥ ॥ 13 ॥ anūkaṁ trayastriṁśaḥ । dvātriṁśad≠vā etasya karūkarāṇy≠anūkaṁ trayastriṁśaṁ, tasmād≠anūkaṁ trayastriṁśaḥ ॥ 14 ॥

For the translation, see § 42, cl. 3.

[1] The last line is omitted in Bd[1], Bd[2], IO[2] and Jīvānanda's edition; but it occurs in IO[1] and has the support of Gayadāsa's commentary, Cambridge MS., Add. 2491, fol. 36 *a*.

The Śatapatha Brāhmaṇa on Costal Cartilages

4. The statement in the *Śatapatha Brāhmaṇa*, VIII, 6, 2, 7. 10 (Weber's ed., p. 682), on *jatru*, or the costal cartilages, referred to in §§ 42, cl. 4, 62, cl. 6, runs as follows:

Uras≠triṣṭubhaḥ । tā retaḥsicor≠velay≠opadadhāti, pṛṣṭayo vai retaḥsicā, uro vai prati pṛṣṭayaḥ ॥ 7 ॥ parśavo bṛhatyaḥ । kīkasāḥ kakubhaḥ, so 'ntareṇa triṣṭubhaś≠ca kakubhaś≠ca bṛhatīr≠upadadhāti, tasmād≠imā ubhayatra parśavo baddhāḥ kīkasāsu ca jatruṣu ॥ 10 ॥

For the translation, see § 42, cl. 4.

NOTE: The osteological terms mentioned in Nos. 3 and 4 have been much misunderstood in dictionaries and translations. Considered in the light of Indian anatomical doctrine it is not so difficult to interpret them correctly. *Pṛṣṭi* is a synonym of *pṛṣṭha*, and means back-bone or vertebra. *Kīkasa* denotes the transverse processes of the thoracic vertebrae. *Jatru* is a costal cartilage. *Karūkara* is another term for the transverse processes of the cervical and thoracic vertebrae. *Kuntāpa* does not refer to any gland in the abdomen, but to the transverse processes of the lumbar vertebrae. *Udara* does not mean the abdomen simply, but the lower or abdominal portion of the vertebral column, while *anūka* refers to the upper or thoracic portion of that column. The whole vertebral column is divided into three parts: *grīvā*, cervical, *anūka*, thoracic, and *udara*, lumbar. This is practically the same as our modern division. *Vīrya*, vital force, or strength, which is said to be the fifteenth neck-bone, obviously represents the median line of the cervical column, considered as forming a single bone, and imparting to the whole set of neck-bones its peculiar strength by which heavy loads are supported. The osteological principles implied in the use of these terms are explained in § 42, cl. 7 and 8, and in my article on 'Anatomical Terms' in the *Journal of the Royal Asiatic Society* for 1907, pp. 1–18.

§ 100. *The Atharva Veda on the Skeleton*

The hymn on the creation of man in the Atharva Veda, X, 2, verses 1–8, referred to in § 2, cl. 4, and § 43, and extracted from the edition of Roth and Whitney, runs as follows:

1. Kena pārṣṇī ābhṛte pūruṣasya, kena māṁsaṁ saṁbhṛtam, kena gulphau ।
ken≠āṅgulīḥ peśanīḥ, kena khāni, ken≠ochlakhau madhyataḥ, kaḥ pratiṣṭhām ॥
2. Kasmān≠nu gulphāv≠adharāv≠akṛṇvan≠n≠aṣṭhīvantāv≠uttarau pūruṣasya ।
jaṅghe nirṛtya nyadadhuḥ kva svij, jānunoḥ sandhī ka u tac≠ciketa ॥
3. Catuṣṭayaṁ yujyate saṁhit-āntaṁ, jānubhyām≠ūrdhvaṁ śithiraṁ kabandham ।
śroṇī yad≠ūrū ka u taj≠jajāna yābhyāṁ kusindhaṁ su-dṛḍhaṁ babhūva ॥
4. Kati devāḥ katame ta āsanya uro grīvāś≠cikyuḥ pūruṣasya ।
kati stanau vyadadhuḥ, kaḥ kaphoḍau, kati skandhān, kati pṛṣṭīr≠acinvan ॥
5. Ko asya bāhū samabharad≠'vīryaṁ karavād'≠iti ।
aṁsau ko asya tad≠devaḥ kusindhe adhyādadhau ॥
6. Kaḥ sapta khāni vi tatarda śīrṣaṇi, karṇāv≠imau nāsike cakṣaṇī mukham ।
yeṣāṁ purutrā vijayasya mahmani catuṣpādo dvipado yānti yāmam ॥
7. Hanvor≠hi jihvām≠adadhāt, purūcīm≠adhā mahīm≠adhi śiśrāya vācam ।
sa ā varīvarti bhuvaneṣv≠antar≠apo vasānaḥ, ka u tac≠ciketa ॥
8. Mastiṣkam≠asya yatamo lalāṭaṁ kakāṭikāṁ prathamo yaḥ kapālam ।
citvā cityaṁ hanvoḥ pūruṣasya divaṁ ruroha, katamaḥ sa devaḥ ॥

For the translation, see § 43, cl. 2; also my article in the *Journal of the Royal Asiatic Society* for 1907, pp. 10–12.

INDEX

The numbers refer to the pages. Sanskrit terms are in italics, proper names in capitals.

J.

K.

L.